Years 6–8
Maths
FOR
STUDENTS

Years 6–8 Maths FOR STUDENTS

by Ingrid Kemp
Mark Zegarelli
Colin Beveridge

Made by the people who make the **FOR DUMMIES** books!

A Wiley Brand

Years 6–8 Maths for Students®

Published by
Wiley Publishing Australia Pty Ltd
42 McDougall Street
Milton, Qld 4064
www.dummies.com

Copyright © 2016 Wiley Publishing Australia Pty Ltd

The moral rights of the authors have been asserted.

National Library of Australia
Cataloguing-in-Publication data:

Author:	Colin Beveridge
Contributors:	Mark Zegarelli, Ingrid Kemp
Title:	Years 6–8 Maths for Students
ISBN:	9780730326731 (pbk.)
	9780730326809 (ebook)
Series:	For Dummies
Notes:	Includes index.
Subjects:	Mathematics—Textbooks
	Mathematics—Study and teaching (Secondary)
	Mathematics—Problems, exercises, etc.

Dewey Number: 510.76

Cover: Wiley Creative Services

Illustrations by Wiley, Composition Services Graphics

Typeset by diacriTech, Chennai, India

Printed in Australia by
Ligare Book Printer

10 9 8 7 6 5 4 3 2 1

Contents at a Glance

Table of Contents

Introduction

· ·

Once upon a time, you loved numbers. This isn't the first line of a fairy tale. Once upon a time, you really did love numbers. Remember?

Maybe you were three years old and your grandparents were visiting. You sat next to them on the couch and recited the numbers from 1 to 10. Grandma and Grandpa were proud of you and — be honest — you were proud of yourself, too. Or maybe you were five and discovering how to write numbers, trying hard not to print your 2 and 7 backward.

Learning was fun. *Numbers* were fun. So what happened? Maybe the trouble started with long division. Or sorting out how to change fractions to decimals. Could it have been figuring out how to take away a 25 per cent discount from the cost of a purchase? Reading a graph? Converting miles to kilometres? Trying to find that most dreaded value of *x*? Wherever it started, you began to suspect that maths didn't like you — and you didn't like maths very much, either.

Why do people often enter kindergarten excited about learning how to count and, somewhere along the line, become convinced that they can't do maths? The answer to this question would probably take 20 books this size, but solving the problem can begin right here.

I ask you to put aside any doubts. Remember, just for a moment, an innocent time — a time before maths inspired panic attacks or, at best, induced irresistible drowsiness. In this book, I take you from an understanding of the basics to the place where you're ready to enter any mathematics class and succeed.

About This Book

Along the road from counting to algebra, most people experience the Great Maths Breakdown. This feels something like when your car begins smoking and sputtering on a 43°C highway somewhere between Noplace and Not Much Else.

Please consider this book your personal roadside helper, and think of me as your friendly maths mechanic (only much cheaper!). Stranded on the freeway, you may feel frustrated by circumstances and betrayed by your vehicle, but for the person holding the toolbox, it's all in a day's work. The tools for fixing the problem are in this book.

Not only does this book help you with the basics of math, but it also helps you get past any aversion you may feel toward maths in general. I've broken down the concepts into easy-to-understand sections. And because *Years 6–8 Maths for Students* is a reference book, you don't have to read the chapters or sections in order — you can look over only what you need. So feel free to jump around. Whenever I cover a topic that requires information from earlier in the book, I refer you to that section or chapter, in case you want to refresh yourself on the basics.

Here are two pieces of advice I give all the time — remember them as you work your way through the concepts in this book:

- ✔ **Take frequent breaks.** Every 20 to 30 minutes, stand up and push in your chair. Then feed the cat, tidy your room (yeah, right!), take a walk, juggle tennis balls, try on last year's Santa's hat — do something to distract yourself for a few minutes. You'll come back to your books more productive than if you just sat there hour after hour with your eyes glazing over.

- ✔ **After you've read through an example and think you understand it, copy the problem, close the book, and try to work it through.** If you get stuck, steal a quick look — but later, try that same example again to see whether you can get through it without opening the book. (Remember that, on any tests you're preparing for, peeking is probably not allowed!)

Although every author secretly (or not-so-secretly) believes that each word she pens is pure gold, you don't have to read every word in this book unless you really want to. Feel free to skip over sidebars (those shaded grey boxes) where I go off on a tangent — unless you find tangents interesting, of course.

Foolish Assumptions

Making assumptions is always a risky business, but knowing where I'm coming from may put you at ease. So, in writing this book, I assume that:

- ✔ You know how to count and are familiar with the symbols for the numbers.

- ✔ You understand the idea of money and changing a banknote for an equivalent value of coins.

✔ You know what some basic shapes look like.

✔ You're prepared to think fairly hard about maths and want either to pass an upcoming test or exam or to simply improve your maths skills.

Icons Used in This Book

Throughout the book, I use three icons to highlight what's hot and what's not:

This icon points out key ideas that you need to know. Make sure you understand before reading on! Remember this info even after you close the book.

Theories are fine, but anything marked with a Tip icon in this book tells you something practical to help you get to the right answer. These are the tricks of the mathematical trade.

The Warning icon highlights errors and mistakes that can cost you marks or your sanity, or both.

Where to Go From Here

This book is set up so you can jump right into the topics that interest you. If you feel like an absolute beginner in maths, I recommend you read Parts I and II to build a foundation for the other topics. If you're pretty comfortable with the mechanics of maths, use the table of contents and index to find the subject you have questions about right now. This book is a reference — keep it with your maths kit and turn to it whenever you have a question about maths.

Part I
Whole Numbers: The Building Blocks of Maths

getting started with
Years 6–8 Maths for

STUDENTS

In this part . . .

- ✔ Set yourself up for maths success — and understand what maths you're already good at.

- ✔ Work with number sequences, addition and subtraction.

- ✔ Multiply with style and divide with ease.

- ✔ Get your head around negative numbers.

- ✔ Understand how to solve word problems — and why doing so can be useful.

Chapter 1

Ready, Set ... Success!

- -

In This Chapter

▶ Realising you already use maths every day

▶ Understanding how you use whole and part numbers, measurements, shapes, and even algebra

▶ Getting ready for maths success and maintaining motivation

▶ Keeping a positive attitude and organising your notes

- -

Before you read any more of this book, take a big, deep breath. I know what taking on something difficult or frightening feels like — I feel just the same about taking a class at the gym, and I still have to steel myself a bit when I go into a shopping centre.

I start this chapter by saying thanks — thanks for giving maths a try and thanks for listening to me. I'm not the kind of maths teacher who wears tweed jackets with leather patches and yells at you when you don't pick up on her mumbles straightaway. I want to help you get past the fear and the mind blanks and show you not just that you can do maths well, but that you already do maths well and can use that base to build upon. I show you how, with a bit of work, you can master the bits and pieces of maths you don't have down to a tee. You're smart. I believe in you.

Perhaps you find the maths you do in day-to-day life so easy you don't even notice you're doing sums. I spend some time in this chapter showing you what you already know and then introduce the topics I cover in the rest of the book.

You're Already Good at Maths

Put your hand up if you've ever said something like, 'I'm no good at maths.' I promise I won't yell at you. Now imagine saying, 'I'm no good at talking' or, 'I'm no good at walking.' Those things may be true at times — I get tongue-tied once in a while, and I've been known to trip over invisible objects — but most of the time my mumbling and stumbling are perfectly adequate to get by. I bet the same thing applies with your maths. Maybe you freeze up when you see a fraction or just nod and smile politely when someone shows you a pie chart. This doesn't mean you're bad at maths, just that you trip up once in a while.

If you can shift your self-talk on maths from 'I'm no good at this' to 'I'm still getting to grips with this', you'll create a self-fulfilling prophecy and begin to understand maths.

Part of the problem may be that you don't realise how much of what you do every day involves doing maths in your head. You may not think you're doing maths when you judge whether to cross the road on a red light, but your brain is really doing a series of complex calculations and asking questions such as:

- ✔ How fast is that bus going, and how far away is it? How long will the bus take to get here?

- ✔ How wide is the road, and how long will it take for me to get across?

- ✔ What's the probability of that driver slowing down to avoid me if I'm in the road?

- ✔ How badly do I want to avoid being honked at or run over?

- ✔ What are the survival and recovery rates for my local hospital?

- ✔ How soon do I need to be where I'm going?

- ✔ How much time will crossing now save over waiting for the light to change?

You do all of these calculations — very roughly — in your head, without a calculator, and without freezing up and saying, 'I'm no good at maths.' If you regularly got any of those sums wrong — the speed–distance–time analysis, the probability or the game theory — you'd be reading this in hospital and trying to figure out what the jagged line graph at the end of the bed means. (Turn to Chapter 13 if this really is the case — and get well soon!)

So before you cross the road on your way to school or walking the dog, you solve as many as six 'impossible' sums in your head, maybe before you've even had breakfast.

Your first homework assignment

I'm not a big one for setting homework, but I'm going to ask you to do one thing for me (and, more importantly, for yourself): If you ever find yourself in a situation where you feel like saying, 'I'm no good at maths', catch yourself and say something else. Try 'I used to struggle with maths, but I'm discovering that maths is easier than I thought', or 'I'm fine with day-to-day maths', or 'I really recommend *Years 6–8 Maths For Students*: This book turned me into a mathematical genius.'

Although mathematicians traditionally wear rubbish clothes, thick glasses and a bad comb-over, this fashion isn't compulsory. The tweed generation is dying out, and most of the maths geeks I know are now just a bit scruffy. So, don't worry: Being good at maths won't turn you into a fashion disaster with no friends.

I appreciate my homework assignment is tremendously difficult — asking you to change your entire way of thinking is a big ask. To assist you I enlist the help of a rubber band and ask you to treat yourself with something I call Dunford Therapy, after the genius who told me about it:

1. **Find a rubber band big enough to go around your wrist comfortably.**

   Put the rubber band around one of your wrists — either one, it doesn't matter.

2. **Every time you catch yourself saying anything along the lines of 'I'm no good at maths', snap the rubber band really hard against the bony bit of your wrist.**

   This will hurt. That's the idea.

3. **After you catch yourself a few times, your brain will start to rewire itself to avoid thinking such filthy and disgusting thoughts, and you'll find yourself capable of extraordinary feats of mathematics.**

 If you have particularly fragile wrists or any inkling that you might do yourself more damage with a rubber band than swearing and shaking your hand in pain, don't use Dunford Therapy. The rubber band is supposed to hurt just enough to help you change your way of thinking, not to injure you.

Getting the odd maths sum wrong doesn't mean you are stupid — far from it, in fact, because you're immediately and obviously smarter than someone who doesn't even try the sum.

Talking yourself up

Encouraging yourself is a recurring theme in this book — the more you give yourself credit for the things you can do, the easier the things you're still working on become. Be sensible about things: Don't rush to the library and check out the *Journal of Differential Equations*. But when you see something that's a bit tricky-looking, try to avoid saying, 'I can't do that' or, 'I haven't been taught that' as a response. Maybe say, 'I can't do that yet' or, 'I need to do some work on this.' Better still, say, 'What would I need to find out to be able to solve this?'

The section 'Setting Yourself Up for Success', later in this chapter, is all about ways to build your confidence and set yourself up to get on top of your maths studies quickly, effectively, and with a great big goofy grin. (Best of all, Dunford Therapy isn't part of this section.)

Whole Numbers: Party Time!

Everyone likes parties. Balloons! Silly hats! Cheese-and-kabana sticks arranged in a potato to look like an echidna! (Or is that just your parents?) But these things don't spring into existence on their own. If you want to plan a party, you may need to put your maths skills to work to make sure you buy enough snacks for everyone.

Maybe you want to bake a cake for 12 people coming to celebrate your birthday. But disaster! The recipe book only has a recipe for a cake that serves four people. What can you possibly do?

I'm sure you can come up with a few solutions. I've also got a few ideas, which I explain here in excruciating detail:

- ✔ **Let people go hungry:** You have 12 guests and only enough cake for four. How many will have to forgo your delicious chocolate sponge? Twelve people take away four lucky cake-eaters leaves eight guests, who perhaps would prefer the chips anyway.

- ✔ **Make extra cakes:** One cake feeds four people and you want to feed 12. How many cakes do you need? Twelve people divided by four per cake gives you three cakes.

- ✔ **Cut your slices into smaller pieces:** If you cut four slices each into three smaller bits, you have 4 times 3 equals 12.

- ✔ **Make a bigger cake:** This is the kind of approach that you typically get asked about in an exam. You need to figure out how much bigger to make the cake — just like before, $12 \div 4 = 3$ times as big. To make the cake three times bigger, you multiply all of the ingredients in the recipe by three.

My suggestion in the preceding list is a bit of a 'don't try this at home' moment: Although the last option is the most 'mathsy', it may not work out quite as well in real life. Unless the recipe in your cookery book gives instructions on how to adjust the cooking time of your humungous new cake, the physics of cake-baking may conspire against you and leave you with something inedible. Try my idea if you like, but don't blame me if your cake doesn't rise.

Forgive me if you already knew how to do all of that. That's actually a good sign. The point wasn't to bamboozle you with tricky maths but to say that sometimes you do maths without even thinking about what you're doing.

One of the points from my cake example is to think about which sum is appropriate for each idea, so you can adapt the concept to different situations. What if your cake recipe serves six people? What if you're expecting 48 guests? What if the recipe is for quiche instead of cake?

In Part I of this book I look at exactly this kind of question. What kind of sum is the right one to do? How can you figure out roughly what the answer should be? How do you work out the arithmetic to get a precise answer? I look at the 'basic' operations — adding, subtracting, multiplying and dividing — along with turning words into numbers (and solving word problems) and working with negative numbers.

Parts of the Whole: Fractions, Decimals, Percentages and More

Public speaking ... death ... spiders ... fractions. Are you scared? Adding 10 per cent GST! Are you scared now?

I understand. Seeing how whole numbers fit together is relatively easy, but then suddenly the evil maths guys start throwing fractions and percentages at you — and things aren't so intuitive. Fractions (at least, proper fractions) are just numbers that are smaller than whole numbers — they follow the same rules as regular numbers but sometimes need a bit of adjusting before you can apply them to everyday situations.

I have two main aims in this section: To show you that fractions, decimals, percentages and ratios are nothing like as fearsome as you may believe; and to show you that fractions, decimals, percentages and ratios are all different ways of writing the same thing — therefore, if you understand one of them, you can understand all of them.

I won't promise that you'll emerge from this section deeply in love with fractions, but I hope I can help you make peace with fractions so you can work through the questions likely to come up in exams and in real life. The chapters in Part II go into these areas in a lot more detail.

Mmmm, pizza! Everyday fractions

You use fractions and decimals in real life all the time — any time you slice a pizza into smaller bits ... any time you say you'll be somewhere at quarter past six ... any time you say or read the price of a product in the supermarket and, in fact, any time at all when you use money.

A fraction is really just two numbers, one on top of the other, that describe an amount (usually, anyway) between zero and one. A fraction is a part of a whole one. The bottom number tells you how finely you've divided the whole thing (the bigger the number, the finer or smaller the 'slice') and the top number tells you how many slices you have.

For example, think about a quarter of an hour. A quarter is written as $\frac{1}{4}$: The 4 says, 'Split your hour into four equal bits', and the 1 says, 'Then think about one of the bits.' A quarter of an hour is a whole hour (or 60 minutes) divided into four parts, making 15 minutes. Three-quarters of an hour ($\frac{3}{4}$) is three times as long: 45 minutes.

You already use decimals all the time as well. When you write down an amount of money using dollars and cents, you use a decimal point to show where the whole number (of dollars) ends and where the parts of a dollar (cents) begin. If you look at your mobile phone bill or your shopping receipt, you see decimal points all over the place. Don't be afraid of decimals: As far as you're concerned, decimal points are just dots in a number that you can leave in place and otherwise ignore. For example, you work out a sum like 5.34 ÷ 2 (with a dot) in exactly the same way as you work out 534 ÷ 2 (without a dot) — the only difference is that you have to remember to put the dot back in, in the same place, when you finish the sum.

Percentages are easier than you think: Introducing the Table of Joy

What if I told you I had a simple, reliable method for working out the sums you need to do in somewhere between a quarter and a half of questions in a typical maths test? Such a method exists — the Table of Joy. I go into serious detail about this table in Chapter 8, but I also dot it about here and there in other chapters.

You can use the Table of Joy in all of the following topics:

- **Converting metric units:** Working in either direction, and finding the conversion rate.
- **Currency conversion:** Converting to and from any currency, and working out the exchange rate.

- ✔ **Finding a fraction of a number:** Without making you cry.

- ✔ **Percentages:** Both regular and reverse percentages.

- ✔ **Pie charts:** How big a slice should be, the value a slice represents, and what the total value of the slices in the chart should be.

- ✔ **Ratios:** Pretty much any ratio sum you can imagine, and more besides.

- ✔ **Recipe scaling:** How much you need to adjust your recipe by, and how many people it now feeds.

- ✔ **Scale drawing:** Finding the size of the real thing, or the sketch, or the scale.

- ✔ **Speed/distance/time questions:** And pretty much anything you could possibly want to do (at least, in the tests you're likely to face in the next few years).

The idea of the Table of Joy is simple: Write down the information you need to use in a labelled table, and do a simple sum to work out the answer to your question. Follow these steps to use the Table of Joy:

1. **Draw out a noughts-and-crosses grid, with squares big enough to label.**

2. **Put the *units* of what you're dealing with in the top-middle and top-right squares.**

   For example, if you want to convert currencies, your units may be 'euros' and 'dollars'. If you want to work out a sale percentage, your units may be 'dollars' and 'per cent'.

3. **Put the *contexts* of the information you have in the middle-left and bottom-left squares.**

   Again, with currencies, you may have 'exchange rate' and 'money changed'. With percentages, you may have 'full price' and 'sale price'.

   Each time the Table of Joy comes up in this book, I show you how to label the relevant table, but after a while you'll probably do it instinctively.

4. **Put the relevant numbers in the correct cells, with reference to the labels.**

   For example, 100 per cent is the same as the full price, so 100 goes in the square with 'per cent' at the top and 'full price' at the side.

5. **Put a question mark in the remaining square, and write out the Table of Joy sum.**

   In the Table of Joy you always start with three numbers and then have to work out the fourth.

The sum is the other number in the same row as the question mark, multiplied by the other number in the same column as the question mark, divided by the remaining number.

6. After you work out the sum, you have your answer.

This may seem like a lot of work, but after you get into the routine of using the Table of Joy, you'll work out your sums quite quickly. In Figure 1-1 I show you how to create an example Table of Joy to answer the following question:

The Australian dollar is worth 0.75 US dollars. I want to buy trainers on sale in America for US$75. How much is that in Australian dollars?

Don't worry if the calculation in the Table of Joy looks tricky. In Chapter 7 I take you through decimal sums in detail. I just want to show you here how easily you can figure out what sum you need to do.

Figure 1-1:
The steps of the Table of Joy. (a) Draw a big noughts-and-crosses grid. (b) Label the rows and columns. (c) Fill in the numbers. (d) Do the Table of Joy sum. The answer is AU$100.

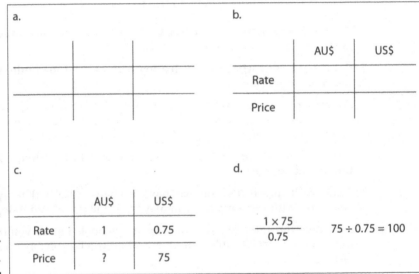

Sizing Up Time, Weights, Measures and Shapes

I bet you're perfectly comfortable with at least one of the following topics: Telling the time, taking a temperature, weighing yourself or other objects, counting money, measuring distances, or playing with shapes. You may even be comfortable with all of them.

Even if you just feel okay with one of these topics, you can build on your knowledge with the other subjects. For example, if you know how to use a thermometer, you can use exactly the same skills to read a scale or a ruler.

This is all useful, day-to-day stuff — and the reason I'm confident you know something about these topics is that they're all around us, all the time. On the way to the shopping centre, you may check the train timetable to see when you need to leave or the weather forecast to see whether you need to take a coat. At the shops, you weigh your bananas to see how much they cost, decide between 50 and 100 metres of dental floss, and then pay the bill at the checkout — before packing the whole lot into your bag and making sure it fits nicely.

All of that is maths. And I bet you do most of it without really thinking. Similarly, a lot of students freeze up when I ask them to work out the change from $20 on paper, but given Monopoly money they do the same sum without any trouble. All I want you to do is make sure you link your everyday experiences with the numbers you juggle on the page. The chapters in Part III help with this.

Weights and measures you already know

You have four topics to master that are to do with measuring things other than distance:

- **Time:** You need to be able to work with a clock, read timetables, fill in timesheets and work with speed — which, after you appreciate the pitfalls, are all pretty easy.

- **Money:** You're probably already familiar with money sums. You need to be able to do regular arithmetic with money and change one currency into another (the Table of Joy can help with this — refer to the section 'Percentages are easier than you think: Introducing the Table of Joy', earlier in this chapter).

- **Weight:** Even if you don't use scales regularly, you've probably seen somebody else use them. I take you through using and reading the various types of scales, and I show you how to convert between different units of weight.

- **Temperature:** You're probably quite happy with most aspects of temperature, although I do introduce a few tricky bits that you may not get straightaway — converting between temperature scales and using negative numbers are two areas where some people end up scratching their heads. Don't worry: I take things slowly.

Getting yourself into shape

You need to understand how to deal with lengths, areas, volumes and shapes. Some people find visualising shapes really easy — if you're one of those people, you'll find the shape sections (in Chapter 11) pretty straightforward. If not, don't worry — I explain things as simply as possible.

The shape topics are split into two groups: Measuring (where I talk about how big a shape is) and the actual shapes (where I help you with angles, symmetry and so on). I also have a quick look at maps and plans. You can measure an object in several different ways. For example, you can measure how tall or wide or deep the object is (length), how much floor space it takes up or how much paper you need to cover it up (area), and how much room space it takes up or how much stuff it holds (volume).

Why bother with graphs and tables?

In my spare room I have a shoebox full of receipts, bills, statements and handwritten notes saying things like '$8.75 on curry' and 'Class with Jenny, $55'. This box is a shambles of an accounting system, and if anyone wants to exchange a few hours of sorting it out for a few hours of maths tuition, please get in touch with me.

But if I want to understand my financial position better, I don't want a shoebox of randomly arranged bits of paper. I want my numbers neatly arranged on a few pages of paper or — better yet — in a graph so I can see at a glance how long I need to work before I pay off my loans and can afford a holiday.

The strength of tables and graphs is that they take a mess of numbers and make them tidier or easier to understand, or both. In the last chapter of Part III (Chapter 13), I show you how to read and make tables and graphs, and help you see which is best to use in which situation.

Seeing How x Marks the Spot

In maths, x stands for a number — any number. Any letter that you use to stand for a number is a variable, which means that its value can vary — that is, its value is uncertain. In contrast, a number in algebra is often called a constant because its value is fixed.

Sometimes you have enough information to find out the identity of x. For example, consider the following:

$$2 + 2 = x$$

Obviously, in this equation, x stands for the number 4. But other times, what the number x stands for stays shrouded in mystery. The chapters in Part IV help you remove some of this mystery, covering algebraic expressions, isolating and solving for x, and solving algebra word problems.

Setting Yourself Up for Success

Don't worry if you're not looking forward to studying (I know that feeling!) — you can make things easier for yourself. You don't have to enjoy learning maths, but I won't tell anyone if you suddenly find yourself thinking, *This isn't so bad after all*. In this section, I show you how you can set yourself up so that maths is a bit less intimidating, a lot less stressful and (whisper it) more enjoyable. Like most things, success boils down to preparation and positivity — in this section, I help you on both of these fronts.

I start off with a few ideas about setting up somewhere to work where you can be comfortable and concentrate with as few distractions as possible, and where everything you need is to hand.

Getting properly equipped

I don't like running. Actually, that's not quite true. I don't mind the running part. But I don't like going outside in the cold and wet (or heat and humidity). I can make myself more likely to go running — and reap its benefits — if I prepare properly. I put my trainers and running clothes beside my bed so I see them as soon as I get up. I plan a route that takes me through my favourite parts of town. And I promise myself the treat of a good cup of coffee when I get home.

The key is setting myself up properly. I keep the things I know I'll need handy, I make the task as enjoyable as possible, and I reward myself for completing the job.

You can do the same for your maths. By keeping your equipment somewhere convenient, making your workspace comfortable and inviting, and rewarding yourself after each maths session, I bet you soon find studying isn't quite such a chore as you thought.

Tools of the trade

You don't need much stuff to get going with *Years 6–8 Maths For Students* — you can do an awful lot with just a pen and paper. But you may want to pick up a few extra bits and pieces along the way. Here are the things I strongly recommend you buy the next time you're in a stationery shop or online:

- ✔ **A notebook:** I find having a single place to keep track of all the things I want to remember makes it easier to look them up when I want to remember them — otherwise, you end up scrambling through reams of paper to find the brilliant idea you had three weeks ago but can't remember now.

- ✔ **Pencils, pens and markers:** Having a notebook isn't much use without something to write in it with. I like to work in pencil if I'm drawing pictures or doing something I'm not confident in. I move on to ink when I'm happy with what I'm doing. The markers are mainly for making bright memorable notes and highlighting the important things I want to remember.

- ✔ **A calculator:** In a lot of this book I show you how to work things out without using a calculator — after all, trying to figure out sums by hand is always a good exercise. That said, calculators are extremely useful for checking your answers. Your school has probably already recommended the correct calculator for your year level.

- ✔ **A rubbish bin:** Maths isn't like philosophy. It's not all worth saving.

- ✔ **A geometry set:** A ruler, a set of compasses and a protractor are all useful — as is some of the other stuff that's usually bundled in with those sets ... although I'm pretty sure no-one has used a stencil since about 1994. Some of the processes you may need to be able to do to pass your tests require something from the geometry set, so maybe make this the first bit of equipment you buy.

If you don't have some of this stuff, don't use that as an excuse not to get started! You can make a start on one of the chapters that doesn't need any equipment. For example, in Chapter 12, where I talk about time, you don't need anything more than a pen and paper.

A space of your own

Nothing in the rules of maths says you have to study at a desk. Or at home. Or indoors. In fact, changing your scenery can help put you into a different frame of mind and provide the inspiration you need. I often pick up my notebook and decamp to my local coffee shop or park in search of a breakthrough.

Discovering where you work best

Try out several places to see where you work best. Does the local library have quiet tables you could work at? Can you spread out on a bed? (This was always my favourite when I was a teenager, because I could claim I'd worked myself to sleep.) Maybe the kitchen table is a good place for you, or you work best with a notebook on your lap, half-distracted by the TV.

Try studying in different locations and at different times of the day. Get creative about mixing it up, and see what feels best for you.

Improving your workspace

After you figure out where your favourite workspace is, you can tweak it to make the area even more conducive to effective studying. Here are three ways to improve where you work:

- **Minimise distractions:** Maths is a lot easier when you have undisturbed focus and you know you don't have to stop for any reason. When I need to concentrate, I turn off my phone and email, crank up some music and completely shut out the outside world for as long as I need. Sometimes I set a timer for 30 minutes or so, and sometimes I leave my study time open-ended.

   If you have family members or friends who constantly demand your attention, you may need to cajole, bribe or intimidate them into leaving you alone when you study. I find a 'CAUTION: FRACTIONS!' sign tends to do the trick. Alternatively, you could just ask them nicely.

- **Maximise comfort:** If you're not physically comfortable when you study, relaxing mentally is tough. If your brain says, 'I don't want to sit in that horrible plastic chair — it makes my back hurt,' persuading yourself to start studying is hard. Do all you can to make your workspace welcoming and cosy — make sure you can sit up straight, stay at the right temperature and have a drink.

- **Keep things tidy:** Your experience may vary with this, but when my desk is a shambles — which it quite frequently is — the mess distracts me ... as does the nagging suspicion somewhere in my mind that my mum's going to visit and tell me to tidy up. I make a point of decluttering my desk before I start anything that needs my full attention.

   Of course, you might prefer to work in a mess. But don't come crying to me when my mum shows up and calls your room a bombsite.

Staying Motivated

Whenever I begin a new project, I start off with the enthusiasm of a small puppy with a new toy. After a while, though — sometimes minutes, sometimes months — I start to lose interest a bit. If I'm not careful, I start skipping days and before long the project dies a quiet death.

Fortunately, I have a few schemes up my sleeve for avoiding the death of projects. The cheap psychological tricks that I describe in the following sections either keep you in the saddle or help you get back on the horse after you fall off.

Remembering why you're studying

The human brain loves the word 'because'. You're a (largely) rational creature, and having a reason for doing something makes you more likely to do it — for example, saving up cash without a goal is harder than saving up for a new bike.

Think about why you're studying. Maybe you want to improve your overall grade average. Maybe you want to keep yourself on track to get into uni. Maybe you want to eventually open your own hairdressing salon when you leave school and know you'll need maths skills to keep your accounts in good order.

Now take a big bit of paper, write 'I want to understand maths because I want to improve my grades/get into uni/open a hairdressing salon', sign your statement and put the paper somewhere you can't help but see it. Whenever you struggle with your studying, look at your note and remind yourself why you're learning maths. Your brain doesn't really care what your reason is. If you try to jump the queue at the photocopier, you may say, 'Do you mind if I jump in, because I need to copy this page for my class in 10 minutes?' But the person in front of you is just as likely to agree if you say, 'Do you mind if I jump in, because I desperately need to make some copies?'

Using the 'calendar of crosses'

When American comedian Jerry Seinfeld was an up and coming comic, he faced a problem that many comedians (and writers) have: Not enough material. To put this problem straight, he decided he was going to write something every day without fail. He picked up a cheap calendar and every day he wrote something, he marked the date with a big red cross.

After a few days, he found the crosses were making a chain — and the last thing he wanted to do was break the chain. The calendar helped motivate him to keep on writing and was probably a big factor in his success in his field.

You can apply this idea to any habit you want to form — doing more exercise, going to bed on time, drinking five glasses of water a day ... or doing a few minutes of maths. You soon get into the habit of doing a few minutes a day just to avoid breaking the chain, even when you don't feel like studying.

Buy a cheap calendar or find one online to print out. Stick the calendar next to your reason for doing maths, and draw a cross on the calendar every day you do some maths work. Don't break the chain!

Rewarding yourself

Life coaches talk about the difference between 'towards goals' and 'away-from goals'. This is the same thing as carrots and sticks — if you want a donkey to move forward, you can bribe her with carrots or threaten her with sticks. Some donkeys — and people — respond better to bribes than to threats.

The 'calendar of crosses' (which I describe in the previous section) is a mixture of carrots and sticks — you have the reward of seeing a nice long unbroken chain, but you also have the threat that if you don't do something today, you'll break that chain.

Today, I'm tricking myself into writing on my birthday, which in any reasonable world would be a national holiday. I need to get this chapter finished, but after I reach my prescribed word count, I'll reward myself with a trip to my favourite coffee shop for a large cappuccino and some carrot cake. I'm drooling at the thought — but I'm writing a lot faster than I would without a (literal and metaphorical) carrot.

Getting Your Head On Straight

I have seen normal intelligent adults suffer full-blown panic attacks when asked to solve a maths problem. I've seen people freeze completely, and I've seen people deny they know how to add two and two.

Being intimidated by maths isn't unusual. I have moments where I look at a topic I'm not familiar with and tense up. Panic isn't the best place to be if you want to learn something, however — so I've discovered how to get myself into the right frame of mind for absorbing information and doing good work. In this section, I describe a few of the tricks I use to sort myself out.

I like to think of the first three tactics as POPS: Posture, Oxygen and Positive Self-talk. Whenever you panic, try using POPS to calm yourself.

Sitting up straight

You know when your teachers point out your slouching? They may have a point. Try the following exercise one day: Go for a walk with your shoulders hunched and your head down, a frown of concentration on your face, hands deep in your pockets. Then walk with your shoulders back, head up, a big smile and arms swinging freely. Feels better, doesn't it? People tell you to smile when you pick up the phone for a reason.

Your posture plays a big part in how you approach a task and how well you do in that task. Sitting up straight, throwing back your shoulders and working with a smile all make it easier for you to work quickly and effectively. Try it and see!

Getting a breath of fresh air

I used to suffer from panic attacks — they're horrible and I wouldn't wish them on anyone. One of the tricks I was taught for dealing with panic attacks involved diaphragmatic breathing.

What breathing? Yeah, I asked that too. Diaphragmatic means pertaining to the diaphragm, a muscle somewhere in your lower chest. The idea is that instead of taking shallow breaths into the top of your lungs, you take deep breaths as far down as possible and then breathe out slowly. Singers use diaphragmatic breathing before they go on stage: It has the twin benefits of helping lung capacity so they can sing better, and calming them down so stage fright doesn't hit so hard.

Here's how to do it:

1. **Put one hand on the top of your chest and the other hand on your belly.**

2. **Breathe in as deeply as you can, trying not to move your upper hand. Your lower hand should move out as your lungs fill with air.**

3. **Breathe in for a count of seven, but don't hold your breath.**

4. **Breathe out very slowly for a count of 11.**

   Don't worry if you can't manage all the way up to 11 — just breathe out for as long as you can and make a note to breathe more slowly next time.

5. **Keep doing this for a minute or so and you'll feel your heart rate drop and your head start to clear.**

   A clear head makes maths a lot easier.

Talking to yourself — not as crazy as it sounds

One of my most effective tactics as a teacher is to convince students not to say, 'I can't do this' but to say, 'I can't do this yet' or, 'I'm still learning this.' Describing yourself as being on the way somewhere really helps you carry on moving.

The way you express your thoughts can revolutionise how you work. People who go into a Monday thinking Mondays are rubbish tend to have rubbish Mondays. Sportspeople who think about losing win less often than those who think about winning. People who say, 'I can do this when I've got the pieces in place' do better at maths than those who say, 'I'm useless at maths. I'm stupid.'

You're not stupid. You've picked up this book, which makes you a very smart person.

Learning from your mistakes

I was rubbish at learning to drive. I was sure I couldn't drive and used the mistakes I made in every lesson as evidence that I wasn't cut out for the whole car nonsense. The problem was not that I was rubbish at driving but that I was beating down my confidence by focusing on my mistakes.

About the same time, I was learning to play guitar. I adopted a 'Right! I'll show you!' attitude after my parents told me I wasn't dexterous enough to play guitar and my music teacher decided I'd never amount to much. In that mindset, every chord I hit that sounded good was a small victory — and never mind the 12 bum notes that came before it. I was willing to try new ideas just to see what happened. I lapped up anything that could possibly make me a better guitarist.

A simple change of thinking can make all the difference — by accepting you'll make mistakes on the way to mastery and determining to learn from those mistakes, you may find your confidence grows by leaps and bounds. (And to the cyclist I, uh, encountered on my driving test? Apologies. I'll leave more room next time.)

Keeping Good Notes

When I start working with a student, I can usually tell how interested they are in maths by taking a look at their notebook or exercise book. This isn't a foolproof rule (some of my brightest students have the same kind of messy scrawl as I do), but the neater — and more attractive — you make your notes, the easier you can read them, the easier you can see what you've done and the easier you can pick up on mistakes.

Deciding on a notebook or a computer

Where you keep your notes is up to you. Have a think about the following and see what sounds best for your way of working:

- **Notebook:** The advantage of working on paper is that your only limit is what you can do with pens and pencils. If you need a picture of a duck, you draw a duck. If you need to do some long division, you write out the sum. Maths isn't like English: The notes you take are completely different. Maths thrives on pictures and sums more than on sentences — although there is always some explaining to do. A notebook is pretty easy to carry around with you too.

- **Loose paper:** Working on loose sheets of paper can avoid the two negative issues associated with working in a notebook: Organising your notes if you revisit a topic is difficult in a notebook, and 'I forgot my notebook' is a bit too easy to use as an excuse for not doing any work. Working on loose sheets of paper still has a drawback: Losing sheets of paper or finding notes all over the house happens quite a bit. If you're much better at staying neat and organised than I am, using loose paper can be a really good approach.

- **Computer:** Taking notes on a computer is a bit trickier than using paper because drawing pictures and writing formulas on screen isn't easy. But working on a computer has advantages: If you have bad handwriting (like I do), typed notes are much easier to read — and you can search and edit your work without too many headaches.

I use a mixture of these approaches. When I learn something new, I take notes on paper or in a notebook. When I revise a topic, I type up notes on my computer.

Recording the language of maths

In some ways, maths is like a foreign language. Dutch, maybe. It has a lot of words in common with English, and some of it even looks enough like English for you to read it ... but then in other places it descends into unpronounceable chaos that makes no sense at all. Worse yet, some of the words you think you recognise aren't quite as they seem or have more precise meanings than you think.

Unfortunately, I don't know of anywhere you can go to immerse yourself in maths culture and language for a few months until you speak the lingo fluently. (And you can only watch *Good Will Hunting* or *A Beautiful Mind* so many times before you go crazy.)

Instead, I suggest you keep a vocabulary book at the back of your notebook or on your computer. Whenever you come across a maths word that you don't know or don't quite understand, write down the word on one side of the page and write its definition on the other side.

Record cards are an excellent way to learn maths vocab. Write the word on one side of a card and the meaning on the other. Run through the cards every so often until you can rattle off the definition without thinking.

Chapter 2

Getting Bigger and Smaller: Sequences, Addition and Subtraction

. . . .

In This Chapter

▶ Tuning into number sequences

▶ Starting to get your head around addition and subtraction

▶ Working with the number line

▶ Understanding some simple tricks to remember simple sums

▶ Working up to adding and subtracting bigger numbers

. . . .

*O*ne useful characteristic about numbers is that they're *conceptual,* which means that, in an important sense, they're all in your head. (This fact probably won't get you out of having to know about them, though — nice try!) For example, you can picture three of anything: Three cats, three cricket balls, three cannibals, three planets. But just try to picture the concept of three all by itself, and you find it's impossible. Oh, sure, you can picture the numeral 3, but the *threeness* itself — much like love or beauty or honour — is beyond direct understanding. But when you understand the *concept* of three (or four, or a million), you have access to an incredibly powerful system for understanding the world of mathematics.

In this chapter, I discuss a few common *number sequences* and show you how these connect with simple math *operations* like addition and subtraction.

Adding things up and taking them away are the two most fundamental skills in arithmetic. If you master these skills — just two sides of the same coin — you'll find the rest of this book much, much easier than it would be without them.

This chapter covers adding and taking away using a number line for small values. I also give you some hints on memorising some important sums. After all, counting on your fingers is totally acceptable — but it's much slower than being able to recall facts straightaway.

Finally in this chapter, you get some practice at dealing with big numbers. I take some time to show you not only how to add and subtract big numbers but also why the methods work.

Understanding Number Sequences

Historians believe that the first number systems came into being at the same time as agriculture and commerce. Before that, people in prehistoric, hunter-gatherer societies were pretty much content to identify bunches of things as 'a lot' or 'a little'. Moving on from counting commodities, humans soon put numbers to use in a wide range of applications. Numbers were useful for measuring distances, counting money, amassing an army, levying taxes, building pyramids, and lots more.

But beyond their many uses for understanding the external world, numbers have an internal order all their own. So numbers are not only an *invention*, but equally also a *discovery*: A landscape that seems to exist independently, with its own structure, mysteries and even perils.

One path into this new and often strange world is the *number sequence*: An arrangement of numbers according to a rule. In the following sections, I introduce you to a variety of number sequences that are useful for making sense of numbers.

Evening the odds

One of the first facts you probably heard about numbers is that all of them are either even or odd. For example, you can split an even number of marbles *evenly* into two equal piles. But when you try to divide an odd number of marbles the same way, you always have one *odd*, leftover marble. Here are the first few even numbers:

> 2 4 6 8 10 12 14 16 ...

You can easily keep the sequence of even numbers going as long as you like. Starting with the number 2, keep adding 2 to get the next number.

Similarly, here are the first few odd numbers:

1 3 5 7 9 11 13 15 ...

The sequence of odd numbers is just as simple to generate. Starting with the number 1, keep adding 2 to get the next number.

Patterns of even or odd numbers are the simplest number patterns around, which is why kids often figure out the difference between even and odd numbers soon after learning to count.

When I planned this chapter, I thought there could be hardly any real-life use for knowing about even and odd numbers. Then, this morning, I went out to try to find a new student's house. Wandering down the student's road, I noticed a sign saying 'ODD NUMBERS 15–37' — so I knew Eric's house (number 29) was in that particular side street. But odd and even numbers have more use than simply finding a friend's house. You can also use the concept of odd and even numbers to check whether your answer to an addition or take-away sum makes sense.

Try adding two numbers of the same 'flavour' — an odd number plus an odd number, or an even number plus an even number. Here are a few examples:

$$7 + 5 = 12$$
$$14 + 6 = 20$$
$$9 + 9 = 18$$

The answer is always an even number.

The same happens if you take away an odd number from an odd number, or an even number from an even number:

$$7 - 5 = 2$$
$$14 - 6 = 8$$
$$9 - 9 = 0$$

The answer is always an even number.

Now see what happens when we work with numbers of mixed flavours:

$$4 + 7 = 11$$
$$16 - 7 = 9$$
$$12 + 3 = 15$$

You get odd numbers. Perhaps you saw that coming. Whenever you add or take away numbers of different flavours, you get an odd number.

Counting by threes, fours, fives and so on

When you get used to the concept of counting by numbers greater than 1, you can run with it. For example, here's what counting by threes, fours and fives looks like:

Threes: 3 6 9 12 15 18 21 24 ...

Fours: 4 8 12 16 20 24 28 32 ...

Fives: 5 10 15 20 25 30 35 40 ...

Counting by a given number is a good way to begin learning the multiplication table for that number, especially for the numbers you're kind of sketchy on. (In general, people seem to have the most trouble multiplying by 7, but 8 and 9 are also unpopular.) In Chapter 3, I show you a few tricks for memorising the multiplication table once and for all.

Getting square with square numbers

When you study maths, sooner or later, you probably want to use visual aids to help you see what numbers are telling you. (Later in this book, I show you how one picture can be worth a thousand numbers when I discuss geometry in Chapter 12 and graphing in Chapter 13.)

The tastiest visual aids you'll ever find are those little square cheese-flavoured crackers. (You probably have a box sitting somewhere in the pantry. If not, plain crackers or any other square food works just as well.) Shake a bunch out of a box and place the little squares together to make bigger squares. Figure 2-1 shows the first few.

Figure 2-1:
Square
numbers.

| 1 |

| 1 | 2 |
| 3 | 4 |

1	2	3
4	5	6
7	8	9

1	2	3	4
5	6	7	8
9	10	11	12
13	14	15	16

1	2	3	4	5
6	7	8	9	10
11	12	13	14	15
16	17	18	19	20
21	22	23	24	25

Voilà! The square numbers:

1 4 9 16 25 36 49 64 ...

TIP

You get a *square number* by multiplying a number by itself, so knowing the square numbers is another handy way to remember part of the multiplication table. Although you probably remember without help that $2 \times 2 = 4$, you may be sketchy on some of the higher numbers, such as $7 \times 7 = 49$. Knowing the square numbers gives you another way to etch that multiplication table forever into your brain, as I show you in Chapter 3.

Square numbers are also a great first step on the way to understanding exponents, which I introduce later in this chapter and explain in more detail in Chapter 3.

Composing yourself with composite numbers

Some numbers can be placed in rectangular patterns. Mathematicians probably should call numbers like these 'rectangular numbers', but instead they chose the term *composite numbers*. For example, 12 is a composite number because you can place 12 objects in rectangles of two different shapes, as in Figure 2-2.

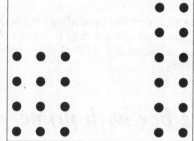

Figure 2-2: The number 12 laid out in two rectangular patterns.

As with square numbers, arranging numbers in visual patterns like this tells you something about how multiplication works. In this case, by counting the sides of both rectangles, you find out the following:

$3 \times 4 = 12$

$2 \times 6 = 12$

Similarly, other numbers such as 8 and 15 can also be arranged in rectangles, as in Figure 2-3.

Figure 2-3: Composite numbers, such as 8 and 15, can form rectangles.

As you can see, both these numbers are quite happy being placed in boxes with at least two rows and two columns. And these visual patterns show this:

$$2 \times 4 = 8$$
$$3 \times 5 = 15$$

The word *composite* means that these numbers are *composed of* smaller numbers. For example, the number 15 is composed of 3 and 5 — that is, when you multiply these two smaller numbers, you get 15. Here are all the composite numbers from 1 to 16:

   4 6 8 9 10 12 14 15 16

Notice that all the square numbers (refer to the preceding section) also count as composite numbers, because you can arrange them in boxes with at least two rows and two columns. Additionally, a lot of other non–square numbers are also composite numbers.

Stepping out of the box with prime numbers

Some numbers are stubborn. Like certain people you may know, these numbers — called *prime numbers* — resist being placed in any sort of a box. Look at how Figure 2-4 depicts the number 13, for example.

Figure 2-4:
Unlucky
13, a prime
example of
a number
that refuses
to fit in
a box.

Try as you may, you just can't make a rectangle out of 13 objects. (That fact may be one reason the number 13 got a bad reputation as unlucky.) Here are all the prime numbers fewer than 20:

2 3 5 7 11 13 17 19

As you can see, the list of prime numbers fills the gaps left by the composite numbers (refer to the preceding section). Therefore, every counting number is either prime or composite. The only exception is the number 1, which is neither prime nor composite.

Multiplying quickly with exponents

Here's an old question with an answer that may surprise you: Suppose you took a job that paid you just 1 cent the first day, 2 cents the second day, 4 cents the third day, and so on, doubling the amount every day, like this:

1 2 4 8 16 32 64 128 256 512 ...

As you can see, in the first ten days of work, you would've earned a little more than $10 (actually, $10.23 — but who's counting?). How much would you earn in 30 days? Your answer may well be, 'I wouldn't take a lousy job like that in the first place.' At first glance, this looks like a good answer, but here's a glimpse at your second ten days' earnings:

... 1,024　2,048　4,096　8,192　6,384　32,768　65,536　131,072
262,144　524,288 ...

By the end of the second 10 days, your total earnings would be over $10,000. And by the end of 30 days, your earnings would top out around $10,000,000! How does this happen? Through the magic of exponents (also called *powers*). Each new number in the sequence is obtained by multiplying the previous number by 2:

$$2^1 = 2$$
$$2^2 = 2 \times 2 = 4$$
$$2^3 = 2 \times 2 \times 2 = 8$$
$$2^4 = 2 \times 2 \times 2 \times 2 = 16$$

As you can see, the notation 2^4 means *multiply 2 by itself 4 times.*

You can use exponents on numbers other than 2. Here's another sequence you may be familiar with:

1   10   100   1,000   10,000   100,000   1,000,000   ...

In this sequence, every number is 10 times greater than the number before it. You can also generate these numbers using exponents:

$$10^1 = 10$$
$$10^2 = 10 \times 10 = 100$$
$$10^3 = 10 \times 10 \times 10 = 1,000$$
$$10^4 = 10 \times 10 \times 10 \times 10 = 10,000$$

This sequence is important for defining *place value,* the basis of the decimal number system, which shows up when I discuss decimals in Chapter 7. You find out more about exponents in Chapter 3.

It All Adds Up: Addition and Subtraction

Adding is what happens when you combine two groups of similar objects together. If I own four books and I buy two more, I end up with six of them: $4 + 2 = 6$. You add up when you gain or increase something.

One of the neat things about maths is that the rules hold whatever you add — it doesn't have to be books. If you start with four cups of coffee and drink two more, you've drunk six cups of coffee. If you walk 4 kilometres and then walk two more, you've walked 6 kilometres. Whatever the things are, if you start with four of them and add two more, you end up with six.

You have to be careful when you're adding and taking away that the things you're working with are similar — you can't really add two apples to four oranges and get a meaningful answer without bending the rules (you could say it makes six pieces of fruit, but that's a bit of a cheat). It really doesn't make sense to add two clouds to four phones, or to add 2 kilometres to 4 grams.

You probably have a good idea about taking away too. Taking away, or subtracting, happens when you decrease, lose or spend things. If I have six books and my cheapskate friend borrows two of them, I wind up with four books: $6 - 2 = 4$.

Adding things up

Addition is the first operation you find out about, and it's almost everybody's favourite. It's simple, friendly and straightforward. No matter how much you worry about maths, you've probably never lost a minute of sleep over addition. Addition is all about bringing things together, which is a positive goal. For example, suppose you and I are standing in line to buy tickets for a movie. I have $30 and you have only $10. I could lord it over you and make you feel crummy that I can go to the movies and you can't. Or, instead, you and I can join forces, adding together my $30 and your $10 to make $40. Now, not only can we both see the movie, but we may even be able to buy some popcorn, too.

Addition uses only one sign — the plus sign (+): Your equation may read $2 + 3 = 5$, or $12 + 2 = 14$, or $27 + 44 = 71$, but the plus sign always means the same thing.

When you add two numbers together, those two numbers are called *addends*, and the result is called the *sum*. So, in the first example, the addends are 2 and 3, and the sum is 5.

Take it away: Subtracting

Subtraction is usually the second operation you discover, and it's not much harder than addition. Still, there's something negative about subtraction — it's all about who has more and who has less. Suppose you and I have been running on treadmills at the gym. I'm happy because I ran 5 kilometres, but then you start bragging that you ran 12 kilometres. You subtract and tell me that I should be very impressed that you ran 7 kilometres farther than I did. (But with an attitude like that, don't be surprised if you come back from the showers to find your running shoes filled with liquid soap!)

As with addition, subtraction has only one sign: The minus sign (–). You end up with equations such as $4 - 1 = 3$, and $14 - 13 = 1$, and $93 - 74 = 19$.

When you subtract one number from another, the result is called the *difference*. This term makes sense when you think about it: When you subtract, you find the difference between a higher number and a lower one.

One of the first facts you probably heard about subtraction is that you can't take away more than you start with. In that case, the second number can't be larger than the first. And if the two numbers are the same, the result is always 0. For example, $3 - 3 = 0$; $11 - 11 = 0$; and $1,776 - 1,776 = 0$. Later someone breaks the news that you *can* take away more than you have. When you do, though, you need to place a minus sign in front of the difference to show that you have a negative number — that is, a number below 0:

$$4 - 5 = -1$$
$$10 - 13 = -3$$
$$88 - 99 = -11$$

When subtracting a larger number from a smaller number, remember the words *switch* and *negate*: You *switch* the order of the two numbers and do the subtraction as you normally would, but at the end, you *negate* the result by attaching a minus sign. For example, to find $10 - 13$, you switch the order of these two numbers, giving you $13 - 10$, which equals 3; then you negate this result to get –3. That's why $10 - 13 = -3$.

The minus sign does double duty, so don't get confused. When you stick a minus sign between two numbers, it means the first number minus the second number. But when you attach it to the front of a number, it means that this number is a negative number.

I also go into more detail on negative numbers in Chapter 4.

Looking at the number line

As kids outgrow counting on their fingers (and use them only when trying to remember the names of all seven dwarfs), teachers often substitute a picture of the first ten numbers in order, like the one in Figure 2-5.

This way of organising numbers is called the *number line*. People often see their first number line — usually made of brightly coloured construction paper — pasted above the blackboard in school. The basic number line

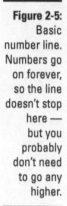

Figure 2-5:
Basic
number line.
Numbers go
on forever,
so the line
doesn't stop
here —
but you
probably
don't need
to go any
higher.

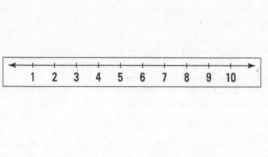

provides a visual image of the *counting numbers* (also called the *natural numbers*), the numbers greater than 0. You can use it to show how numbers get bigger in one direction and smaller in the other.

Some people like to draw the number line vertically, starting with zero at the bottom of the page and counting up the line, like counting floors in a skyscraper. In this book, I work from left to right, mainly because it takes up less space.

I like to remember which way round the number line goes by saying 'the left is less (or lower)' — the three Ls.

You don't actually need to draw a number line. A ruler serves as a perfectly good substitute. A 30-centimetre ruler has all the numbers from 0 to 30 written out ready for you to count on as you please.

In this section, I show you how to use the number line to understand a few basic but important ideas about numbers.

Adding and subtracting on the number line

You can use the number line to demonstrate simple addition and subtraction. These first steps in maths become a lot more concrete with a visual aid. Here's the main point to remember:

✔ As you go *right*, the numbers go *up*, which is *addition* (+).

✔ As you go *left*, the numbers go *down*, which is *subtraction* (–).

For example, $2 + 3$ means you *start at* 2 and *jump up* 3 spaces to 5, as Figure 2-6 illustrates.

Figure 2-6:
Moving through the number line from left to right.

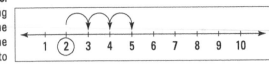

Here, in full, is the method for adding:

1. **Put your pen on the number line on the first number in your sum.**

2. **Move to the right by the number of spaces indicated by the second number in your sum.**

3. **Where you end up on the number line is the answer.**

As another example, $6 - 4$ means *start at* 6 and *jump down* 4 spaces to 2. That is, $6 - 4 = 2$. See Figure 2-7.

Figure 2-7:
Moving through the number line from right to left.

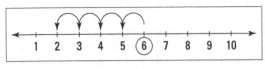

Here, in full, are the steps for taking away:

1. **Put your pen on the number line on the first number in your sum.**

2. **Move to the left by the number of spaces indicated by the second number in your sum.**

3. **Where you end up on the number line is the answer.**

The steps for adding and taking away are very similar — the only difference is the direction in which you move.

You can use these simple up and down rules repeatedly to solve a longer string of added and subtracted numbers. For example, $3 + 1 - 2 + 4 - 3 - 2$

means 3, *up* 1, *down* 2, *up* 4, *down* 3 and *down* 2. In this case, the number line shows you that $3 + 1 - 2 + 4 - 3 - 2 = 1$.

Getting a handle on nothing, or zero

An important addition to the number line is the number 0, which means *nothing, zilch, nada*. Step back a moment and consider the bizarre concept of nothing. For one thing — as more than one philosopher has pointed out — by definition, *nothing* doesn't exist! Yet we routinely label it with the number 0, as in Figure 2-8.

Figure 2-8:
The number line starting at 0 and continuing with 1, 2, 3, ... 10.

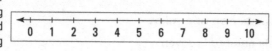

Actually, mathematicians have an even more precise labelling of *nothing* than zero. It's called the *empty set*, which is sort of the mathematical version of a box containing nothing.

Nothing sure is a heavy trip to lay on little kids, but they don't seem to mind. They understand quickly that when you have three toy trucks and someone else takes away all three of them, you're left with zero trucks. That is, $3 - 3 = 0$. Or, placing this on the number line, $3 - 3$ means start at 3 and go down 3, as in Figure 2-9.

Figure 2-9:
Starting at 3 and moving down three.

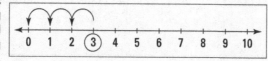

Seeing how close numbers are

Using the number line for taking away lets you see how far apart two numbers are. Some people call taking away 'finding the difference' — this method shows you why.

If you need to figure out 19 – 17, you don't really want to have to count back 17 spaces. Instead, look at the number line and see directly that you'd need to take two steps to get from 17 to 19 — so 19 – 17 = 2.

This technique works only with taking away. Don't be tempted to try it with adding.

Adding and subtracting with two rulers

You can, with a bit of work, use two rulers to add and take away small numbers. To add two numbers (let's say 7 + 5, as in Figure 2-10), here's what you do:

1. **Find the first number on one ruler.**

   For our sum, this number is seven.

2. **Find the second number on the other ruler.**

   For our sum, this number is five.

3. **Put the two numbers next to each other.**

4. **Find the zero on either ruler and read the number it's next to.**

   For our sum, this number is 12. So, 7 + 5 = 12.

Some rulers have centimetres on one side and inches on the other — make sure you use the centimetre side of both rulers!

Figure 2-10:
Adding
seven and
five with the
help of two
rulers.

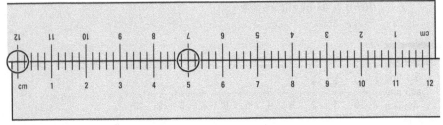

Taking away two numbers is slightly different. Let's do 7 – 5, as in Figure 2-11:

1. **Find the first number on one ruler.**

   For our sum, this number is seven.

2. **Put the zero of the other ruler next to the first number.**

   For our sum, put the zero next to the seven.

3. **Find the second number on the second ruler.**

   For our sum, this number is five.

4. **Read off the number the second number is next to.**

   For our sum, this number is 2. So, $7 - 5 = 2$.

Figure 2-11:
Doing the
sum $7 - 5$
with two
rulers.

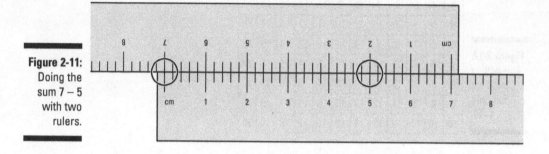

Remembering Some Simple Sums

Using the number line or the ruler method that I describe in the preceding sections is all well and good if you have all the time in the world. But when your sums involve big numbers, you may need to do several small-number sums one after the other. Before you know it, you've spent hours on a sum when you could have been taking a walk in the park.

I don't usually recommend remembering things you can easily look up, but you can save yourself literally days of work if you know your number facts — that is, all of the adding sums up to $10 + 10$.

If you think this sounds like a lot of work, I'm afraid you're right: There are 100 of those pesky sums. I have some good news, though: Addition is symmetrical — it doesn't matter which way round you add things. For example, $4 + 7$ is the same as $7 + 4$ (they both make 11). So at least you only have to remember about half as many facts as you thought.

Meeting the adding table

Figure 2-12 shows an adding table to help you learn your number facts. Adding with the table is easy — you find the first number you want to add in the top row and the second number you want to add in the far-left column, and then follow down and across with your fingers until they meet.

+	0	1	2	3	4	5	6	7	8	9	10
0	0	1	2	3	4	5	6	7	8	9	10
1	1	2	3	4	5	6	7	8	9	10	11
2	2	3	4	5	6	7	8	9	10	11	12
3	3	4	5	6	7	8	9	10	11	12	13
4	4	5	6	7	8	9	10	11	12	13	14
5	5	6	7	8	9	10	11	12	13	14	15
6	6	7	8	9	10	11	12	13	14	15	16
7	7	8	9	10	11	12	13	14	15	16	17
8	8	9	10	11	12	13	14	15	16	17	18
9	9	10	11	12	13	14	15	16	17	18	19
10	10	11	12	13	14	15	16	17	18	19	20

Figure 2-12:
The adding
table for
numbers
1–10.

You can take away with the table too, but this takes a little more practice: Find the first number in the body of the table, and notice how that number is repeated through the grid in a diagonal stripe. Go along the stripe until the column you're in has the second number at the top of it. Read across to the left — the answer is at the start of the row. I show you how to solve 16 – 8 using this method in Figure 2-13.

+	0	1	2	3	4	5	6	7	8	9	10
0	0	1	2	3	4	5	6	7	8	9	10
1	1	2	3	4	5	6	7	8	9	10	11
2	2	3	4	5	6	7	8	9	10	11	12
3	3	4	5	6	7	8	9	10	11	12	13
4	4	5	6	7	8	9	10	11	12	13	14
5	5	6	7	8	9	10	11	12	13	14	15
6	6	7	8	9	10	11	12	13	14	15	16
7	7	8	9	10	11	12	13	14	15	16	17
8	8	9	10	11	12	13	14	15	16	17	18
9	9	10	11	12	13	14	15	16	17	18	19
10	10	11	12	13	14	15	16	17	18	19	20

Figure 2-13:
Solving
16 – 8 using
the adding
table.

Unfortunately, you won't always have the adding table with you. So you really do need to learn all the sums in it.

You might think that spending time on adding and taking away small numbers seems a bit basic. Don't beat yourself up about having to learn stuff that seems simple. If you ever watch a football team training, you'll see the players spend hours making simple kicks and passes to each other and running back and forth. Most of the players have done this stuff since they were six (or younger), but they still practise so that kicking, marking and running is natural and easy when they play in a real match. Spending time reminding yourself how to do the basics of maths is absolutely fine. In fact, I wish all my students would spend some time on this!

Learning your adding facts

Luckily, you can break down the adding table a bit. Start with the first column — adding one. You already know how to do that without thinking: You just go to the next number. So you hardly need to learn that column of the table.

Now look at the last row — adding ten. Adding ten is simple: You just put a one in front of the original number. For example, $2 + 10 = 12$. And $7 + 10 = 17$. (The exception is $10 + 10 = 20$, but you probably know that.)

If you're happy to count backwards, you can add nine — just add ten and count back by one. So, to do $6 + 9$, you can say '6 + 10 is 16. Count back 1 to get 15.' You can check this idea works with some of the other sums in the adding table.

So, now you actually only have 28 number facts to learn — but you may wonder how you will learn them.

I suspect that if you enjoy sitting in rows at school reciting 'seven plus one equals eight, seven plus two equals nine ...' for hours on end, you probably aren't reading this chapter. That method is effective ... but deadly dull.

My way of teaching makes things a bit more interesting: I want you to play some cards:

1. **Find a pack of cards.**

2. **Deal two cards.**

3. **Find the score of each of the cards.**

   An ace is worth one, and the court cards (jack, queen and king) are all worth ten.

4. **Add up the scores of the two cards.**

   If you can work out the score in your head without looking at the adding table or counting, pat yourself on the back. If not, write the sum in your notebook to look back at later.

5. **Go back to Step 2 until you run out of cards.**

Play this card game every day for a week or so. The more you do it, the fewer questions you will need to write down in your book — which means you're learning. Go you!

Tackling your take-away facts

To learn the take-away facts, I need you to play some more cards — with a twist (see what I did there?):

1. **Find a pack of cards.**

2. **Deal three cards — two of them together and one below them.**

3. **Figure out the score of each of the cards.**

   An ace is worth one and the court cards are worth ten each.

4. **Add up the scores on the first two cards.**

5. **If the third card is smaller than your two-card total from Step 4, take away the third card score from the two-card score. If the third card is bigger than your two-card total, take away the two-card score from the third card score.**

   For example, if you deal 6, 7 and 4, your sums are $6 + 7 = 13$, and then $13 - 4 = 9$. If you deal 2, 3 and a king, your sums are $2 + 3 = 5$, and then $10 - 5 = 5$.

   If you work out the score in your head without looking at the adding table or counting, pat yourself on the back. If not, write down the sum in your notebook.

6. **Go back to Step 2 until you run out of cards.**

   You'll have one card left over, so just ignore that one. Do this subtraction game every day for a week — you'll quickly get the hang of taking away.

Increasing your success with flash cards

I like to use flash cards — little cards with a question or sum on one side and the answer on the back. You can buy ready-made flash cards, find free printable ones online, or make your own out of index cards or cut-up paper.

Here's how to use your flash cards to help your adding and taking away sums:

1. **Shuffle all the flash cards you want to practise.**

2. **Answer the question on the top one.**

3. **Check the answer.**

   If you get it right straightaway, put that card to one side; if not, put the card to the back of the pile.

4. **Go back to Step 2 until you've put all the cards to one side.**

The neat thing about the flash-card method is that it makes you practise the sums you need to practise more than the ones you know by heart.

Try working with flash cards against the clock. Seeing how quickly you get through the pack as you practise can be a great motivator.

What to do when you forget

Even with all the preparation in the world, you sometimes forget your sums. It happens to me, it'll happen to you, it happens to Stephen Hawking. Instead of getting upset or frustrated, finding other ways to approach a question is a good idea.

The best strategy is probably to go back to the two-rulers method or simply count on your fingers. But although these are perfectly good once-in-a-while strategies, you probably don't want to be doing them every time — otherwise, your sums take hours.

When you forget a sum, write it down in your notebook. Simply writing down the sum and flagging it up as something you'd like to know better helps your brain get hold of the information.

Don't beat yourself up about forgetting or making mistakes! Very few people are lucky enough to learn everything perfectly the first time, or even the tenth.

Super-Size Me: Working with Bigger Numbers

The sums up to 10 + 10 are so important. Most of the sums you do involve small numbers (checking you haven't lost a finger in a washing-up accident, figuring out whether you have enough eggs for an omelette — the sums you do without even thinking about them). Importantly, these small-number sums are key building blocks to working with bigger numbers.

When you have more of a handle on simple addition and subtraction, and some tools for remembering simple sums, you're ready to move on to larger numbers. The following sections show you how.

Adding and taking away bigger numbers

For the purposes of this section, imagine travelling in a country where only three types of banknote are available: $100, $10 and $1.

In your cash drawer you have $125 — a $100 note, two $10 notes and five $1 notes. You can read the first number of $125 as how many $100s you have, the second number as how many $10s and the third as how many $1s. For your birthday a generous friend gives you $213 to celebrate. He gives you two $100 notes, one $10 note and three $1 notes.

You had one $100 and have just added two, so now you have $1 + 2 = 3$; three $100 notes. You can do the same for the $10s: You had two and your friend gave you one, so now you have $2 + 1 = 3$; three $10 notes. Likewise, you had five $1 notes. Your friend gave you three, so now you have $5 + 3 = 8$; eight $1 notes.

Altogether, you have three $100s, three $10s and eight $1s, making a grand total of $338. Notice how you can just write down the numbers of each note to give you your final answer.

Taking away uses the same kind of idea. You have $275 saved up and you want to buy a new game for your Xbox, which costs $64. In your cash drawer you find two $100 notes. The game doesn't need any of them, so you have $2 - 0 = 2$ left.

You have seven $10s. You need six of them, so you have $7 - 6 = 1$ left.

And you have five $1 notes, of which you have to use four, so you have $5 - 4 = 1$ left.

Altogether, that leaves you with $211.

Knowing your adding and taking-away facts up to $10 + 10$ and $20 - 10$ will be extremely useful in this section. If you're not confident, keep practising — it'll soon come!

The basic recipe for adding numbers is to split them up into hundreds, tens and units — or $100 notes, $10 notes and $1 notes, as per the preceding examples — and add each type (or each kind of banknote) separately.

In line: Adding larger numbers in columns

When you want to add larger numbers, stack them on top of each other so that the ones digits line up in a column, the tens digits line up in another column, and so on. Then add column by column, starting from the ones column on the right. Not surprisingly, this method is called *column addition*. Here's how you add 55 + 31 + 12. First add the ones column:

$$
\begin{array}{r}
55 \\
31 \\
+12 \\
\hline
8
\end{array}
$$

Next, move to the tens column:

$$
\begin{array}{r}
55 \\
31 \\
+12 \\
\hline
98
\end{array}
$$

This problem shows you that 55 + 31 + 12 = 98.

For the sake of your sums, try to keep your columns neat. Give yourself plenty of space so you don't mix up columns. Use grid paper if it helps.

Carry on: Dealing with two-digit answers

Sometimes when you're adding a column, the sum is a two-digit number. In that case, you need to write down the ones digit of that number and carry the tens digit over to the next column to the left — that is, write this digit above the column so you can add it with the rest of the numbers in that column. For example, suppose you want to add 376 + 49 + 18. In the ones column, 6 + 9 + 8 = 23, so write down the 3 and carry the 2 over to the top of the tens column:

$$
\begin{array}{r}
2 \\
376 \\
49 \\
+\ 18 \\
\hline
3
\end{array}
$$

Now continue by adding the tens column. In this column, $2 + 7 + 4 + 1 = 14$, so write down the 4 and carry the 1 over to the top of the hundreds column:

```
  12
 376
  49
+18
----
  43
```

Continue adding in the hundreds column:

```
  12
 376
  49
+ 18
----
 443
```

This problem shows you that $376 + 49 + 18 = 443$.

Columns and stacks: Subtracting larger numbers

To subtract larger numbers, stack one on top of the other as you do with addition. (For subtraction, however, don't stack more than two numbers — put the larger number on top and the smaller one underneath it.)
For example, suppose you want to subtract $386 - 54$. To start, stack the two numbers and begin subtracting in the ones column: $6 - 4 = 2$:

```
 386
 -54
----
   2
```

Next, move to the tens column and subtract $8 - 5$ to get 3:

```
 386
 -54
----
  32
```

Finally, move to the hundreds column. This time, $3 - 0 = 3$:

```
 386
 -54
----
 332
```

This problem shows you that $386 - 54 = 332$.

Can you spare a ten? Borrowing to subtract

Sometimes the top digit in a column is smaller than the bottom digit in that column. In that case, you need to borrow from the next column to the left. Borrowing is a two-step process:

1. **Subtract 1 from the top number in the column directly to the left.**

   Cross out the number you're borrowing from, subtract 1, and write the answer above the number you crossed out.

2. **Add 10 to the top number in the column you were working in.**

For example, suppose you want to subtract 386 − 94. The first step is to subtract 4 from 6 in the ones column, which gives you 2:

$$\begin{array}{r} 38\mathbf{6} \\ -94 \\ \hline 2 \end{array}$$

When you move to the tens column, however, you find that you need to subtract 8 − 9. Because 8 is smaller than 9, you need to borrow from the hundreds column. First, cross out the 3 and replace it with a 2, because 3 − 1 = 2:

$$\begin{array}{r} 2 \\ \cancel{3}86 \\ -\;94 \\ \hline 2 \end{array}$$

Next, place a 1 in front of the 8, changing it to an 18, because 8 + 10 = 18:

$$\begin{array}{r} 2 \\ \cancel{3}\mathbf{1}86 \\ -\;94 \\ \hline 2 \end{array}$$

Now you can subtract in the tens column: 18 − 9 = 9:

$$\begin{array}{r} 21\mathbf{8}6 \\ -\;\mathbf{9}4 \\ \hline \mathbf{9}2 \end{array}$$

The final step is simple: $2 - 0 = 2$:

$$\begin{array}{r} 2186 \\ -\ 94 \\ \hline 292 \end{array}$$

Therefore, $386 - 94 = 292$.

In some cases, the column directly to the left may not have anything to lend. Suppose, for instance, that you want to subtract $1,002 - 398$. Beginning in the ones column, you find that you need to subtract $2 - 8$. Because 2 is smaller than 8, you need to borrow from the next column to the left. But the digit in the tens column is a 0, so you can't borrow from there because the cupboard is bare, so to speak:

$$\begin{array}{r} 10\mathbf{02} \\ -3\mathbf{98} \end{array}$$

When borrowing from the next column isn't an option, you need to borrow from the nearest non-zero column to the left.

In this example, the column you need to borrow from is the thousands column. First, cross out the 1 and replace it with a 0. Then place a 1 in front of the 0 in the hundreds column:

$$\begin{array}{r} \mathbf{0} \\ \cancel{1}\ 10\ 0\ 2 \\ -3\ 9\ 8 \\ \hline \end{array}$$

Now cross out the 10 and replace it with a 9. Place a 1 in front of the 0 in the tens column:

$$\begin{array}{r} 0\ \ \ \mathbf{9} \\ \cancel{1}\ \cancel{10}\ 102 \\ -3\ \ \ 98 \\ \hline \end{array}$$

Finally, cross out the 10 in the tens column and replace it with a 9. Then place a 1 in front of the 2:

$$\begin{array}{r} 0\ \ 9\ \ \mathbf{9} \\ \cancel{1}\ \cancel{10}\ \cancel{10}\ 12 \\ -3\ \ 9\ \ 8 \\ \hline \end{array}$$

At last, you can begin subtracting in the ones column: $12 - 8 = 4$:

```
 0   9   9
 1  10  10  12
    -3   9   8
 ─────────────
              4
```

Then subtract in the tens column: $9 - 9 = 0$:

```
 0   9   9
 1  10  10  12
    -3   9   8
 ─────────────
          0   4
```

Then subtract in the hundreds column: $9 - 3 = 6$:

```
 0   9   9
 1  10  10  12
    -3   9   8
 ─────────────
      6   0   4
```

Because nothing is left in the thousands column, you don't need to subtract anything else. Therefore, $1,002 - 398 = 604$.

Chapter 3

Equal Piles: Multiplying and Dividing

. . . .

In This Chapter

▶ Understanding the basics behind multiplication and division

▶ Reintroducing yourself to the times table and multiplying with bigger numbers

▶ Working through short and long division

▶ Getting your head around the order to follow with multiple sums

. . . .

*I*magine you're at the supermarket and buy four cartons of eggs, each containing 12 eggs. You need to work out how many eggs you have altogether.

The long way to do it is to start with 12 + 12 (making 24), then add another 12 (making 36), and then add a fourth 12 — giving a total of 48.

Working like that is okay if you have only a few cartons of eggs. But if you go on to own the supermarket one day and get an order for 75 cartons of eggs, you may not want to spend your whole morning adding things up.

Instead, you can multiply or times 12 by 75 — which we write as 12 × 75. In this chapter, I show you how to multiply small numbers and then how to use that skill to multiply bigger numbers.

Multiply and times mean exactly the same thing and you can use the terms interchangeably. 'Multiply' is more technical but 'times' is easier to say.

Now imagine you have 3,600 eggs and need to put them into cartons of 12. To work out how many cartons you need, you could simply count down 12 at a time until you get to zero — but that may take all day. Instead, you can divide 3,600 by 12. In this chapter, I also tell you all you need to know about dividing.

Towards the end of the chapter, I introduce you to the idea of *order of operations* — basically, this tells you what to do first (and second) in a sum with multiple operations.

Meeting the Basics of Multiplication and Division

The prefix *multi-* means 'many' — think 'multi-player game' or 'multiplex cinema'. The suffix *-ply* means 'times' — for example, two-ply tissues. Multiply, then, means 'many times'.

'Nine times seven' simply means 'add up a list of nine sevens' — or 'add up a list of seven nines'. You can see any multiplication sum as a number of equal piles of things: The first number is how many piles you have, and the second number is how many things you have in each pile.

You may have memories of reciting times tables in earlier years at school. I was terrified of my maths teacher at primary school, even though I was good at my times tables. Every Friday, he spent half the lesson marching up and down barking out 20 questions from the times tables. We learnt them soon enough, but teaching by intimidation is hardly the method I'd recommend.

Instead, in this chapter, I show you the times tables and — just like with the adding tables (refer to Chapter 2) — give you some games to play to remember them. The times tables usually only go up to ten, so I also show you how to work with bigger numbers.

Dividing is exactly the opposite of multiplying: You take a number of things and split them into equal piles. Armies are split up into divisions. So are Aussie Rules football leagues.

So '92 divided by four' just means 'split up 92 into 4 piles and tell me how big the piles are'. Or, 'split up 92 into piles of 4, and tell me how many piles there are'. In this chapter, I show you some games to help you remember your division sums up to 100 ÷ 10, and then show you how to do division when you have bigger numbers. Again, you just need to split up piles.

In math beyond arithmetic, using parentheses without another operator stands for multiplication. The parentheses can enclose the first number, the second number, or both numbers. For example:

$$3(5) = 15 \quad \text{means } 3 \times 5 = 15$$
$$(8)7 = 56 \quad \text{means } 8 \times 7 = 56$$
$$(9)(10) = 90 \text{ means } 9 \times 10 = 90$$

This switch makes sense when you stop to consider that the letter x, which is often used in algebra, looks a lot like the multiplication sign $\times$. So in this book, when I start using x in Part IV, I also stop using $\times$ and begin using parentheses without another sign to indicate multiplication.

Remembering Your Times Tables

You may consider yourself among the multiplicationally challenged. That is, you consider being called upon to remember 9×7 a tad less appealing than being dropped from an airplane while clutching a parachute purchased from the trunk of some guy's car. If so, this section is for you.

In Chapter 2 I show you how to add big numbers by adding up a series of smaller adding sums. In this chapter, I show you how to multiply big numbers by adding a series of multiplication sums. So, first of all, you need to know your times tables — all the times sums up to 10×10. You may think this sounds like a lot to remember — 100 sums! But you have to do a lot less than you think. The times table, which I show in Figure 3-1, is symmetrical, so 4×8 is the same as 8×4 (both sums make 32).

x	0	1	2	3	4	5	6	7	8	9	10
0	0	0	0	0	0	0	0	0	0	0	0
1	0	1	2	3	4	5	6	7	8	9	10
2	0	2	4	6	8	10	12	14	16	18	20
3	0	3	6	9	12	15	18	21	24	27	30
4	0	4	8	12	16	20	24	28	32	36	40
5	0	5	10	15	20	25	30	35	40	45	50
6	0	6	12	18	24	30	36	42	48	54	60
7	0	7	14	21	28	35	42	49	56	63	70
8	0	8	16	24	32	40	48	56	64	72	80
9	0	9	18	27	36	45	54	63	72	81	90
10	0	10	20	30	40	50	60	70	80	90	100

Figure 3-1:
The times
tables up
to ten.

Follow these steps to multiply with the times table:

1. **Find the first number you want to times in the top row.**

2. **Find the second number you want to times in the far-left column.**

3. **Follow down and across with your fingers until they meet.**

4. **Where your fingers meet is your answer.**

If you've used the addition tables in Chapter 2, the times tables work just the same way.

You can divide with the times tables too — but this is a bit harder:

1. **Find the second number (the number you want to divide by) in the far-left column.**

2. **Move to the right along the table until you find the first number in the sum, the one before the divide sign.**

3. **Go up from there and find the number at the top of the column — that's your answer.**

If the first number isn't there, the sum doesn't come out exactly — so if you try to split the number into that many piles, you have some left over. For example, if you try to split 13 lollies between three children, everyone gets 4 lollies (using up 12 of the lollies) and there's 1 lolly left over. In real life, you may eat that yourself to save on arguments. In maths, you might write 13 ÷ 4 = 3 r 1. The 'r' means 'remainder' — or 'what's left over'. So 3 r 1 means 'Everyone gets three, and there's one left over.'

To find the answer when a divide doesn't come out exactly, here's what you do:

1. **Find the second number (the number you want to divide by) in the far-left column.**

2. **Find the biggest number in that row that's smaller than the number you're trying to find.**

3. **Take away the smaller number from the bigger.**

   This gives you the remainder: How much smaller it is.

4. **Write down r and then whatever the remainder is.**

5. **Read up from your smaller number.**

6. **Write the number at the top of the column in front of the r.**

I give an example of this in Figure 3-2, where I work out 70 ÷ 8. In this example, 64 is the biggest number in the row less than 70, so I read up and find the 8. This is 6 less than 70, so the answer is 8 r 6 — or eight with remainder six.

x	0	1	2	3	4	5	6	7	8	9	10
0	0	0	0	0	0	0	0	0	0	0	0
1	0	1	2	3	4	5	6	7	8	9	10
2	0	2	4	6	8	10	12	14	16	18	20
3	0	3	6	9	12	15	18	21	24	27	30
4	0	4	8	12	16	20	24	28	32	36	40
5	0	5	10	15	20	25	30	35	40	45	50
6	0	6	12	18	24	30	36	42	48	54	60
7	0	7	14	21	28	35	42	49	56	63	70
8	0	8	16	24	32	40	48	56	64	72	80
9	0	9	18	27	36	45	54	63	72	81	90
10	0	10	20	30	40	50	60	70	80	90	100

Figure 3-2:
Working out
70 ÷ 8 using
the times
tables.

Practising your times tables

Ideally, you need to remember all of the times tables. I know — it's an insufferable chore and a terrible amount of work and so unfair (at least, so my students tell me). Things aren't so bad, though.

The one times table is just the numbers themselves. So, $1 \times 1 = 1$, and $1 \times 2 = 2$, and $1 \times 3 = 3$, and so on. The ten times table is similar, but with a zero stuck on the end — so $10 \times 1 = 10$, and $10 \times 2 = 20$, and $10 \times 3 = 30$.

For the other numbers, I need you to play some cards:

1. **Find a pack of cards.**

2. **Deal two cards and find the score for each.**

   Aces count as one, and jacks, queens and kings are all ten each.

   To make the game harder but shorter, whenever you get an ace, jack, queen or king, deal another card on top straightaway.

3. **Times the numbers of the two cards together.**

   If you get the answer quickly, smile broadly. If not, write down the sum in your notebook.

4. **Go back to Step 2 until you run out of cards.**

   Try playing this game once a day for a week or two and see how it gets easier the more you play.

Introducing the short multiplication table

If the multiplication table from Figure 3-1 were smaller and a little more manageable, I'd like it a lot more. So here's my short multiplication table, in Table 3-1.

Table 3-1	The Short Multiplication Table						
	3	**4**	**5**	**6**	**7**	**8**	**9**
3	9	12	15	18	21	24	27
4		16	20	24	28	32	36
5			25	30	35	40	45
6				36	42	48	54
7					49	56	63
8						64	72
9							81

As you can see, I've gotten rid of a bunch of numbers. In fact, I've reduced the table from 100 numbers to 28. I've also shaded 11 of the numbers I've kept.

Is just slashing and burning the sacred multiplication table wise? Is it even legal? Well, of course it is! After all, the table is just a tool, like a hammer. If a hammer's too heavy to pick up, you need to buy a lighter one. Similarly, if the multiplication table is too big to work with, you need a smaller one. Besides, I've removed only the numbers you don't need. For example, the condensed table doesn't include rows or columns for 0, 1, or 2. Here's why:

- ✔ Any number multiplied by 0 is 0 (people call this trait the *zero property of multiplication*).

- ✔ Any number multiplied by 1 is that number itself (which is why mathematicians call 1 the *multiplicative identity* — because when you multiply any number by 1, the answer is identical to the number you started with).

- ✔ Multiplying by 2 is fairly easy; if you can count by 2s — 2, 4, 6, 8, 10, and so forth — you can multiply by 2.

The rest of the numbers I've gotten rid of are redundant. (And not just redundant, but also repeated, extraneous and unnecessary!) For example, any way you slice it, 3×5 and 5×3 are both 15. In my condensed table, I've simply removed the clutter.

So what's left? Just the numbers you need. These numbers include a grey row and a grey diagonal. The grey row is the 5 times table, which you probably know pretty well. (In fact, the 5s may evoke an early-childhood memory of running to find a hiding place on a warm day while one of your friends counted in a loud voice: 5, 10, 15, 20, . . .)

The numbers on the grey diagonal are the square numbers. As I discuss in Chapter 2, when you multiply any number by itself, the result is a square number. You probably know these numbers better than you think.

Getting to know the short multiplication table

In about an hour, you can make huge strides in memorising the multiplication table. To start, make a set of flash cards that give a multiplication problem on the front and the answer on the back. They may look like Figure 3-3.

Remember, you need to make only 28 flash cards — one for every example in Table 3-1. Split these 28 into two piles — a 'grey' pile with 11 cards and a 'white' pile with 17. (You don't have to colour the cards grey and white; just keep track of which pile is which, according to the shading in Table 3-1.) Then begin:

1. **5 minutes:** Work with the grey pile, going through it one card at a time. If you get the answer right, put that card on the bottom of the pile.

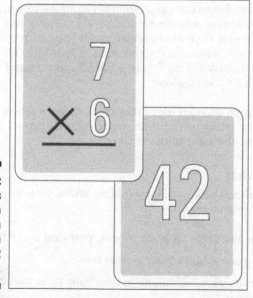

Figure 3-3: Both sides of a flash card, with 7×6 on the front and 42 on the back.

If you get it wrong, put it in the middle so you get another chance at it more quickly.

2. **10 minutes:** Switch to the white pile and work with it in the same way.

3. **15 minutes:** Repeat Steps 1 and 2.

Now take a break. Really — the break is important to rest your brain. Come back later in the day and do the same thing.

When you're done with this exercise, you should find going through all 28 cards with almost no mistakes to be fairly easy. At this point, feel free to make cards for the rest of the standard times table — you know, the cards with all the 0, 1 and 2 times tables on them and the redundant problems — mix all 100 cards together, and amaze your family and friends.

Working around mind blanks

I'm supposed to be a hot-shot maths genius. Every so often, if I'm tired or distracted or over-confident, I write down something like $2 \times 3 = 5$ and my students laugh at me. It's okay to laugh at your teacher (or tutor) when they do that. The point is, even experts forget their times tables once in a while.

So don't panic if you have a mind blank every so often. The important thing is to be able to work out the sum numbers if you blank.

The most common way to figure out (say) your seven times table is to count up in sevens while counting on your fingers: 1 times 7 is 7, 2 times 7 is 14, 3 times 7 is 21, and so on. If you're confident with your adding (which I cover in Chapter 2), this is a reliable (but slow) way to do it. This method also has the advantage that by saying '5 times 7 is 35', you remind yourself of your times-table facts as you go along.

I also have a couple of nice ways to remember certain times tables using my fingers. Luckily, these tricks work for the more difficult times tables (towards the bottom and the right of the table).

Folding under your nines

You can figure out your nine times table by folding under your fingers as you go along. Here's how it works:

1. **Put both hands on the table in front of you, pointing away from you.**

2. **Mentally number your fingers from one to ten.**

   Your left pinky is one, your left thumb is five, your right thumb is six and your right pinky is ten.

3. Ask the question 'What am I multiplying nine by?'

For example, for 9×7, you multiply nine by seven.

4. Fold the finger with that number under your hand.

In this example, the number is seven, so you fold your right index finger. (I show what I mean in Figure 3-4.)

5. Write down how many fingers and thumbs are to the left of your folded finger. This is how many tens are in the answer.

In this example, you have six fingers to the left — all of your left hand plus your right thumb.

6. Write down how many fingers and thumbs are to the right of your folded finger. This is how many singles are in the answer.

In this example, you have three fingers to the right.

7. You've just written down the answer. Awesome.

In this example, your answer is 63.

The finger-folding method works only with the nine times table. If you try it with other times tables, you get the wrong answer.

For more help when multiplying by nine, see the sidebar 'To the nines: A slick trick'.

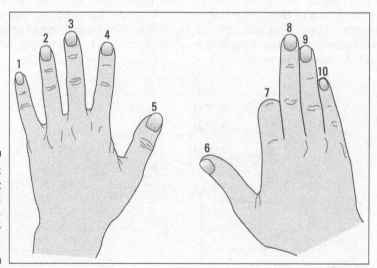

Figure 3-4:
Working out
7×9 with
the folding-
finger
method.

Pointing at the big ones

The neat little trick I describe here works for the sums from 6×6 up to 10×10. Here are the steps:

1. **Put your hands on the table, with your fingers pointing towards each other.**

2. **Mentally number the fingers on each hand.**

   Your thumbs are six and your little fingers ten.

3. **Touch the two fingers you want to multiply together to each other.**

4. **Count how many fingers on your left hand are above (on the pinky side) your touching fingers.**

5. **Count how many fingers on your right hand are above (on the pinky side) your touching fingers.**

6. **Times those two numbers together and write down the answer.**

7. **Count up the remaining fingers on both hands, including the touching ones.**

   This is how many tens you have, so write down that number with a zero after it.

8. **Bingo! Add the two numbers and you have your answer.**

If this sounds ridiculously complicated, have a look at Figure 3-5, where I show you an example for the sum 7×8. Above the touching fingers are two fingers on one hand and three on the other; these times together to make six. Including the touching fingers, five fingers are below, so you add 50 and find the answer to be 56.

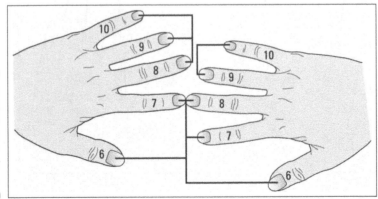

Figure 3-5:
Working
out 7×8
with the
touching-
finger
method.

You count up the fingers below and including your touching fingers to get the tens and times together the numbers above to get the singles.

Working backwards

A useful strategy for working out a forgotten times sum is to work backwards from a sum that you do know. For example, if you know that $7 \times 6 = 42$, you know that 7×7 is simply one more 7 — making 49. You can also see that 8×6 is one more 6 — making 48.

Here's the recipe when you can't remember a sum in the times table but know the one above it or below it:

1. **Work out which number is common to both of the sums.**

   For example, if you use 5×8 to work out 4×8, 8 is the common number.

2. **Work out whether the number you want is higher or lower than the one you know.**

   If you want a higher number, you need to add something on; if you want a smaller number, you need to take away.

3. **Either add or take away the common number from the answer you know.**

To the nines: A slick trick

Here's a trick to help you remember the 9 times table. To multiply any one-digit number by 9:

1. **Subtract 1 from the number being multiplied by 9 and jot down the answer.**

   For example, suppose you want to multiply 7×9. Here, $7 - 1 = \mathbf{6}$.

2. **Jot down a second number so that, together, the two numbers you wrote add up to 9. You've just written the answer you were looking for.**

Adding, you get $6 + 3 = \mathbf{9}$. So $7 \times 9 = 63$.

As another example, suppose you want to multiply 8×9:

$$8 - 1 = \mathbf{7}$$
$$7 + 2 = \mathbf{9}$$

So $8 \times 9 = 72$.

This trick works for every one-digit number except 0 (but you already know that $0 \times 9 = 0$).

Multiplying Bigger Numbers

Just like with adding (which I talk about in Chapter 2), learning your multiplication facts is a step towards working with bigger numbers. Think how frustrating it would be if you had to stop multiplying just because a sum went all the way up to 11.

In this section, I describe two stages of difficulty: Multiplying a big number by a smallish number (from one to ten), and multiplying two big numbers — which isn't difficult but is quite involved. And repetitive. And fiddly. It takes a while, which is why it's called *long multiplication*.

I give you a couple of ways of working with large times sums. Choose the one you find more useful and appealing.

Multiplying a big number by a small number

Most ways of multiplying numbers together work much the same way: You think of the bigger number as money and the smaller number as piles. You split the money into 'banknotes' and coins (ones, tens, hundreds and so on) and figure out what you end up with when you pile up each banknote the right number of times.

Piling up the money

Say your parents want to give each of your four cousins $123 for Christmas. You offer to work out how much money they need.

Start by splitting $123 into one $100 note, two $10 notes and three $1 coins. You have four cousins so you need four times as many of each note.

So, you need four $100 notes, eight $10 notes and 12 $1 coins. The $100s add up to $400, the $10s add up to $80 and the $1s add up to $12. When you add those up, you get $492.

Ignore the zeros until the end. When you want to work out 4×20, think of four piles, each with two $10 notes. That way, you just work out $4 \times 2 = 8$; so you have eight $10 notes, making $80.

Using the grid method

Another way of doing bigger times sums is to use the grid method — which happens to be my favourite. The grid method is also called the lattice method. Here's the recipe:

1. **Draw out a grid as many squares wide as the bigger number has digits, and as tall as the number of digits in the smaller number.**

   For example, for 123×4, the grid is three squares wide and one square tall. Give yourself plenty of room to work.

2. **Split the big number into banknotes as I describe in the previous section and write the amount of each at the top of each row.**

   For our example, you write 100 at the top of the first column, 20 at the top of the second column, and 3 at the top of the third column.

3. **Write the small number at the far left of the row.**

4. **In each square of the grid, write down what you get if you times the number at the top of the column by the number at the far left of the row.**

   Remember to ignore the zeros until the end.

5. **Add up all of the amounts you have to see your answer.**

I show an example of the using the grid method in Figure 3-6.

Figure 3-6:
Doing
123×4
using the
grid method.

x	100	20	3
4			

x	100	20	3	
4	400	80	12	400
				80
				+ 12
				492

Working the way you (and your parents) were likely taught

The standard way you were likely taught in class looks like this:

1. **Set the question out correctly, lining up the columns.**

   Grid paper can be really helpful as carrying is involved.

2. **Working from right to left, times each digit in the big number by the small number, and carry over any double-digits.**

In this example, multiply the 3 by 4, which equals 12. Write down the 2 and carry the one to be in front of the 2.

Multiply the 2 by 4, which equals 8. Add the one that was carried over to this total, which gives 9 and write it underneath the tens digit in the first row.

Multiply the 1 by 4, this equals 4. Write it underneath the hundreds digit in the first row.

Figure 3-7 shows how to work through 123×4 the standard way to arrive at the answer (492).

Figure 3-7:
Doing
123×4 the
standard
way.

$$
\begin{array}{r} 1\ 2\ 3 \\ \times 4 \\ \hline \end{array}
\qquad
\begin{array}{r} 1\ {}^{1}2\ 3 \\ \times 4 \\ \hline 2 \end{array}
\qquad
\begin{array}{r} 1\ {}^{1}2\ 3 \\ \times 4 \\ \hline 9\ 2 \end{array}
\qquad
\begin{array}{r} 1\ {}^{1}2\ 3 \\ \times 4 \\ \hline 4\ 9\ 2 \end{array}
$$

Working the really old-fashioned way

The old-fashioned way for multiplying a bigger number — the way I was taught at school — looks like this:

1. **Write down the big number.**

2. **Below the big number, write down the smaller number.**

   Make the ends of the two numbers match up, as in Figure 3-6.

3. **Working from right to left, times each digit in the big number by the small number.**

   Write down the answer so that the last digit lines up with the digit in the top number. Remember to add a zero to the row where you are multiplying by the tens digit and two zeros to the row where you are multiplying by a hundreds digit.

4. **Add up the numbers you've written in each column, carrying as necessary.**

   I explain carrying in detail in Chapter 2.

5. **There's your answer!**

Figure 3-8 shows how to work out 123×4 the old-fashioned way to arrive at the answer (492).

Figure 3-8:
Doing
123 × 4
the old-
fashioned
way.

```
        1   2   3
×               4
            1   2
        8
+   4
        4   9   2
```

Generating a times table

I can see that frown of confusion on your face after you read that heading.
Why would anyone want to generate a times table? Because you can create
a times table for multiplying and dividing big numbers. In the preceding
section I show you to times repeatedly by the small number. If you need to
multiply by a bigger number, you save yourself a bit of time if you work out
the times tables before you begin and then simply look up the number you
need to write down.

One way to do this is to work out the sums by multiplying in your head.
Sit still for ten minutes doing 47×1, 47×2, 47×3 and so on until your
brain melts. (I don't really recommend this method, but you can do it if
you need to.)

The second way is a bit quicker and less brain-melty: Write down the
number you want to create the table for next to a number one in a circle.
Then add the number to itself and write the answer next to a circled two.
Add the original number on again and keep going until you get to a circled
ten. You should have the original number with a zero on the end — if not,
you've made a mistake somewhere and need to go back and check.

Multiplying two big numbers

Multiplying two big numbers is very similar to multiplying a big number by a
small number, except one of the numbers is bigger than before.

Think about taking the bigger number, splitting it up into 'banknotes', work
out how much money is in each of the piles, and add those up. I describe
this idea in more detail in the section 'Piling up the money', earlier in this
chapter.

Expanding the grid

Have a look at the earlier section 'Using the grid method'. You can apply this method to multiplying two big numbers. Here's what you do:

1. **Draw out a grid as many squares wide as the bigger number has digits, and as tall as the number of digits in the smaller number.**

   If you want to do 456 × 78, you need a three-by-two grid. Give yourself plenty of space.

2. **Change the big number into banknotes and write them across the top.**

   In our example, write 400, 50 and 6.

3. **Do the same with the smaller number, but at the far-left end of the rows.**

   Here you have 70 and 8.

4. **In each square, times the first digit from the top of the column by the first digit at the start of the row and follow it by as many zeros as they have between them.**

   For 400 × 70, you do 4 × 7 = 28 and then follow it with three zeros (two from the 400 and one from the 70). Your answer for that square is 28,000.

5. **After you fill all the squares, add up the totals in the squares to reach your final answer.**

I show you an example of multiplying two large numbers using a grid in Figure 3-9.

x	400	50	6		28000
70	28000	3500	420		3200
8	3200	400	48		3500
					400
					420
					+ 48
					35568

Figure 3-9:
Long multi-
plication
with a grid.

How you (and your parents) were likely taught

The standard way for multiplying larger numbers (the one your teachers probably passed on) is as follows:

1. Set the question out correctly, lining up the columns.

   Grid paper can be really helpful as carrying is involved.

2. Multiply through by the first digit, much like you are multiplying by a single digit.

   In this example, multiply through by the 8. Remember to add any carried values.

3. Write the answers in the first row under the answer line.

   Crossing out your carried numbers as you add them can help you remember where you're up to.

4. Add a zero to the next row and multiply through by the ten digit, as if it is a short multiplication problem.

   I always write the zero in a different colour so I don't forget!

   In this example, you multiply through by the tens digit in 78: 7. If you need to carry any numbers use a different colour and remember to cross them out as you go.

5. Add a new line underneath the two lines of working and then add the two lines together to find your answer.

Figure 3-10 shows the workings using the standard method for multiplying larger numbers.

Figure 3-10: Doing 456 × 78 the standard way.

456	$^{+}4\ ^{+5}6$	$^{+}4\ ^{+5}6$	$^{+}4\ ^{+}5\ 6$	$^{+}4\ ^{+}5\ 6$
×78	×78	×78	×78	×78
	3 6 4 8	3 6 4 8	3 6 4 8	3 6 4 8
		0	3 1 9 2 0	3 1 9 2 0
				3 5 5 6 8

Going back a long way in time

In the olden days, when shell suits were the height of fashion and *Big Brother* was still new, I learned to do long multiplication at school. Here's how it works:

1. **Write the bigger number above the smaller number and line up the last digits.**

2. Work out the times table for the smaller number.

3. Times each digit of the bigger number by the smaller number by looking it up in the times table.

4. Write the answer underneath.

Line up the end of the new number with the digit you were multiplying by — you should get a staircase effect, as in the example in Figure 3-11. In this example, you need to look up 6×78, 5×78 and 4×78 in the grid and write them below.

5. Add up the numbers that result to see your answer.

			4	5	6
		×		7	8
	1	4	6	8	
	3	9	0		
3	1	2			
3	5	5	6	8	

Working with all of the zeros

Adding and taking away things with lots of zeros hanging around is easy enough: Just make sure the ends of the numbers are lined up before you do the sum as normal.

Multiplying and dividing numbers with zeros at the end is a bit different. Think about the sum $10 \times 10 = 100$. Each of the numbers you multiply has one zero on the end, making two zeros altogether — and it's no coincidence that the answer has two zeros on the end. When you have zeros at the end of a number that you need to times, you end up with all of the zeros at the end of the new number:

1. To times two numbers ending in lots of zeros together, write down how many zeros are on the end of the first number.

If you want to do $30,000 \times 300$, the first number (30,000) has four zeros.

2. Write down how many zeros are on the end of the second number, and add up the total number of zeros.

Ooooh! Dividing numbers with loads of zeros

You probably won't have to divide numbers with lots of zeros at the end in your numeracy exam, but here's how to do it:

1. Write the divide sum as a fraction. For example, write 400 × 200 ÷ 8,000 as (400 × 200)/8,000.

2. If the top of the fraction is an add or take-away sum, work out the sum. This is surprisingly important. You can leave a times sum alone though.

3. If you have a number on top that ends in a zero and a number on the bottom that ends in a zero, cross out one of each.

4. Keep doing this until you run out of zeros on top or bottom.

5. Now do the sum. It should be easier now.

What you're really doing here is cancelling a factor of 10 from the top and bottom of a fraction. I go into cancelling in more detail in Chapter 6.

In this example, the second number (300) has two zeros. Four zeros and two zeros gives six zeros altogether.

3. **Ignore the zeros for a moment and do the times sum with the digits left at the start of the numbers.**

   For example, do 3 × 3 = 9.

4. **Add to the end of this number as many zeros as you worked out in Step 2.**

   In our example, add six zeros after 9, to give 9,000,000.

One for You, One for Me: Handling Division

You do a divide sum whenever you want to split a quantity into smaller, equal parts. Division is the exact opposite of multiplication. If 123 × 4 = 492 means 'if you make four piles of 123, you need 492', then 492 ÷ 4 means 'if you split 492 into four piles, how big is each?' — the answer is 123.

As with multiplication, division also has more than one sign: The division sign (÷) and the fraction slash (/) or fraction bar (—). So some other ways to write 12 ÷ 3 are

$$\frac{12}{3} = 4 \text{ and}$$

$$12/3 = 4$$

When you divide one number by another, the first number is called the *dividend,* the second is called the *divisor,* and the result is the *quotient.* For example, in the division from the preceding example, the dividend is 12, the divisor is 3, and the quotient is 4.

Dividing and conquering

As with all of the sums you tackle in this book, division is much easier if you break it down into smaller pieces. And, just like with much of what I cover in this book, I find the sums are easier if you think of numbers as representing money — $1 coins, $10 notes, $100 notes and so on.

Imagine you have $126 you want to split between seven people. You begin with one $100 note, two $10 notes and six $1 coins.

You try to divide the $100 note fairly between seven people, but you can't do this because you have only one $100 note. Instead, you turn the $100 note into ten $10 notes. With the two $10 notes you had before, you now have 12 $10 notes altogether.

Twelve is more than $1 \times 7 = 7$ but less than $2 \times 7 = 14$, so you can give everybody one $10 note. They all say thank you, and you have five $10 notes left over. You change the five $10 notes into 50 $1s, making $56 altogether because you also have six $1 coins. Fifty-six is 8×7, so everyone gets eight $1 coins.

Each person now has a $10 and eight $1s, making a total of $18, which is your answer.

Taking one step at a time

When you divide, you work from left to right, the complete opposite of what you do with all other sums in this book.

Here's the process for doing a division sum:

1. **Write the big number (the one you want to split up) under a 'bus stop' like the one in Figure 3-12.**

   Leave plenty of space between your numbers — you'll probably be writing more numbers in between them.

2. **Write the smaller number in front of the bus stop.**

3. **Somewhere nearby, write out the times table for the small number.**

4. **Find the first number under the bus stop that you haven't worked on yet.**

   Remember to work from left to right.

5. **Look for the biggest number in the times table that's smaller than your target, and the single-digit number beside it in the list.**

   Write the single-digit number above your target, on the roof of the bus shelter.

6. **Figure out how many are 'left over'.**

   Find the difference between the number you found in the times table and your target number. Write this just to the left of the next number under the bus stop to make a new number — for example, if you have six left over and the next number is three, the next number you work with is 63.

7. **Go back to Step 4 and repeat until you run out of numbers.**

8. **The number above the bus stop is your answer.**

Figure 3-12: Division by a single-digit number.	$7\overline{)1 \quad 2 \quad 6}$ $\dfrac{0}{7\overline{)1 \quad {}^12 \quad 6}}$ $\dfrac{0 \quad 1}{7\overline{)1 \quad {}^12 \quad {}^56}}$ $\dfrac{0 \quad 1 \quad 8}{7\overline{)1 \quad {}^12 \quad {}^56}}$

 As with all of your sums, keep your working clear and tidy so you can spot and correct any mistakes. Leave plenty of space between the numbers so you can fit in any extra digits you need. You can use grid paper to help keep everything in straight lines.

Whatever happened to the division table?

Considering how much time teachers spend on the multiplication table, you may wonder why you've never seen a division table. For one thing, the multiplication table focuses on multiplying all the one-digit numbers by each other. This focus doesn't work too well for division because division usually involves at least one number that has more than one digit.

Besides, you can use the multiplication table for division, too, by reversing the way you normally use the table. For example, the multiplication table tells you that $6 \times 7 = 42$. You can reverse this equation to give you these two division problems:

$$42 \div 6 = 7$$
$$42 \div 7 = 6$$

Making short work of long division

In the olden days, knowing how to divide large numbers — for example, $62,997 \div 843$ — was important. People used *long division*, an organised method for dividing a large number by another number. The process involved dividing, multiplying, subtracting and dropping numbers down.

But face it — one of the main reasons the pocket calculator was invented was to save 21st-century humans from ever having to do long division again.

Having said that, I need to add that your teacher and math-crazy friends may not agree. Perhaps they just want to make sure you're not completely helpless if your calculator disappears somewhere into your backpack or your desk drawer or the Bermuda Triangle. But if you do get stuck doing page after page of long division against your will, you have my deepest sympathy.

Long division seems to be the most feared and dreaded part of numeracy. I understand why: Long division is fiddly, tedious and unforgiving — one tiny slip and your answer goes terribly, horribly wrong. But after you get into a routine and you do your sums the same way every time, long division suddenly clicks and you realise you can do it and it's not all bad. So, take a deep breath and say after me: 'Long division is just like the division I did earlier in this chapter, only with bigger numbers.'

Understanding how to do long division with some not-too-horrible numbers is a good idea. In this section, I give you a good start with long division, using the long division process to show you how to do a division problem that has a one-digit divisor.

Recall that the *divisor* in a division problem is the number that you're dividing by. When you're doing long division, the size of the divisor is your main concern: Small divisors are easy to work with, and large ones are a royal pain.

Suppose you want to find $860 \div 5$. Start off by writing the problem like this:

$$5 \overline{)860}$$

Long division moves from left to right. In this case, you start with the number in the hundreds column (8). To begin, ask how many times 5 goes into 8 — that is, what's $8 \div 5$? The answer is 1 (with a little bit left over), so write **1** directly above the 8. Now multiply 1×5 to get 5, place the answer directly below the 8, and draw a line beneath it:

$$
\begin{array}{r}
1 \\
5 \overline{)860} \\
5
\end{array}
$$

Subtract $8 - 5$ to get 3. (**Note:** After you subtract, the result should always be smaller than the divisor. If not, you need to write a higher number above the division symbol.) Then bring down the 6 to make the new number 36:

$$
\begin{array}{r}
1 \\
5 \overline{)860} \\
\underline{-5} \\
36
\end{array}
$$

These steps are one complete cycle — to complete the problem, you just need to repeat them. Now ask how many times 5 goes into 36 — that is, what's $36 \div 5$? The answer is 7 (with a little left over). Write **7** just above the 6, and then multiply 7×5 to get 35; write the answer under 36:

$$
\begin{array}{r}
17 \\
5 \overline{)860} \\
\underline{-5} \\
36 \\
\underline{-35}
\end{array}
$$

Now subtract to get $36 - 35 = 1$; bring down the 0 next to the 1 to make the new number 10:

$$
\begin{array}{r}
172 \\
5\overline{)860} \\
\underline{-5} \\
36 \\
\underline{-35} \\
10
\end{array}
$$

Another cycle is complete, so begin the next cycle by asking how many times 5 goes into 10 — that is, $10 \div 5$. The answer this time is 2. Write down the **2** in the answer above the 0. Multiply to get $2 \times 5 = 10$, and write this answer below the 10:

$$
\begin{array}{r}
172 \\
5\overline{)860} \\
\underline{-5} \\
36 \\
\underline{-35} \\
10 \\
\underline{-10}
\end{array}
$$

Now subtract $10 - 10 = 0$. Because you have no more numbers to bring down, you're finished, and here's the answer (that is, the quotient):

$$
\begin{array}{r}
172 \\
5\overline{)860} \\
\underline{-5} \\
36 \\
\underline{-35} \\
10 \\
\underline{-10} \\
0
\end{array}
$$

So $860 \div 5 = 172$.

Just like when you divide by a small number, if you're dividing by a double-digit divisor, I suggest you make a times table for this number. If you're not sure how to make a times table, read the section 'Generating a times table', earlier in this chapter — you'll save a great deal of time in the long run.

The preceding problem divides evenly, but many don't. The following section tells you what to do when you run out of numbers to bring down, and Chapter 7 explains how to get a decimal answer.

Dealing with the left overs: Remainders

Imagine your baker has sold you a baker's dozen of doughnuts — that is, 13 — for your brother's party, where you plan to feed six people. Naturally, in the interests of fairness, everyone gets two doughnuts — but one is left over.

Realistically, you can take two approaches: You can dispose of the doughnut and pretend it's not part of the sum (perhaps by eating it on the sly); or you can try to split up the doughnut into six equal pieces.

The first approach (leaving it alone) is one way of dealing with the problem of left-over numbers when you divide mathematically. You may say '13 ÷ 6 = 2, with one left over', or even '2, remainder 1' (or 2r1). Remainder (or r) just means 'what's left over'.

Checking your answer

When you divide, get into the habit of checking your answer is right. The quick-and-easy but not-very-good-for-learning way is to redo the sum on a calculator.

Alternatively, if you want to practise a little more, try multiplying your answer by the small number and check you get back to the big number you started with.

In either case, you get a big burst of self-esteem every time you get a sum right. If you happen to get a sum not so right, don't worry — keep at it! Try the sum again, or try another sum and come back to the original sum later.

TIP

In long division, the remainder is the number that's left when you no longer have numbers to bring down. The following equation shows that $47 \div 3 = 15r2$:

$$
\begin{array}{r}
15 \\
3\overline{)\,47} \\
\underline{-3} \\
17 \\
\underline{-15} \\
2
\end{array}
$$

Depending on what question you're trying to answer, this is often a perfectly good answer. Sometimes, though, you need to do some more with the remainder and turn it into a fraction. Don't cry, they really don't bite, honestly.

Indeed, if proof were needed that professional mathematicians are not like normal people, pretty much everyone I've ever worked with would go for the 'chop the remainder up into equal slices' solution.

This is to say, they'd all turn the remainder into a fraction. This is honestly a really easy process:

1. **Working from left to right: Write down the remainder.**

2. **Write down a slash (/).**

3. **Write down the number you divided by.**

4. **You've written down the remainder as a fraction.**

For the example above, that works out to be 1/6 — one-sixth. Everyone gets an extra sixth of a doughnut, just in case they don't have enough sugar already.

I look at fractions in much more detail in Chapter 6.

Introducing Order of Operations

When you were younger, did you ever try putting on your shoes first and then your socks? If you did, you probably discovered this simple rule:

1. **Put on socks.**

2. **Put on shoes.**

Thus, you have an order of operations: The socks have to go on your feet before your shoes. So in the act of putting on your shoes and socks, your socks have precedence over your shoes. A simple rule to follow, right?

In this section, I outline a similar set of rules for evaluating expressions, called the *order of operations*. Don't let the long name throw you. Order of operations is just a set of rules to make sure you get your socks and shoes on in the right order, mathematically speaking, so you always get the right answer.

Note: Through most of this book, I introduce overarching themes at the beginning of each section and then explain them later in the chapter instead of building them and finally revealing the result. But order of operations is a bit too confusing to present that way. Instead, I start with a list of four rules and go into more detail about them later in the chapter. Don't let the complexity of these rules scare you off before you work through them!

Evaluate arithmetic expressions from left to right according to the following order of operations:

1. **Parentheses**

2. **Exponents**

3. **Multiplication and division**

4. **Addition and subtraction**

Don't worry about memorising this list right now. I break it to you slowly in the remaining sections of this chapter, starting from the bottom and working toward the top, as follows:

✔ In 'Applying order of operations to simple expressions', I show Steps 3 and 4 — how to evaluate expressions with any combination of addition, subtraction, multiplication, and division.

✔ In 'Using order of operations in expressions with exponents', I show you how Step 2 fits in — how to evaluate expressions with simple operations plus exponents, square roots and absolute value.

✔ In 'Understanding order of operations in expressions with parentheses', I show you how Step 1 fits in — how to evaluate all the expressions I explain plus expressions with parentheses.

Applying order of operations to simple expressions

In this section, I get you started on the basics of evaluating expressions that contain any combination of the main four operations — adding, subtracting, multiplying, and dividing. Generally speaking, these four expressions come in the three types in Table 3-2.

Table 3-2	The Three Types of Simple Expressions	
Expression	*Example*	*Rule*
Contains only addition and subtraction	$12 + 7 - 6 - 3 + 8$	Evaluate left to right.
Contains only multiplication and division	$18 \div 3 \times 7 \div 14$	Evaluate left to right.
Mixed-operator expression: Contains a combination of addition/subtraction and multiplication/division	$9 + 6 \div 3$	1. Evaluate multiplication and division left to right. 2. Evaluate addition and subtraction left to right.

Here, I show you how to identify and evaluate all three types of expressions.

Expressions with only addition and subtraction

Some expressions contain only addition and subtraction. When this is the case, the rule for evaluating the expression is simple.

When an expression contains only addition and subtraction, evaluate it step by step from left to right. For example, suppose you want to evaluate this expression:

$$17 - 5 + 3 - 8$$

Because the only operations are addition and subtraction, you can evaluate from left to right, starting with $17 - 5$:

$$= 12 + 3 - 8$$

As you can see, the number 12 replaces $17 - 5$. Now the expression has three numbers instead of four. Next, evaluate $12 + 3$:

$$= 15 - 8$$

This step breaks down the expression to two numbers, which you can evaluate easily:

$= 7$

So $17 - 5 + 3 - 8 = 7$.

Expressions with only multiplication and division

Some expressions contain only multiplication and division. When this is the case, the rule for evaluating the expression is pretty straightforward.

When an expression contains only multiplication and division, evaluate it step by step from left to right. Suppose you want to evaluate this expression:

$9 \times 2 \div 6 \div 3 \times 2$

Again, the expression contains only multiplication and division, so you can move from left to right, starting with 9×2:

$= 18 \div 6 \div 3 \times 2$

$= 3 \div 3 \times 2$

$= 1 \times 2$

$= 2$

Notice that the expression shrinks one number at a time until all that's left is 2. So $9 \times 2 \div 6 \div 3 \times 2 = 2$

Mixed-operator expressions

Often an expression contains

✔ At least one addition or subtraction operator

✔ At least one multiplication or division operator

I call these *mixed-operator expressions*. To evaluate them, you need some stronger medicine.

Evaluate mixed-operator expressions as follows:

1. **Evaluate the multiplication and division from left to right.**

2. **Evaluate the addition and subtraction from left to right.**

For example, suppose you want to evaluate the following expression:

$$5 + 3 \times 2 + 8 \div 4$$

As you can see, this expression contains addition, multiplication and division, so it's a mixed-operator expression. To evaluate it, start by underlining the multiplication and division in the expression:

$$5 + \underline{3 \times 2} + \underline{8 \div 4}$$

Now evaluate what you've underlined from left to right:

$$= 5 + 6 + \underline{8 \div 4}$$
$$= 5 + 6 + 2$$

At this point, you're left with an expression that contains only addition, so you can evaluate it from left to right:

$$= 11 + 2$$
$$= 13$$

Thus, $5 + 3 \times 2 + 8 \div 4 = 13$.

Using order of operations in expressions with exponents

Here's what you need to know to evaluate expressions that have exponents. *Exponents* (also called powers) are shorthand for repeated multiplication. For example, 2^3 means to multiply 2 by itself three times. In this example, 2 is the *base number* and 3 is the *exponent*. The most common exponent is the number 2. When you take any whole number to the power of 2, the result is a square number. (For more information on square numbers, see Chapter 2.) For this reason, taking a number to the power of 2 is called *squaring* that number. You can read 3^2 as 'three squared', 4^2 as 'four squared' and so forth.

Evaluate exponents from left to right *before* you begin evaluating simple operations (adding, subtracting, multiplying and dividing).

The trick here is to turn the expression into a more simple expression and then use what I show you earlier in 'Applying order of operations to simple expressions'. For example, suppose you want to evaluate the following:

$3 + 5^2 - 6$

First, evaluate the exponent:

$3 + 25 - 6$

At this point, the expression contains only addition and subtraction, so you can evaluate it from left to right in two steps:

$= 28 - 6$

$= 22$

So $3 + 5^2 - 6 + 22$.

Understanding order of operations in expressions with parentheses

In maths, parentheses — ( ) — are often used to group together parts of an expression. When it comes to evaluating expressions, here's what you need to know about parentheses.

To evaluate expressions that contain parentheses:

1. **Evaluate the contents of parentheses from the inside out.**
2. **Evaluate the rest of the expression.**

Simple expressions with parentheses

Similarly, suppose you want to evaluate $(1 + 15 + 5) + (6 - 3) \times 5$. This expression contains two sets of parentheses, so evaluate these from left to right. Notice that the first set of parentheses contains a mixed-operator expression, so evaluate this in two steps, starting with the division:

$= (1 + 3) + (6 - 3) \times 5$

$= 4 + (6 - 3) \times 5$

Now evaluate the contents of the second set of parentheses:

$$= 4 + 3 \times 5$$

Now you have a mixed-operator expression, so evaluate the multiplication (3×5) first:

$$= 4 + 15$$

Finally, evaluate the addition:

$$= 19$$

So $(1 + 15 \div 5) + (3 - 6) \times 5 = 19$.

Expressions with exponents and parentheses

As another example, try this out:

$$1 + (3 + 6^2 \div 9) \times 2^2$$

Start by working with *only* what's inside the parentheses. The first part to evaluate there is the exponent, 6^2:

$$1 + (3 + 36 \div 9) \times 2^2$$

Continue working inside the parentheses by evaluating the division $36 \div 9$:

$$1 + (3 + 4) \times 2^2$$

Now you can get rid of the parentheses altogether:

$$1 + 7 \times 2^2$$

At this point, what's left is an expression with an exponent. This expression takes three steps, starting with the exponent:

$$= 1 + 7 \times 4$$
$$= 1 + 28$$
$$= 29$$

So $1 + (3 + 6^2 \div 9) \times 2^2 = 29$.

Expressions with parentheses raised to an exponent

Sometimes the entire contents of a set of parentheses are raised to an exponent. In this case, evaluate the contents of the parentheses *before* evaluating the exponent, as usual. Here's an example:

$$(7 - 5)^3$$

First, evaluate $7 - 5$:

$$= 2^3$$

With the parentheses removed, you're ready to evaluate the exponent:

$$= 8$$

Once in a rare while, the exponent itself contains parentheses. As always, evaluate what's in the parentheses first. For example:

$$21^{(19+3\times-6)}$$

This time, the smaller expression inside the parentheses is a mixed-operator expression. I've underlined the part that you need to evaluate first:

$$= 21^{(19 - 18)}$$

Now you can finish off what's inside the parentheses:

$$= 21^1$$

At this point, all that's left is a very simple exponent:

$$= 21$$

So $21^{(19+3\times-6)} = 21$

Note: Technically, you don't need to put parentheses around the exponent. If you see an expression in the exponent, treat it as though it has parentheses around it. In other words, $21^{19+3\times-6} = 21$ means the same as $21^{(19+3\times-6)} = 21$.

Expressions with nested parentheses

Occasionally, an expression has *nested parentheses*, or one or more sets of parentheses inside another set. Here I give you the rule for handling nested parentheses.

When evaluating an expression with nested parentheses, evaluate what's inside the *innermost* set of parentheses first and work your way toward the *outermost* parentheses.

For example, suppose you want to evaluate the following expression:

$2 + (9 - (\underline{7} - \underline{3}))$

I underlined the contents of the innermost set of parentheses, so evaluate these contents first:

$= 2 + (9 - 4)$

Next, evaluate what's inside the remaining set of parentheses:

$= 2 + 5$

Now you can finish things off easily:

$= 7$

So $2 + (9 - (7 - 3)) = 7$.

As a final example, here's an expression that requires everything from this whole section on order of operations:

$4 + (7 \times (2^{5-1} + 4 \times 6))$

This expression is about as complicated as you're ever likely to see in pre-algebra: One set of parentheses containing another set, with an exponent. You first look at the exponent. This is where you begin evaluating:

$4 + (7 \times (2^4 + 4 \times 6))$

What's left is one set of parentheses inside another set. Again, work from the inside out. The smaller expression here is $2^4 + 4 \times 6$, so evaluate the exponent first, then the multiplication and finally the subtraction:

$= 4 + (7 \times (2^4 + 4 \times 6))$
$= 4 + (7 \times (16 + 4 \times 6))$
$= 4 + (7 \times (16 + 24))$
$= 4 + (7 \times 40)$

Only one more set of parentheses to go:

$$= 4 + 280$$

At this point, finishing up is easy:

$$= 284$$

Therefore, $4 + (7 \times (2^{5-1} + 4 \times 6)) = 284$.

As I say earlier in this section, this problem is about as hard as they come at this stage of maths. Copy it down and try solving it step by step with the book closed.

Chapter 4

Going Backwards with Negative Numbers

In This Chapter

▶ Staying positive when working with negative numbers

▶ Working out how to add and subtract when negative numbers are involved

▶ Multiplying and dividing with negative numbers

*I*n most of this book I talk about *positive numbers*, or numbers bigger than zero. But things also happen below zero.

Negative numbers (sometimes called minus numbers) are numbers that are below zero. For example, you get the number –3 ('negative three' or 'minus three') when you take three away from nothing: A temperature of –3 degrees is three degrees below zero.

In Chapter 2, I cover the number line. But if you flick back to the number line I include in that chapter, you see that I have chopped a bit off it. The number line actually carries on forever in both directions — to the right, the numbers get bigger; to the left, the numbers become negative.

In this chapter, I provide some tips for understanding negative numbers more clearly. I then take you through using negative numbers within the main four operations.

Taking a Negative Turn: Negative Numbers

When people first find out about subtraction, they often hear that you can't take away more than you have. For example, if you have four pencils, you can take away one, two, three or even all four of them, but you can't take away more than that.

It isn't long, though, before you find out what any credit card holder knows only too well: You can, indeed, take away more than you have — the result is a negative number. For example, if you have $4 and you owe your friend $7, you're $3 in debt. That is, $4 - 7 = -3$. The minus sign in front of the 3 means that the number of dollars you have is three less than 0. Figure 4-1 shows how you place negative whole numbers on the number line.

Figure 4-1: Negative whole numbers on the number line.

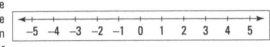

Adding and subtracting on the number line works pretty much the same with negative numbers as with positive numbers. For example, Figure 4-2 shows how to subtract $4 - 7$ on the number line.

Figure 4-2: Subtracting $4 - 7$ on the number line.

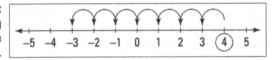

The interesting — by which I mean slightly difficult — thing with negative numbers is the bigger the number looks, the smaller it actually is. If you go outside in –10 degree weather, you get colder than if you go out in –5 degree weather, even though the number ten looks bigger than the number five.

The negative sign turns things around — so what looks bigger is actually smaller. Negative numbers are always smaller than positive numbers.

You won't need to do too much maths with negative numbers in day-to-day life, but here are some contexts where you may meet them:

- ✔ **Temperatures:** Temperatures are by far the most common reason you use negative numbers in day-to-day life. At zero degrees Celsius, water freezes and things get frosty. As the temperature gets colder, the frost gets worse and the number gets bigger. Last night, where I live, the temperature dropped to –2 degrees. But that's not as cold as things got when I lived in Montana in the US — one night there, the temperature dropped to –35 degrees, so cold I had to install a heater in my car engine to stop it freezing solid. A typical freezer has a temperature of about –20 degrees, which is warmer than the Montana winter but cooler than the Australian one.

✔ **Goal differences:** You find negative numbers in soccer league tables. A team's goal difference is how many more goals it scores than it concedes. A team towards the bottom of the league usually concedes more goals than it scores, so the team has a negative goal difference — the bigger the negative number, the worse the team is doing, so –30 is a worse goal difference than –5, and both are worse than a goal difference of 1.

✔ **Money:** You may see 'less than no money' written as a negative number. When my bank balance drops below zero and I am overdrawn (something my account allows me to do), my statement shows my balance as a negative number. The bigger the negative number, the worse my finances: A balance of –$500 ($500 overdrawn) is worse than a balance of –$50 ($50 overdrawn), and both are worse than a balance of $1 ($1 in credit).

✔ **Changes:** When a number decreases over time, you may see it written as a negative change. For example, if house prices in a particular area go down by 2 per cent, you may see this written as '–2%' rather than '2 per cent down'. A price change of –10% is worse for the seller than a change of –5%, and both are worse than no change (0%) or a small increase (1%).

In the following sections, I give you a closer look at how to perform the main four operations with negative numbers.

Addition and Subtraction with Negative Numbers

The great secret to adding and subtracting negative numbers is to turn every problem into a series of ups and downs on the number line. When you know how to do this, you find that all these problems are quite simple.

So in this section, I explain how to add and subtract negative numbers on the number line. Don't worry about memorising every little bit of this procedure. Instead, just follow along so you get a sense of how negative numbers fit onto the number line.

Starting with a negative number

When you're adding and subtracting on the number line, starting with a negative number isn't much different from starting with a positive number. For example, suppose you want to calculate $-3 + 4$. Using the up and down rules, you start at -3 and go up 4:

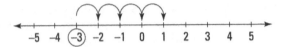

So $-3 + 4 = 1$.

Similarly, suppose you want to calculate $-2 - 5$. Again, the up and down rules help you out. You're subtracting, so move to the left: Start at -2, down 5:

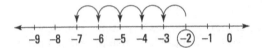

So $-2 - 5 = -7$.

Adding a negative number

Suppose you want to calculate $-2 + -4$. You already know to start at -2, but where do you go from there? Here's the up and down rule for adding a negative number.

Adding a negative number is the same as subtracting a positive number — go *down* on the number line.

By this rule, $-2 + -4$ is the same as $-2 - 4$, so start at -2, down 4:

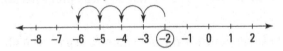

So $-2 + (-4) = -6$.

Note: The problem −2 + −4 can also be written as −2 + (−4). Some people prefer to use this convention so that two operation symbols (- and +) aren't side by side. Don't let it trip you up. The problem is the same.

If you rewrite a subtraction problem as an addition problem — for instance, rewriting 3 − 7 as 3 + (−7) — you can switch the order of the equation. Just remember to keep the negative sign attached to the number when you rearrange: (−7) + 3.

Subtracting a negative number

The last rule you need to know is how to subtract a negative number. For example, suppose you want to calculate 2 − (−3). Here's the up and down rule:

Subtracting a negative number is the same as adding a positive number — go *up* on the number line.

This rule tells you that 2 − (−3) is the same as 2 + 3, so start at 2, up 3:

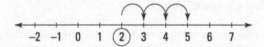

So 2 − (−3) = 5.

When subtracting negative numbers, you can think of the two minus signs as cancelling each other out to create a positive.

Combining addition and subtraction operations

When an equation using negative numbers asks you to combine addition and subtraction, just keep in mind that adding a number means moving *up* and subtracting a number means moving *down*. So if you go *up* 2 steps, then *up* 1 more step and then *down* 6 steps, you've gone a total of 3 steps *down*; therefore, 2 + 1 − 6 = −3.

Here's another example: −3 + 8 − 1 means *down* 3, *up* 8, *down* 1.

This time, go *down* 3 steps, then *up* 8 steps and then *down* 1 step. You've gone a total of 4 steps *up*, so $-3 + 8 - 1 = 4$.

Combining signs

You can turn every problem involving negative numbers into an up-and-down example. The way to do this is by combining adjacent signs:

- ✔ Combine a plus and minus as a *minus* sign.

- ✔ Combine two minus signs as a *plus* sign.

For example:

$$-5 + (-3) - (-9)$$

In this example, you see a plus sign and a minus sign together (between the 5 and the 3), which you can combine as a minus sign. You also see two minus signs (between the 3 and the 9), which you can combine as a plus sign:

$$-5 -3 +9 \text{ means } down \text{ 5, } down \text{ 3, } up \text{ 9}$$

This technique allows you use your up-and-down skills to solve the problem: *Down* 5 steps, then *down* 3 steps and *up* 9 steps leaves you 1 step *up*, so $-5 + (-3) - (-9) = 1$.

Multiplication and Division with Negative Numbers

Multiplication and division with negative numbers is virtually the same as with positive numbers. The presence of one or more minus signs (–) doesn't change the numerical part of the answer. The only question is whether the sign is positive or negative:

Just remember that when you multiply or divide two numbers

- ✔ If the numbers have the *same sign*, the result is always positive.

- ✔ If the numbers have *opposite signs*, the result is always negative.

For example,

$$2 \times 3 = 6 \quad 2 \times -3 = -6$$
$$-2 \times -3 = 6 \quad -2 \times 3 = -6$$

As you can see, the numerical portion of the answer is always 6. The only question is whether the complete answer is 6 or –6. That's where the rule of same or opposite signs comes in.

Another way of thinking of this rule is that the two negatives cancel each other out to make a positive.

Similarly, look at these four division equations:

$$10 \div 2 = 5 \quad 10 \div -2 = -5$$
$$-10 \div -2 = 5 \quad -10 \div 2 = -5$$

In this case, the numerical portion of the answer is always 5. When the signs are the same, the result is positive, and when the signs are different, the result is negative.

Chapter 5

Say What? Turning Words into Numbers

In This Chapter

▶ Getting rid of a couple of myths about word problems

▶ Knowing the four steps to solving a word problem

▶ Attacking more complex word problems with confidence

The very mention of word problems —or story problems, as they're sometimes called — is enough to send a cold shiver of terror into the bones of maths students. Many would rather swim across a moat full of hungry crocodiles than 'figure out how many baskets of corn Farmer Brown picked' or 'help Aunt Sylvia decide how many cookies to bake'. But word problems help you understand the logic behind setting up equations in real-life situations, making maths actually useful — even if some of the scenarios in the word problems you practise on are pretty far-fetched.

In this chapter, I dispel a few myths about word problems. Then I show you how to solve a word problem in four simple steps. After you understand the basics, I show you how to solve more-complex problems. Some of these problems have longer numbers to calculate, and others may have more complicated stories. In either case, you can see how to work through them step by step.

Dispelling Two Myths about Word Problems

Here are two common myths about word problems:

✔ Word problems are always hard.

✔ Word problems are only for school — after that, you don't need them.

Both of these ideas are untrue. But they're so common that I want to address them head-on.

Word problems aren't always hard

Word problems don't have to be hard. For example, here's a word problem that you may have run into in first grade:

> Adam had 4 apples. Then Brenda gave him 5 more apples. How many apples does Adam have now?

You can probably do the maths in your head, but when you were starting out in maths, you may have written it down:

$$4 + 5 = 9$$

Finally, if you had one of those teachers who made you write out your answer in complete sentences, you wrote 'Adam has 9 apples.' (Of course, if you were the class clown like I was, you probably wrote, 'Adam doesn't have any apples because he ate them all.')

Word problems seem hard when they get too complex to solve in your head and you don't have a system for solving them. In this chapter, I give you a system and show you how to apply it to problems of increasing difficulty. And in Chapters 10 and 16, I give you further practice solving more difficult word problems.

Word problems are useful

In the real world, maths rarely comes in the form of equations. It comes in the form of situations that are very similar to word problems.

Once you leave school, you'll still need maths in many situations. Whenever you paint a room, prepare a budget, bake a double batch of chocolate cookies, estimate the cost of a vacation, buy wood to build a shelf, do your taxes, or weigh the pros and cons of buying a car versus leasing one, you'll need maths. And the maths skill you'll need most is understanding how to turn the _situation_ you're facing into numbers that you calculate.

Word problems give you practice turning situations — or stories — into numbers.

Solving Basic Word Problems

Generally, solving a word problem involves four steps:

1. **Read through the problem and set up a *word equation*— that is, an equation that contains words as well as numbers.**

2. **Plug in numbers in place of words wherever possible to set up a regular maths equation.**

3. **Use maths to solve the equation.**

4. **Answer the question the problem asks.**

Most of this book is about Step 3. This chapter and Chapters 10 and 16 are all about Steps 1 and 2. I show you how to break down a word problem sentence by sentence, jot down the information you need to solve the problem, and then substitute numbers for words to set up an equation.

When you know how to turn a word problem into an equation, the hard part is done. Then you can use the rest of what you find in this book to figure out how to do Step 3 — solve the equation. From there, Step 4 is usually pretty easy, though at the end of each example, I make sure you understand how to do it.

Turning word problems into word equations

The first step to solving a word problem is reading it and putting the information you find into a useful form. In this section, I show you how to squeeze the juice out of a word problem and leave the pits behind!

Jotting down information as word equations

Most word problems give you information about numbers, telling you exactly how much, how many, how fast, how big and so forth. Here are some examples:

Nunu is spinning 17 plates.

The width of the house is 20 metres.

If the local train is going 40 kilometres per hour ...

You need this information to solve the problem. And you can easily grab some paper, so don't be afraid to use it. (If you're concerned about trees, write on the back of all that junk mail you get.) Have a piece of scrap paper handy and jot down a few notes as you read through a word problem.

For example, here's how you can jot down 'Nunu is spinning 17 plates':

Nunu = 17

Here's how to note that 'the width of the house is 20 metres':

width = 20

The third example tells you, 'If the local train is going 40 kilometres per hour ...' So you can jot down the following:

local = 40

Don't let the word *if* confuse you. When a problem says 'If so-and-so were true ...' and then asks you a question, assume that it *is* true and use this information to answer the question.

When you jot down information this way, you're really turning words into a more useful form called a *word equation*. A word equation has an equals sign like a maths equation, but it contains both words and numbers.

Writing relationships: Turning more-complex statements into word equations

When you start doing word problems, you notice that certain words and phrases show up over and over again. For example:

Bobo is spinning five fewer plates than Nunu.

The height of a house is half as long as its width.

The express train is moving three times faster than the local train.

You've probably seen statements such as these in word problems since you were first doing maths. Statements like these look like English, but they're really maths, so spotting them is important. You can represent each of these types of statements as word equations that also use the main four operations (addition, subtraction, multiplication and division). Look again at the first example:

Bobo is spinning five fewer plates than Nunu.

You don't know the number of plates that either Bobo or Nunu is spinning. But you know that these two numbers are related.

You can express this relationship like this:

Bobo + 5 = Nunu

This word equation is shorter than the statement it came from. And as you see in the next section, word equations are easy to turn into the maths you need to solve the problem.

Here's another example:

The height of a house is half as long as its width.

You don't know the width or height of the house, but you know that these numbers are connected. You can express this relationship between the width and height of the house as the following word equation:

height = width ÷ 2

With the same type of thinking, you can write 'The express train is moving three times faster than the local train' as this word equation:

express = 3 × local

As you can see, each of the examples allows you to set up a word equation using one of the main four operations — adding, subtracting, multiplying and dividing.

Figuring out what the problem's asking

The end of a word problem usually contains the question you need to answer to solve the problem. You can use word equations to clarify this question so you know right from the start what you're looking for.

For example, you can write the question, 'All together, how many plates are Bobo and Nunu spinning?' as

Bobo + Nunu = ?

You can write the question, 'How tall is the house' as:

height = ?

Finally, you can rephrase the question, 'What's the difference in speed between the express train and the local train?' in this way:

express − local = ?

Plugging in numbers for words

After you've written out a bunch of word equations, you have the facts you need in a form you can use. You can often solve the problem by plugging numbers from one word equation into another. In this section, I show you how to use the word equations you built in the last section to solve three problems.

Example: Send in the clowns

Some problems involve simple addition or subtraction. Here's an example:

> Bobo is spinning five fewer plates than Nunu. (Bobo dropped a few.) Nunu is spinning 17 plates. Altogether, how many plates are Bobo and Nunu spinning?

Here's what you have already, just from reading the problem:

Nunu = 17

Bobo + 5 = Nunu

Plugging in the information gives you the following:

Bobo + 5 = 17

If you see how many plates Bobo is spinning, feel free to jump ahead. If not, here's how you rewrite the addition equation as a subtraction equation:

Bobo = 17 − 5 = 12

The problem wants you to find out how many plates the two clowns are spinning together. So you need to find out the following:

Bobo + Nunu = ?

Just plug in the numbers, substituting 12 for Bobo and 17 for Nunu:

12 + 17 = 29

So Bobo and Nunu are spinning 29 plates.

Example: Our house in the middle of our street

At times, a problem notes relationships that require you to use multiplication or division. Here's an example:

> The height of a house is half as long as its width, and the width of the house is 20 metres. How tall is the house?

You already have a head start from what you determined earlier:

> width = 20
>
> height = width ÷ 2

You can plug in information as follows, substituting 20 for the word *width*:

> height = 20 ÷ 2 = 10

So you know that the height of the house is 10 metres.

Example: I hear the train a-comin'

Pay careful attention to what the question is asking. You may have to set up more than one equation. Here's an example:

> The express train is moving three times faster than the local train. If the local train is going 40 kilometres per hour, what's the difference in speed between the express train and the local train?

Here's what you have so far:

> local = 40
>
> express = 3 × local

Plug in the information you need:

> express = 3 × 40 = 120

In this problem, the question at the end asks you to find the difference in speed between the express train and the local train. Finding the difference between two numbers is subtraction, so here's what you want to find:

> express − local = ?

You can get what you need to know by plugging in the information you've already found:

> 120 − 40 = 80

Therefore, the difference in speed between the express train and the local train is 80 kilometres per hour.

Solving More Complex Word Problems

The skills I show you previously in 'Solving Basic Word Problems' are important for solving any word problem because they streamline the process and make it simpler. What's more, you can use those same skills to find your way through more complex problems. Problems become more complex when

- ✔ The calculations become harder. (For example, instead of a dress costing $50, it costs $49.95.)
- ✔ The amount of information in the problem increases. (For example, instead of two clowns, you have five, all spinning a different number of plates.)

Don't let problems like these scare you. In this section, I show you how to use your new problem-solving skills to solve more-difficult word problems.

When numbers get serious

A lot of problems that look tough aren't much more difficult than the problems I show you in the previous sections. For example, consider this problem:

> Aunt Effie has $732.84 hidden in her pillowcase, and Aunt Jezebel has $234.19 less than Aunt Effie has. How much money do the two women have all together?

One question you may have is how these women ever get any sleep with all that change clinking around under their heads. But moving on to the maths, even though the numbers are larger, the principle is still the same as in problems in the earlier sections. Start reading from the beginning: 'Aunt Effie has $732.84 ...' This text is just information to jot down as a simple word equation:

> Effie = $732.84

Continuing, you read, 'Aunt Jezebel has *$234.19 less than* Aunt Effie has.' It's another statement you can write as a word equation:

> Jezebel = Effie − $234.19

Now you can plug in the number $732.84 where you see Aunt Effie's name in the equation:

> Jezebel = $732.84 − $234.19

So far, the big numbers haven't been any trouble. At this point, though, you probably need to stop to do the subtraction:

$$\begin{array}{r} \$732.84 \\ -\ \$234.19 \\ \hline \$498.65 \end{array}$$

Now you can jot this information down, as always:

Jezebel = $498.65

The question at the end of the problem asks you to find out how much money the two women have all together. Here's how to represent this question as an equation:

Effie + Jezebel = ?

You can plug information into this equation:

$732.84 + $498.65 = ?

Again, because the numbers are large, you probably have to stop to do the maths:

$$\begin{array}{r} \$732.84 \\ +\ \$498.65 \\ \hline \$1231.49 \end{array}$$

So all together, Aunt Effie and Aunt Jezebel have $1,231.49.

As you can see, the procedure for solving this problem is basically the same as for the simpler problems in the earlier sections. The only difference is that you have to stop to do some addition and subtraction.

Too much information

When the going gets tough, knowing the system for writing word equations really becomes helpful. Here's a word problem that's designed to scare you off — but with your new skills, you're ready for it:

> Four women collected money to save the endangered southern hairy-nosed wombat. Keisha collected $160, Bree collected $50 more than Keisha, Amy collected twice as much as Bree, and together Amy and Sophia collected $700. How much money did the four women collect all together?

If you try to do this problem all in your head, you'll probably get confused. Instead, take it line by line and just jot down word equations as I discuss earlier in this chapter.

First, 'Keisha collected $160.' So jot down the following:

Keisha = 160

Next, 'Bree collected $50 dollars more than Keisha,' so write

Bree = Keisha + 50

After that, 'Amy collected twice as much as Bree':

Amy = Bree × 2

Finally, 'together, Amy and Sophia collected $700':

Amy + Sophia = 700

That's all the information the problem gives you, so now you can start working with it. Keisha collected $160, so you can plug in 160 anywhere you find Keisha's name:

Bree = 160 + 50 = 210

Now you know how much Bree collected, so you can plug this information into the next equation:

Amy = 210 × 2 = 420

This equation tells you how much Amy collected, so you can plug this number into the last equation:

420 + Sophia = 700

To solve this problem, change it from addition to subtraction using inverse operations (an operation that undoes this one):

Sophia = 700 − 420 = 280

Now that you know how much money each woman collected, you can answer the question at the end of the problem:

Keisha + Bree + Amy + Sophia = ?

You can plug in this information easily:

$$160 + 210 + 420 + 280 = 1{,}070$$

So you can conclude that the four women together collected $1,070.

Putting it all together

Here's one final example putting together everything from this chapter. Try writing down this problem and working it through step by step on your own. If you get stuck, come back here. When you can solve it from beginning to end with the book closed, you'll have a good grasp of how to solve word problems:

> On a recent shopping trip, Travis bought six shirts for $19.95 each and two pairs of trousers for $34.60 each. He then bought a jacket that cost $37.08 less than he paid for both pairs of trousers. If he paid with three $100 bills, how much change did he receive?

On the first read-through, you may wonder how Travis found a store that prices jackets that way. Believe me — it was quite a challenge. Anyway, back to the problem. You can jot down the following word equations:

> shirts = $19.95 × 6
>
> trousers = $34.60 × 2
>
> jacket = trousers − $37.08

The numbers in this problem are probably longer than you can solve in your head, so they require some attention:

$$
\begin{array}{cc}
\$19.95 & \$34.60 \\
\times\ \ \ 6 & \times\ \ \ 2 \\
\hline
\$119.70 & \$69.20
\end{array}
$$

With this done, you can fill in some more information:

> shirts = $119.70
>
> trousers = $69.20
>
> jacket = trousers − $37.08

Now you can plug in $69.20 for *trousers*:

> jacket = $69.20 − $37.08

Again, because the numbers are long, you need to solve this equation separately:

$$\begin{array}{r} \$69.20 \\ - \$37.08 \\ \hline \$32.12 \end{array}$$

This equation gives you the price of the jacket:

jacket = $32.12

Now that you have the price of the shirts, trousers and jacket, you can find out how much Travis spent:

amount Travis spent = $119.70 + $69.20 + $32.12

Again, you have another equation to solve:

$$\begin{array}{r} \$119.70 \\ \$69.20 \\ + \ \$32.12 \\ \hline \$221.02 \end{array}$$

So you can jot down the following:

amount Travis spent = $221.02

The problem is asking you to find out how much change Travis received from $300, so jot this down:

change = $300 – amount Travis spent

You can plug in the amount that Travis spent:

change = $300 – $221.02

And do just one more equation:

$$\begin{array}{r} \$300.00 \\ - \ \$221.02 \\ \hline \$78.98 \end{array}$$

So you can jot down the answer:

change = $78.98

Therefore, Travis received $78.98 in change.

Part II

Parts of the Whole

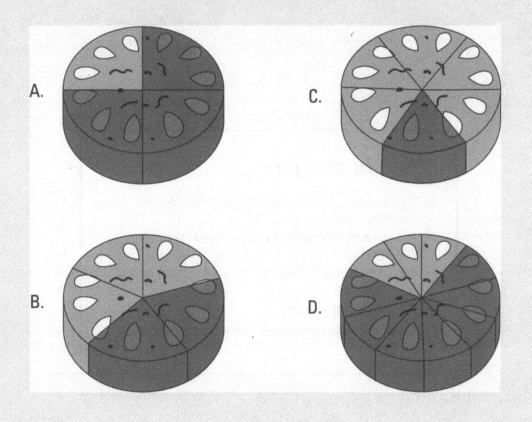

A.

B.

C.

D.

In this part . . .

- ✔ Work with basic fractions, improper fractions, and mixed numbers.

- ✔ Add, subtract, multiply, and divide fractions, decimals and percentages.

- ✔ Convert the form of a rational number to a fraction, a decimal or a percentage.

- ✔ Use ratios and proportions.

- ✔ Solve word problems that involve fractions, decimals and percentages.

Chapter 6

Cake or Death: Fractions without Fear

Suppose that today is your birthday and your family and friends are throwing you a surprise party. After opening all your presents, you finish blowing out the candles on your cake, but now you have a problem: Eight of you want some cake, but you have only *one cake.* Several solutions are proposed:

✔ You can all go into the kitchen and bake seven more cakes.

✔ Instead of eating cake, everyone can eat celery sticks.

✔ Because it's your birthday, you can eat the *whole* cake and everyone else can eat celery sticks. (That idea was yours.)

✔ You can cut the cake into eight equal slices so that everyone can enjoy it.

After careful consideration, you choose the last option. With that decision, you've opened the door to the exciting world of fractions. Fractions represent parts of a thing that can be cut into pieces. In this chapter, I give you some basic information about fractions that you need to know, including the three basic types of fractions: Proper fractions, improper fractions, and mixed numbers.

I move on to increasing and reducing the terms of fractions, and then begin applying the main four operations to fractions. I also show you how to convert between improper fractions and mixed numbers. I show you how to compare fractions using cross-multiplication, and how to multiply and divide fractions. Finally, I provide some help with working with fractions on your calculator. By the time you're done with this chapter, you'll see how fractions really can be a piece of cake!

Slicing a Cake into Fractions

Here's a simple fact: When you cut a cake into two equal pieces, each piece is half of the cake. As a fraction, you write that as $\frac{1}{2}$. In Figure 6-1, the shaded piece is half of the cake.

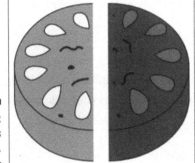

Figure 6-1:
Two halves
of a cake.

Every fraction is made up of two numbers separated by a line, or a fraction bar. The line can be either diagonal or horizontal — so you can write this fraction in either of the following two ways:

$\frac{1}{2}$ or ½

The number above the line is called the *numerator*. The numerator tells you how many pieces you have. In this case, you have one dark-shaded piece of cake, so the numerator is 1.

The number below the line is called the *denominator*. The denominator tells you how many equal pieces the whole cake has been cut into. In this case, the denominator is 2.

Similarly, when you cut a cake into three equal slices, each piece is a third of the cake (see Figure 6-2).

Figure 6-2:
Cake cut
into thirds.

This time, the shaded piece is one-third — $\frac{1}{3}$ — of the cake. Again, the
numerator tells you how many pieces you have, and the denominator tells
you how many equal pieces the whole cake has been cut up into.

Figure 6-3 shows a few more examples of ways to represent parts of the
whole with fractions.

Figure 6-3:
Cakes
cut and
shaded into

(A) $\frac{3}{4}$,

(B) $\frac{2}{5}$,

(C) $\frac{1}{6}$,

and (D) $\frac{7}{10}$

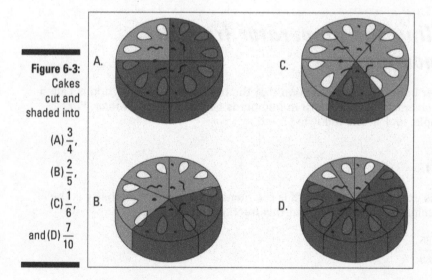

In each case, the numerator tells you how many pieces are shaded, and the
denominator tells how many pieces there are altogether.

The fraction bar can also mean a division sign. In other words,

$$\frac{3}{4}$$

signifies 3 ÷ 4. If you take three cakes and divide them among four people, each person gets

$$\frac{3}{4}$$

of a cake.

Knowing the Fraction Facts of Life

Fractions have their own special vocabulary and a few important properties that are worth knowing right from the start. When you know them, you find working with fractions a lot easier.

Telling the numerator from the denominator

I cover in the preceding section that the top number in a fraction is called the *numerator*, and the bottom number is called the *denominator*. For example, look at the following fraction:

$$\frac{3}{4}$$

In this example, the number 3 is the numerator, and the number 4 is the denominator. Similarly, look at this fraction:

$$\frac{55}{89}$$

The number 55 is the numerator, and the number 89 is the denominator.

Flipping for reciprocals

When you flip over a fraction, you get its reciprocal. For example, the following numbers are reciprocals:

$$\frac{2}{3} \text{ and } \frac{3}{2}$$

$$\frac{11}{14} \text{ and } \frac{14}{11}$$

$$\frac{19}{19}$$

is its own reciprocal.

Using ones and zeros

When the denominator (bottom number) of a fraction is 1, the fraction is equal to the numerator by itself. Conversely, you can turn any whole number into a fraction by drawing a line and placing the number 1 under it. For example:

$$\frac{2}{1} = 2 \qquad \frac{9}{1} = 9 \qquad \frac{157}{1} = 157$$

When the numerator and denominator match, the fraction equals 1. After all, if you cut a cake into eight pieces and you keep all eight of them, you have the entire cake. Here are some fractions that equal 1:

$$\frac{8}{8} = 1 \qquad \frac{11}{11} = 1 \qquad \frac{365}{365} = 1$$

When the numerator of a fraction is 0, the fraction is equal to 0. For example:

$$\frac{0}{1} = 0 \qquad \frac{0}{12} = 0 \qquad \frac{0}{113} = 0$$

The denominator of a fraction can never be 0. Fractions with 0 in the denominator are undefined — that is, they have no mathematical meaning. Earlier in this chapter I outline that placing a number in the denominator is similar to cutting a cake into that number of pieces. You can cut a cake into two, ten or even a million pieces. You can even cut it into one piece (that is, don't cut it at all). But you can't cut a cake into zero pieces. For this reason, putting 0 in the denominator — much like lighting an entire book of matches on fire — is something you should never, never do.

Mixing things up

A mixed number is a combination of a whole number and a proper fraction added together. Here are some examples:

$$1\frac{1}{2} \qquad 5\frac{3}{4} \qquad 99\frac{44}{100}$$

A mixed number is always equal to the whole number plus the fraction attached to it. So

$$1\frac{1}{2} \text{ means } 1+\frac{1}{2}, 5\frac{3}{4} \text{ means } 5+\frac{3}{4}$$

, and so on.

Knowing proper from improper

When the numerator (top number) is less than the denominator (bottom number), the fraction is less than 1:

$$\frac{1}{2}<1 \qquad \frac{3}{5}<1 \qquad \frac{63}{73}<1$$

Fractions like these are called are called proper fractions. Positive proper fractions are always between 0 and 1. However, when the numerator is greater than the denominator, the fraction is greater than 1. Take a look:

$$\frac{3}{2}>1 \qquad \frac{7}{4}>1 \qquad \frac{98}{97}>1$$

Any fraction that's greater than 1 is called an improper fraction. Converting an improper fraction to a mixed number is customary, especially when it's the final answer to a problem.

An improper fraction is always top heavy, as if it's unstable and wants to fall over. To stabilise it, convert it to a mixed number. Proper fractions are always stable.

Later in this chapter, I discuss improper fractions in more detail when I show you how to convert between improper fractions and mixed numbers.

Increasing and Reducing Terms of Fractions

Take a look at these three fractions:

$$\frac{1}{2} \qquad \frac{2}{4} \qquad \frac{3}{6}$$

If you cut three cakes (as I do earlier in this chapter) into these three fractions (see Figure 6-4), exactly half of the cake will be shaded, just like in Figure 6-1, no matter how you slice it. (Get it? No matter how you slice it? You may as well laugh at the bad jokes, too — they're free.) The important point here isn't the humour, or the lack of it, but the idea about fractions.

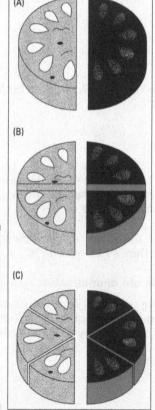

Figure 6-4:
Cakes
cut and
shaded into

(A) $\frac{1}{2}$,

(B) $\frac{2}{4}$,

and (C) $\frac{3}{6}$

The fractions $\frac{1}{2}$, $\frac{2}{4}$, and $\frac{3}{6}$ are all equal in value. In fact, you can write a lot of fractions that are also equal to these. As long as the numerator is exactly half the denominator, the fractions are all equal to $\frac{1}{2}$ — for example,

$$\frac{11}{22} \quad \frac{100}{200} \quad \frac{1,000,000}{2,000,000}$$

These fractions are equal to $\frac{1}{2}$, but their terms (the numerator and denominator) are different. In this section, I show you how to both increase and reduce the terms of a fraction without changing its value.

Increasing the terms of fractions

To increase the terms of a fraction by a certain number, multiply both the numerator and the denominator by that number.

For example, to increase the terms of the fraction $\frac{3}{4}$ by 2, multiply both the numerator and the denominator by 2:

$$\frac{3}{4} = \frac{3 \times 2}{4 \times 2} = \frac{6}{8}$$

Similarly, to increase the terms of the fraction $\frac{5}{11}$ by 7, multiply both the numerator and the denominator by 7:

$$\frac{5}{11} = \frac{5 \times 7}{11 \times 7} = \frac{35}{77}$$

Increasing the terms of a fraction doesn't change its value. Because you're multiplying the numerator and denominator by the same number, you're essentially multiplying the fraction by a fraction that equals 1.

One key point to know is how to increase the terms of a fraction so that the denominator becomes a pre-set number. Here's how you do it:

1. **Divide the new denominator by the old denominator.**

   To keep the fractions equal, you have to multiply the numerator and denominator of the old fraction by the same number. This first step tells you what the old denominator was multiplied by to get the new one.

For example, suppose you want to raise the terms of the fraction $\frac{4}{7}$ so that the denominator is 35. You're trying to fill in the question mark here:

$$\frac{4}{7} = \frac{?}{35}$$

Divide 35 by 7, which tells you that the denominator was multiplied by 5.

2. **Multiply this result by the old numerator to get the new numerator.**

   You now know how the two denominators are related. The numerators need to have the same relationship, so multiply the old numerator by the number you found in Step 1.

   Multiply 5 by 4, which gives you 20. So here's the answer:

   $$\frac{4}{7} = \frac{4 \times 5}{7 \times 5} = \frac{20}{35}$$

Reducing fractions to lowest terms

Reducing fractions is similar to increasing fractions, except that it involves division rather than multiplication. But because you can't always divide, reducing takes a bit more finesse.

In this section, I show you the formal way to reduce fractions, which works in all cases. Then I show you a more informal way you can use when you're more comfortable.

Reducing fractions the formal way

Reducing fractions the formal way relies on understanding how to break down a number into its prime factors. (A number's *prime factors* are the set of prime numbers (including repeats) that equal that number when multiplied together.)

Here's how to reduce a fraction:

1. **Break down both the numerator (top number) and the denominator (bottom number) into their prime factors.**

   For example, suppose you want to reduce the fraction $\frac{12}{30}$. Break down both 12 and 30 into their prime factors:

   $$\frac{12}{30} = \frac{2 \times 2 \times 3}{2 \times 3 \times 5}$$

2. Cross out any common factors.

As you can see, I cross out a 2 and a 3 because they're common factors — that is, they appear in both the numerator and the denominator:

$$\frac{12}{30} = \frac{\cancel{2} \times 2 \times \cancel{3}}{\cancel{2} \times \cancel{3} \times 5}$$

3. Multiply the remaining numbers to get the reduced numerator and denominator.

You can see now that the fraction $\frac{12}{30}$ reduces to $\frac{2}{5}$:

$$\frac{12}{30} = \frac{\cancel{2} \times 2 \times \cancel{3}}{\cancel{2} \times \cancel{3} \times 5} = \frac{2}{5}$$

As another example, here's how you reduce the fraction $\frac{32}{100}$:

$$\frac{32}{100} = \frac{\cancel{2} \times \cancel{2} \times 2 \times 2 \times 2}{\cancel{2} \times \cancel{2} \times 5 \times 5} = \frac{8}{25}$$

This time, cross out two 2s from both the top and the bottom as common factors. The remaining 2s on top and the 5s on the bottom aren't common factors. So the fraction $\frac{32}{100}$ reduces to $\frac{8}{25}$.

Reducing fractions the informal way

Here's an easier way to reduce fractions when you get comfortable with the concept:

1. If the numerator (top number) and denominator (bottom number) are both divisible by 2 — that is, if they're both even — divide both by 2.

For example, suppose you want to reduce the fraction $\frac{36}{60}$. The numerator and the denominator are both even, so divide them both by 2:

$$\frac{36}{60} = \frac{18}{30}$$

2. Repeat Step 1 until the numerator or denominator (or both) is no longer divisible by 2.

In the resulting fraction, both numbers are still even, so repeat the first step again:

$$\frac{18}{30} = \frac{9}{15}$$

3. Repeat Step 1 using the number 3, and then 5, and then 7, continuing testing prime numbers until you're sure that the numerator and denominator have no common factors.

Now, the numerator and the denominator are both divisible by 3, so divide both by 3:

$$\frac{9}{15} = \frac{3}{5}$$

Neither the numerator nor the denominator is divisible by 3, so this step is complete. At this point, you can move on to test for divisibility by 5, 7, and so on, but you really don't need to. The numerator is 3, and it obviously isn't divisible by any larger number, so you know that the fraction $\frac{36}{60}$ reduces to $\frac{3}{5}$.

Converting between Improper Fractions and Mixed Numbers

In 'Knowing the Fraction Facts of Life,' I tell you that any fraction whose numerator is greater than its denominator is an improper fraction. Improper fractions are useful and easy to work with, but for some reason people just don't like them. (The word improper should've tipped you off.) Teachers especially don't like them, and they really don't like an improper fraction to appear as the answer to a problem. However, they love mixed numbers. One reason they love them is that estimating the approximate size of a mixed number is easy.

For example, if I tell you I put $\frac{31}{3}$ of a litre of petrol in my car, you probably find it hard to estimate roughly how much that is: 5 litres, 10 litres, 20 litres?

But if I tell you I put $10\frac{1}{3}$ litres of petrol, you know immediately that this amount is a little more than 10 but less than 11 litres (and probably wasn't going to get me very far). Although $10\frac{1}{3}$ is the same as $\frac{31}{3}$, knowing the mixed number is a lot more helpful in practice. For this reason, you often have to convert improper fractions to mixed numbers.

Knowing the parts of a mixed number

Every mixed number has both a whole number part and a fractional part. So the three numbers in a mixed number are

- ✔ The whole number
- ✔ The numerator
- ✔ The denominator

For example, in the mixed number $3\frac{1}{2}$, the whole number part is 3 and the fractional part is $\frac{1}{2}$. So this mixed number is made up of three numbers: The whole number (3), the numerator (1), and the denominator (2). Knowing these three parts of a mixed number is helpful for converting back and forth between mixed numbers and improper fractions.

Converting a mixed number to an improper fraction

To convert a mixed number to an improper fraction, follow these steps:

1. **Multiply the denominator of the fractional part by the whole number, and add the result to the numerator.**

   For example, suppose you want to convert the mixed number $5\frac{2}{3}$ to an improper fraction. First, multiply 3 by 5 and add 2:

   $$3 \times 5 + 2 = 17$$

2. **Use this result as your numerator, and place it over the denominator you already have.**

   Place this result over the denominator:

   $$\frac{17}{3}$$

   So the mixed number $5\frac{2}{3}$ equals the improper fraction $\frac{17}{3}$. This method works for all mixed numbers. Furthermore, if you start with the fractional part reduced, the answer is also reduced (refer to the earlier 'Increasing and Reducing Terms of Fractions' section).

Converting an improper fraction to a mixed number

To convert an improper fraction to a mixed number, divide the numerator by the denominator. Then write the mixed number in this way:

- ✔ The quotient (answer) is the whole-number part.
- ✔ The remainder is the numerator.
- ✔ The denominator of the improper fraction is the denominator.

For example, suppose you want to write the improper fraction $\frac{19}{5}$ as a mixed number. First, divide 19 by 5:

$$19 \div 5 = 3r4$$

Then write the mixed number as follows:

$$3\frac{4}{5}$$

This method works for all improper fractions. And as is true of conversions in the other direction, if you start with a reduced fraction, you don't have to reduce your answer (refer to 'Increasing and Reducing Terms of Fractions').

Understanding Cross-Multiplication

Cross-multiplication is a handy little technique to know. You can use it in a few different ways, so I explain it here and then show you an immediate application.

To cross-multiply two fractions, follow these steps:

1. **Multiply the numerator of the first fraction by the denominator of the second fraction and jot down the answer.**

2. **Multiply the numerator of the second fraction by the denominator of the first fraction and jot down the answer.**

For example, suppose you have these two fractions:

$$\frac{2}{3} \qquad \frac{4}{7}$$

When you cross-multiply, you get these two numbers:

$$2 \times 7 = 14 \quad 4 \times 3 = 12$$

You can use cross-multiplication to compare fractions and find out which is greater. When you do so, make sure that you start with the numerator of the first fraction.

To find out which of two fractions is larger, cross-multiply and place the two numbers you get, in order, under the two fractions. The larger number is always under the larger fraction. In this case, 14 goes under $\frac{2}{3}$ and 12 goes under $\frac{4}{7}$. The number 14 is greater than 12, so $\frac{2}{3}$ is greater than $\frac{4}{7}$.

For example, suppose you want to find out which of the following three fractions is the greatest:

$$\frac{3}{5} \quad \frac{5}{9} \quad \frac{6}{11}$$

Cross-multiplication works only with two fractions at a time, so pick the first two — $\frac{3}{5}$ and $\frac{5}{9}$ — and then cross-multiply:

$$3 \times 9 = 27 \quad 5 \times 5 = 25$$

Because 27 is greater than 25, you know now that $\frac{3}{5}$ is greater than $\frac{5}{9}$. So you can throw out $\frac{5}{9}$.

Now do the same thing for $\frac{3}{5}$ and $\frac{6}{11}$:

$$3 \times 11 = 33 \quad 5 \times 6 = 30$$

Because 33 is greater than 30, $\frac{3}{5}$ is greater than $\frac{6}{11}$. Pretty straightforward, right? And that set of steps is all you have to know for now. I show you a bunch of great things you can do with this simple skill in the following sections.

All Together Now: Adding Fractions

When you add fractions, one important item to notice is whether their denominators (the numbers on the bottom) are the same. If they're the same — woo-hoo! Adding fractions that have the same denominator is a walk in the park. But when fractions have different denominators, adding them becomes a tad more complex.

To make matters worse, many teachers make adding fractions even more difficult by requiring you to use a long and complicated method when, in many cases, a short and easy one will do.

In this section, I first show you how to add fractions with the same denominator. Then I show you a foolproof method for adding fractions when the denominators are different. It always works, and it's usually the simplest way to go. After that, I show you a quick method that you can use only for certain problems. Finally, I show you the longer, more complicated way to add fractions that usually gets taught.

Finding the sum of fractions with the same denominator

To add two fractions that have the same denominator (bottom number), add the numerators (top numbers) and leave the denominator unchanged.

For example, consider the following problem:

$$\frac{1}{5}+\frac{2}{5}=\frac{1+2}{5}=\frac{3}{5}$$

As you can see, to add these two fractions, you add the numerators (1 + 2) and keep the denominator (5).

Why does this work? Earlier in this chapter I explain that you can think about fractions as pieces of cake. The denominator in this case tells you that the entire cake has been cut into five pieces. So when you add $\frac{1}{5}+\frac{2}{5}$, you're really adding one piece plus two pieces. The answer, of course, is three pieces — that is, $\frac{3}{5}$.

Even if you have to add more than two fractions, as long as the denominators are all the same, you just add the numerators and leave the denominator unchanged:

$$\frac{1}{17}+\frac{3}{17}+\frac{4}{17}+\frac{6}{17}=\frac{1+3+4+6}{17}=\frac{14}{17}$$

Sometimes when you add fractions with the same denominator, you have to reduce your answer to lowest terms (refer to 'Increasing and Reducing Terms of Fractions'). Take this problem, for example:

$$\frac{1}{4}+\frac{1}{4}=\frac{1+1}{4}=\frac{2}{4}$$

The numerator and the denominator are both even, so you know they can be reduced:

$$\frac{2}{4} = \frac{1}{2}$$

In other cases, the sum of two proper fractions is an improper fraction. You get a numerator that's larger than the denominator when the two fractions add up to more than 1, as in this case:

$$\frac{3}{7} + \frac{5}{7} = \frac{8}{7}$$

If you have more work to do with this fraction, leave it as an improper fraction so that it's easier to work with. But if this is your final answer, you may need to turn it into a mixed number:

$$\frac{8}{7} = 8 \div 7 = 1r1 = 1\frac{1}{7}$$

When two fractions have the same numerator, don't add them by adding the denominators and leaving the numerator unchanged.

Adding fractions with different denominators

When the fractions that you want to add have different denominators, adding them isn't quite as easy. At the same time, it doesn't have to be as hard as most teachers make it.

Now, I'm shimmying out onto a brittle limb here, but this needs to be said: Fractions can be added in a very simple way. It always works. It makes adding fractions only a little more difficult than multiplying them. And as you move up the maths food chain into algebra, it becomes the most useful method.

So why doesn't anybody talk about it? I think it's a clear case of tradition being stronger than common sense. The traditional way to add fractions is more difficult, more time-consuming, and more likely to cause an error. But generation after generation has been taught that it's the right way to add fractions. It's a vicious cycle.

But in this book, I'm breaking with tradition. I first show you the easy way to add fractions. Then I show you a quick trick that works in a few special cases. Finally, I show you the traditional way to add fractions.

Using the easy way

At some point in your life, I bet some teacher somewhere told you these golden words of wisdom: 'You can't add two fractions with different denominators.' Your teacher was wrong! Here's the way to do it:

1. **Cross-multiply the two fractions and add the results together to get the numerator of the answer.**

   Suppose you want to add the fractions $\frac{1}{3}$ and $\frac{2}{5}$. To get the numerator of the answer, cross-multiply. In other words, multiply the numerator of each fraction by the denominator of the other:

   $$\frac{1}{3}+\frac{2}{5}$$
   $$1\times5=5$$
   $$2\times3=6$$

   Add the results to get the numerator of the answer:

   $$5+6=11$$

2. **Multiply the two denominators to get the denominator of the answer.**

   To get the denominator, just multiply the denominators of the two fractions:

   $$3\times5=15$$

   The denominator of the answer is 15.

3. **Write your answer as a fraction.**

   $$\frac{1}{3}+\frac{2}{5}=\frac{11}{15}$$

As you discover in the earlier section 'Finding the sum of fractions with the same denominator,' when you add fractions, you sometimes need to reduce the answer you get. Here's an example:

$$\frac{5}{8}+\frac{3}{10}=\frac{(5\times10)+(3\times8)}{8\times10}=\frac{50+24}{80}=\frac{74}{80}$$

Because the numerator and the denominator are both even numbers, you know that the fraction can be reduced. So try dividing both numbers by 2:

$$\frac{74\div2}{80\div2}=\frac{37}{40}$$

This fraction can't be reduced further, so $\frac{37}{40}$ is the final answer.

As you also discover in 'Finding the sum of fractions with the same denominator,' sometimes when you add two proper fractions, your answer is an improper fraction:

$$\frac{4}{5} + \frac{3}{7} = \frac{(4 \times 7) + (3 \times 5)}{5 \times 7} = \frac{28 + 15}{32} = \frac{43}{35}$$

If you have more work to do with this fraction, leave it as an improper fraction so that it's easier to work with. But if this is your final answer, you may need to turn it into a mixed number (refer to 'Converting an improper fraction to a mixed number' for details).

$$\frac{43}{35} = 43 \div 35 = 1r8 = 1\frac{8}{35}$$

In some cases, you have to add more than one fraction. The method is similar, with one small tweak. For example, suppose you want to add $\frac{1}{2} + \frac{3}{5} + \frac{4}{7}$:

1. **Start by multiplying the numerator of the first fraction by the denominators of all the other fractions.**

   $$\frac{1}{2} + \frac{3}{5} + \frac{4}{7}$$
   $$(1 \times 5 \times 7) = 35$$

2. **Do the same with the second fraction, and add this value to the first.**

   $$\frac{1}{2} + \frac{3}{5} + \frac{4}{7}$$
   $$35 + (3 \times 2 \times 7) = 35 + 42$$

3. **Do the same with the remaining fraction(s).**

   $$\frac{1}{2} + \frac{3}{5} + \frac{4}{7}$$
   $$35 + 42 + (4 \times 2 \times 5) = 35 + 42 + 40 = 117$$

   When you're done, you have the numerator of the answer.

4. **To get the denominator, just multiply all the denominators together:**

   $$\frac{1}{2} + \frac{3}{5} + \frac{4}{7}$$
   $$= \frac{35 + 42 + 40}{2 \times 5 \times 7} = \frac{117}{70}$$

As usual, you may need to reduce or change an improper fraction to a mixed number. In this example, you just need to change to a mixed number (refer to 'Converting an improper fraction to a mixed number'):

$$\frac{117}{70} = 117 \div 70 = 1\,r\,47 = 1\frac{47}{70}$$

Trying a quick trick

I show you a way to add fractions with different denominators in the preceding section. It always works, and it's easy. So why do I want to show you another way? It feels like déjà vu.

In some cases, you can save yourself a lot of effort with a little bit of smart thinking. You can't always use this method, but you can use it when one denominator is a multiple of the other. Look at the following problem:

$$\frac{11}{12} + \frac{19}{24}$$

First, I solve it the way I show you in the preceding section:

$$\frac{11}{12} + \frac{19}{24} = \frac{(11 \times 24) + (19 \times 12)}{12 \times 24} = \frac{264 + 228}{288} = \frac{492}{288}$$

Those numbers are pretty big, and I'm still not done because the numerator is larger than the denominator. The answer is an improper fraction. Worse yet, the numerator and denominator are both even numbers, so the answer still needs to be reduced.

With certain fraction addition problems, I can give you a smarter way to work. The trick is to turn a problem with different denominators into a much easier problem with the same denominator.

Before you add two fractions with different denominators, check the denominators to see whether one is a multiple of the other. If it is, you can use the quick trick:

1. **Increase the terms of the fraction with the smaller denominator so that it has the larger denominator.**

   Look at the earlier problem in this new way:

   $$\frac{11}{12} + \frac{19}{24}$$

   As you can see, 12 divides into 24 without a remainder. In this case, you want to raise the terms of $\frac{11}{12}$

   so that the denominator is 24:

$$\frac{11}{12} = \frac{?}{24}$$

To fill in the question mark, the trick is to divide 24 by 12 to find out how the denominators are related; then multiply the result by 11:

$$? = (24 \div 12) \times 11 = 22$$

$$\text{So } \frac{11}{12} = \frac{22}{24}$$

2. **Rewrite the problem, substituting this increased version of the fraction, and add.**

   I cover this earlier in 'Finding the sum of fractions with the same denominator.' Now you can rewrite the problem this way:

   $$\frac{22}{24} + \frac{19}{24} = \frac{41}{24}$$

   As you can see, the numbers in this case are much smaller and easier to work with. The answer here is an improper fraction; changing it to a mixed number is easy:

   $$\frac{41}{24} = 41 \div 24 = 1r17 = 1\frac{17}{24}$$

Relying on the traditional way

In the two preceding sections, I show you two ways to add fractions with different denominators. They both work great, depending on the circumstances. So why do I want to show you yet a third way? It feels like déjà vu all over again.

The truth is that I don't want to show you this way. But they're forcing me to. And you know who they are, don't you? The man — the system — the powers that be. The ones who want to keep you down in the mud, grovelling at their feet. Okay, so I'm exaggerating a little. But let me impress on you that you don't have to add fractions this way unless you really want to (or unless your teacher insists on it).

Here's the traditional way to add fractions with two different denominators:

1. **Find the least common multiple of the two denominators.**

   The *least common multiple* (LCM) of a set of numbers is the lowest positive number that's a multiple of every number in that set.

Suppose you want to add the fractions $\frac{3}{4}+\frac{7}{10}$. First find the LCM of the two denominators, 4 and 10. Here's how to find the LCM using the multiplication table method:

- Multiples of 10: 10, 20, 30, 40

- Multiples of 4: 4, 8, 12, 16, 20

So the LCM of 4 and 10 is 20.

2. **Increase the terms of each fraction so that the denominator of each equals the LCM.**

Increase each fraction to higher terms so that the denominator of each is 20.

$$\frac{3}{4}=\frac{3\times5}{4\times5}=\frac{15}{20} \text{ and } \frac{7}{10}=\frac{7\times2}{10\times2}=\frac{14}{20}$$

3. **Substitute these two new fractions for the original ones and add.**

I show you how to do this in 'Finding the sum of fractions with the same denominator', earlier in this chapter.

At this point, you have two fractions that have the same denominator:

$$\frac{15}{20}+\frac{14}{20}=\frac{29}{20}$$

When the answer is an improper fraction, you still need to change it to a mixed number:

$$\frac{29}{20}=29\div20=1r9=1\frac{9}{20}$$

As another example, suppose you want to add the numbers $\frac{5}{6}+\frac{3}{10}+\frac{2}{15}$.

1. **Find the LCM of 6, 10, and 15.**

Start by decomposing the three denominators to their prime factors:

$$6=2\times3$$
$$10=2\times5$$
$$15=3\times5$$

These denominators have a total of three different prime factors — 2, 3 and 5. Each prime factor appears only once in any decomposition, so the LCM of 6, 10, and 15 is

$$2\times3\times5=30$$

2. **You need to increase the terms of all three fractions so that their denominators are 30:**

$$\frac{5}{6} = \frac{5 \times 5}{6 \times 5} = \frac{25}{30}$$

$$\frac{3}{10} = \frac{3 \times 3}{10 \times 3} = \frac{9}{30}$$

$$\frac{2}{15} = \frac{2 \times 2}{15 \times 2} = \frac{4}{30}$$

3. **Simply add the three new fractions:**

$$\frac{25}{30} + \frac{9}{30} + \frac{4}{30} = \frac{38}{30}$$

Again, you need to change this improper fraction to a mixed number:

$$\frac{38}{30} = 38 \div 30 = 1 \, r \, 8 = 1\frac{8}{30}$$

Because both numbers are divisible by 2, you can reduce the fraction:

$$1\frac{8}{30} = 1\frac{4}{15}$$

Picking your trick: Choosing the best method

As I say earlier in this chapter, I think the traditional way to add fractions is more difficult than either the easy way or the quick trick. Your teacher may require you to use the traditional way, and after you get the hang of it, you'll get good at it. But given the choice, here's my recommendation:

- ✔ Use the easy way when the numerators and denominators are small (say, 15 or under).

- ✔ Use the quick trick with larger numerators and denominators when one denominator is a multiple of the other.

- ✔ Use the traditional way only when you can't use either of the other methods (or when you know the LCM just by looking at the denominators).

Taking It Away: Subtracting Fractions

Subtracting fractions isn't really much different from adding them. As with addition, when the denominators are the same, subtraction is easy. And when the denominators are different, the methods I show you for adding fractions can be tweaked for subtracting them.

So to figure out how to subtract fractions, you can read the section 'All Together Now: Adding Fractions' and substitute a minus sign (–) for every plus sign (+). But it'd be just a little cheesy if I expected you to do that. So in this section, I show you four ways to subtract fractions that mirror what I discuss earlier in this chapter about adding them.

Subtracting fractions with the same denominator

As with addition, subtracting fractions with the same denominator is always easy. When the denominators are the same, you can just think of the fractions as pieces of cake.

To subtract one fraction from another when they both have the same denominator (bottom number), subtract the numerator (top number) of the second from the numerator of the first and keep the denominator the same. For example:

$$\frac{3}{5} - \frac{2}{5} = \frac{3-2}{5} = \frac{1}{5}$$

Sometimes, as when you add fractions, you have to reduce:

$$\frac{3}{10} - \frac{1}{10} = \frac{3-1}{10} = \frac{2}{10}$$

Because the numerator and denominator are both even, you can reduce this fraction by a factor of 2:

$$\frac{2}{10} = \frac{2 \div 2}{10 \div 2} = \frac{1}{5}$$

Unlike addition, when you subtract one proper fraction from another, you never get an improper fraction.

Subtracting fractions with different denominators

Just as with addition, you have a choice of methods when subtracting fractions. These three methods are similar to the methods I show you for adding fractions: The easy way, the quick trick, and the traditional way.

The easy way always works, and I recommend this method for most of your fraction subtracting needs. The quick trick is a great timesaver, so use it when you can. And as for the traditional way — well, even if I don't like it, your teacher and other maths purists probably do.

Knowing the easy way

This way of subtracting fractions works in all cases, and it's easy. (In the next section, I show you a quick way to subtract fractions when one denominator is a multiple of the other.) Here's the easy way to subtract fractions that have different denominators:

1. **Cross-multiply the two fractions and subtract the second number from the first to get the numerator of the answer.**

   For example, suppose you want to subtract $\frac{6}{7} - \frac{2}{5}$. To get the numerator, cross-multiply the two fractions and then subtract the second number from the first number:

   $$\frac{6}{7} - \frac{2}{5}$$
   $$(6 \times 5) - (2 \times 7) = 30 - 14 = 16$$

   After you cross-multiply, be sure to subtract in the correct order. (The first number is the numerator of the first fraction times the denominator of the second.)

2. **Multiply the two denominators to get the denominator of the answer.**

   $$7 \times 5 = 32$$

3. **Putting the numerator over the denominator gives you your answer.**

   $$\frac{16}{35}$$

Here's another example to work with:

$$\frac{9}{10} - \frac{5}{6}$$

This time, I put all the steps together:

$$\frac{9}{10} - \frac{5}{6} = \frac{(9 \times 6) - (5 \times 10)}{10 \times 6}$$

With the problem set up like this, you just have to simplify the result:

$$= \frac{54-50}{60} = \frac{4}{60}$$

In this case, you can reduce the fraction:

$$\frac{4}{60} = \frac{1}{15}$$

Cutting it short with a quick trick

The easy way I show you in the preceding section works best when the numerators and denominators are small. When they're larger, you may be able to take a shortcut.

Before you subtract fractions with different denominators, check the denominators to see whether one is a multiple of the other. If it is, you can use the quick trick:

1. **Increase the terms of the fraction with the smaller denominator so that it has the larger denominator.**

   For example, suppose you want to find $\frac{17}{20} - \frac{31}{80}$. If you cross-multiply these fractions, your results are going to be much bigger than you want to work with. But fortunately, 80 is a multiple of 20, so you can use the quick way.

   First, increase the terms of $\frac{17}{20}$ so that the denominator is 80:

   $$\frac{17}{20} = \frac{?}{80}$$
   $$? = 80 \div 20 \times 17 = 68$$
   $$\text{So } \frac{17}{20} = \frac{68}{80}$$

2. **Rewrite the problem, substituting this increased version of the fraction, and subtract as I show you earlier in 'Subtracting fractions with the same denominator.'**

   Here's the problem as a subtraction of fractions with the same denominator, which is much easier to solve:

   $$\frac{68}{80} - \frac{31}{80} = \frac{37}{80}$$

In this case, you don't have to reduce to lowest terms, although you may have to in other problems (refer to 'Increasing and Reducing Terms of Fractions' for more).

Keeping your teacher happy with the traditional way

As I describe earlier in this chapter in 'All Together Now: Adding Fractions', you want to use the traditional way only as a last resort. I recommend that you use it only when the numerator and denominator are too large to use the easy way and when you can't use the quick trick.

To use the traditional way to subtract fractions with two different denominators, follow these steps:

1. **Find the least common multiple (LCM) of the two denominators.**

   For example, suppose you want to subtract $\frac{7}{8} - \frac{11}{14}$. Here's how to find the LCM of 8 and 14:

   Multiples of 8 : 8, 16, 24, 32, 40, 48, 56

   Multiples of 14 : 14, 28, 42, 54

   So the LCM of 8 and 14 is 56.

2. **Increase each fraction to higher terms so that the denominator of each equals the LCM (refer to 'Increasing and Reducing Terms of Fractions').**

   The denominators of both now are 56:

   $$\frac{7}{8} = \frac{7 \times 7}{8 \times 7} = \frac{49}{56}$$
   $$\frac{11}{14} = \frac{11 \times 4}{14 \times 4} = \frac{44}{56}$$

3. **Substitute these two new fractions for the original ones and subtract as I show you earlier in 'Subtracting fractions with the same denominator.'**

   $$\frac{49}{56} - \frac{44}{56} = \frac{5}{56}$$

   This time, you don't need to reduce because 5 is a prime number and 56 isn't divisible by 5. In some cases, however, you have to reduce the answer to lowest terms.

Multiplying and Dividing Fractions

One of the odd little ironies of life is that multiplying and dividing fractions is easier than adding or subtracting them — just two easy steps and you're done! In fact, you may find multiplying fractions easier than multiplying whole numbers because the numbers you're working with are usually small. More good news is that dividing fractions is nearly as easy as multiplying them. So I'm not even wishing you good luck — you don't need it!

Multiplying numerators and denominators straight across

Everything in life should be as simple as multiplying fractions. All you need for multiplying fractions is a pen or pencil, something to write on (preferably not your hand), and a basic knowledge of the multiplication table. (See Chapter 3 for a multiplication refresher.)

Here's how to multiply two fractions:

1. **Multiply the numerators (the numbers on top) to get the numerator of the answer.**

2. **Multiply the denominators (the numbers on the bottom) to get the denominator of the answer.**

For example, here's how to multiply $\frac{2}{5} \times \frac{3}{7}$:

$$\frac{2}{5} \times \frac{3}{7} = \frac{2 \times 3}{5 \times 7} = \frac{6}{35}$$

Sometimes when you multiply fractions, you have an opportunity to reduce to lowest terms. (For more on when and how to reduce a fraction, refer to 'Reducing fractions to lowest terms', earlier in this chapter.) As a rule, maths people are crazy about reduced fractions, and teachers sometimes take points off a right answer if you could've reduced it but didn't. Here's a multiplication problem that ends up with an answer that's not in its lowest terms:

$$\frac{4}{5} \times \frac{7}{8} = \frac{4 \times 7}{5 \times 8} = \frac{28}{40}$$

Because the numerator and the denominator are both even numbers, this fraction can be reduced. Start by dividing both numbers by 2:

$$\frac{28 \div 2}{40 \div 2} = \frac{14}{20}$$

Again, the numerator and the denominator are both even, so do it again:

$$\frac{14 \div 2}{20 \div 2} = \frac{7}{10}$$

This fraction is now fully reduced.

 When multiplying fractions, you can often make your job easier by cancelling out equal factors in the numerator and denominator. Cancelling out equal factors makes the numbers that you're multiplying smaller and easier to work with, and it also saves you the trouble of reducing at the end. Here's how it works:

✔ When the numerator of one fraction and the denominator of the other are the same, change both of these numbers to 1s. (See the nearby sidebar for why this works.)

✔ When the numerator of one fraction and the denominator of the other are divisible by the same number, factor this number out of both. In other words, divide the numerator and denominator by that common factor.

For example, suppose you want to multiply the following two numbers:

$$\frac{5}{13} \times \frac{13}{20}$$

You can make this problem easier by cancelling out the number 13, as follows:

$$\frac{5}{\cancel{13}\,1} \times \frac{\cancel{13}\,1}{20} = \frac{5 \times 1}{1 \times 20} = \frac{5}{20}$$

You can make it even easier by noticing that 20 and 5 are both divisible by 5, so you can also factor out the number 5 before multiplying:

$$\frac{1\,\cancel{5}}{1} \times \frac{1}{\cancel{20}\,4} = \frac{1}{1} \times \frac{1}{4} = \frac{1}{4}$$

One is the easiest number

With fractions, the relationship between the numbers, not the actual numbers themselves, is most important. Understanding how to multiply and divide fractions can give you a deeper understanding of why you can increase or decrease the numbers within a fraction without changing the value of the whole fraction.

When you multiply or divide any number by 1, the answer is the same number. This rule also goes for fractions, so

$$\frac{3}{8} \times 1 = \frac{3}{8} \text{ and } \frac{3}{8} \div 1 = \frac{3}{8}$$

$$\frac{5}{13} \times 1 = \frac{5}{13} \text{ and } \frac{5}{13} \div 1 = \frac{5}{13}$$

$$\frac{67}{70} \times 1 = \frac{67}{70} \text{ and } \frac{67}{70} \div 1 = \frac{67}{70}$$

And as I discuss earlier in this chapter, when a fraction has the same number in both the numerator and the denominator, its value is 1.

In other words, the fractions are all equal to 1. Look what happens when you multiply the fraction $\frac{3}{4}$ by $\frac{2}{2}$:

$$\frac{3}{4} \times \frac{2}{2} = \frac{3 \times 2}{4 \times 2} = \frac{6}{8}$$

The net effect is that you've increased the terms of the original fraction by 2. But all you've done is multiply the fraction by 1, so the value of the fraction hasn't changed. The fraction $\frac{6}{8}$ is equal to $\frac{3}{4}$.

Similarly, reducing the fraction $\frac{6}{9}$ by a factor of 3 is the same as dividing that fraction by $\frac{3}{3}$ (which is equal to 1):

$$\frac{6}{9} \div \frac{3}{3} = \frac{6 \div 3}{9 \div 3} = \frac{2}{3}$$

So $\frac{6}{9}$ is equal to $\frac{2}{3}$.

Doing a flip to divide fractions

Dividing fractions is just as easy as multiplying them. In fact, when you divide fractions, you really turn the problem into multiplication.

To divide one fraction by another, multiply the first fraction by the reciprocal of the second. (As I discuss earlier in the chapter, the reciprocal of a fraction is simply that fraction turned upside down.)

For example, here's how you turn fraction division into multiplication:

$$\frac{1}{3} \div \frac{4}{5} = \frac{1}{3} \times \frac{5}{4}$$

As you can see, I turn $\frac{4}{5}$ into its reciprocal — $\frac{5}{4}$ — and change the division sign to a multiplication sign. After that, just multiply the fractions as I describe in 'Multiplying numerators and denominators straight across':

$$\frac{1}{3} \times \frac{5}{4} = \frac{1 \times 5}{3 \times 4} = \frac{5}{12}$$

As with multiplication, in some cases, you may have to reduce your result at the end. But you can also make your job easier by cancelling out equal factors (see the preceding section).

Working Properly with Mixed Numbers

All the methods I describe earlier in this chapter work for both proper and improper fractions. Unfortunately, mixed numbers are ornery little critters, and you need to figure out how to deal with them on their own terms.

Adding and subtracting mixed numbers

One way to add and subtract mixed numbers is to convert them to improper fractions, much as I describe earlier in this chapter in 'Multiplying and dividing mixed numbers,' and then to add or subtract them using a method from the 'All Together Now: Adding Fractions' or 'Take It Away: Subtracting Fractions' sections. Doing so is a perfectly valid way of getting the right answer without learning a new method.

Unfortunately, teachers just love to make people add and subtract mixed numbers in their own special way. The good news is that a lot of folks find this way easier than all the converting stuff.

Working in pairs: Adding two mixed numbers

Adding mixed numbers looks a lot like adding whole numbers: You stack them one on top of the other, draw a line, and add. For this reason, some students feel more comfortable adding mixed numbers than adding fractions. Here's how to add two mixed numbers:

 1. **Add the fractional parts using any method you like; if necessary, change this sum to a mixed number and reduce it.**

2. **If the answer you found in Step 1 is an improper fraction, change it to a mixed number, write down the fractional part, and carry the whole number part to the whole number column.**

3. **Add the whole number parts (including any number carried).**

You may also need to reduce your answer to lowest terms (refer to 'Reducing fractions to lowest terms'). In the examples that follow, I show you everything you need to know.

Summing up mixed numbers when the denominators are the same

As with any problem involving fractions, adding is always easier when the denominators are the same. For example, suppose you want to add $3\frac{1}{3} + 5\frac{1}{3}$. Doing mixed number problems is often easier if you place one number above the other:

$$3\frac{1}{3}$$
$$+5\frac{1}{3}$$

As you can see, this arrangement is similar to how you add whole numbers, but it includes an extra column for fractions. Here's how you add these two mixed numbers step by step:

1. **Add the fractions.**

$$\frac{1}{3} + \frac{1}{3} = \frac{2}{3}$$

2. **Switch improper fractions to mixed numbers; write down your answer.**

Because $\frac{2}{3}$ is a proper fraction, you don't have to change it.

3. **Add the whole number parts.**

$$3 + 5 = 8$$

Here's how your problem looks in column form:

$$3\frac{1}{3}$$
$$+5\frac{1}{3}$$
$$8\frac{2}{3}$$

This problem is about as simple as they get. In this case, all three steps are pretty easy. But sometimes, Step 2 requires more attention. For example, suppose you want to add $8\frac{3}{5}+6\frac{4}{5}$. Here's how you do it:

1. **Add the fractions.**

   $$\frac{3}{5}+\frac{4}{5}=\frac{7}{5}$$

2. **Switch improper fractions to mixed numbers, write down the fractional part, and carry over the whole number.**

   Because the sum is an improper fraction, convert it to the mixed number $1\frac{2}{5}$. Write down $\frac{2}{5}$ and carry the 1 over to the whole number column.

3. **Add the whole number parts, including any whole numbers you carried over when you switched to a mixed number.**

   $$1 + 8 + 6 = 15$$

   Here's how the solved problem looks in column form. (Be sure to line up the whole numbers in one column and the fractions in another.)

   $$
   \begin{array}{r}
   1\phantom{\frac{3}{5}} \\
   8\frac{3}{5} \\
   +6\frac{4}{5} \\
   \hline
   15\frac{2}{5}
   \end{array}
   $$

As with any other problems involving fractions, sometimes you need to reduce at the end of Step 1.

The same basic idea works no matter how many mixed numbers you want to add. For example, suppose you want to add $5\frac{4}{9}+11\frac{7}{9}+3\frac{8}{9}+1\frac{5}{9}$:

1. **Add the fractions.**

   $$\frac{4}{9}+\frac{7}{9}+\frac{8}{9}+\frac{5}{9}=\frac{24}{9}$$

2. **Switch improper fractions to mixed numbers, write down the fractional part, and carry over the whole number.**

   Because the result is an improper fraction, convert it to the mixed number $2\frac{6}{9}$ and then reduce it to $2\frac{2}{3}$ (for more on converting

and reducing fractions, refer to sections earlier in this chapter).
I recommend doing these calculations on a piece of scrap paper.

Write down $\frac{2}{3}$ and carry the 2 to the whole number column.

3. **Add the whole numbers.**

   $$2 + 5 + 11 + 3 + 1 = 22$$

Here's how the problem looks after you solve it:

$$
\begin{array}{r}
2 \\
5\dfrac{4}{9} \\
11\dfrac{7}{9} \\
3\dfrac{8}{9} \\
+1\dfrac{5}{9} \\
\hline
22\dfrac{2}{3}
\end{array}
$$

Summing up mixed numbers when the denominators are different

The most difficult type of mixed number addition is when the denominators of the fractions are different. This difference doesn't change Steps 2 or 3, but it does make Step 1 tougher.

For example, suppose you want to add $16\frac{3}{5}$ and $7\frac{7}{9}$.

1. **Add the fractions.**

   Add $\frac{3}{5}$ and $\frac{7}{9}$. You can use any method from earlier in this chapter. Here, I use the easy way:

   $$\frac{3}{5} + \frac{7}{9} = \frac{(3 \times 9) + (7 \times 5)}{5 \times 9} = \frac{27 + 35}{45} = \frac{62}{45}$$

2. **Switch improper fractions to mixed numbers, write down the fractional part, and carry over the whole number.**

   This fraction is improper, so change it to the mixed number $1\frac{17}{45}$.
   Fortunately, the fractional part of this mixed number isn't reducible.

   Write down the $\frac{17}{45}$ and carry over the 1 to the whole number column.

3. Add the whole numbers.

$$1 + 16 + 7 = 24$$

Here's how the completed problem looks:

$$
\begin{array}{r}
1 \phantom{\frac{3}{5}} \\
16\frac{3}{5} \\
+7\frac{7}{9} \\
\hline
24\frac{17}{45}
\end{array}
$$

Subtracting mixed numbers

The basic way to subtract mixed numbers is close to the way you add them. Again, the subtraction looks more like what you're used to with whole numbers. Here's how to subtract two mixed numbers:

1. **Find the difference of the fractional parts using any method you like.**

2. **Find the difference of the two whole number parts.**

Along the way, though, you may encounter a couple more twists and turns. I keep you on track so that, by the end of this section, you can do any mixed-number subtraction problem.

Taking away mixed numbers when the denominators are the same

As with addition, subtraction is much easier when the denominators are the same. For example, suppose you want to subtract $7\frac{3}{5} - 3\frac{1}{5}$. Here's what the problem looks like in column form:

$$
\begin{array}{r}
7\frac{3}{5} \\
-3\frac{1}{5} \\
\hline
4\frac{2}{5}
\end{array}
$$

In this problem, I subtract $\frac{3}{5} - \frac{1}{5} = \frac{2}{5}$. Then I subtract $7 - 3 = 4$. Not too terrible, agreed?

One complication arises when you try to subtract a larger fractional part from a smaller one. Suppose you want to find $11\frac{1}{6} - 2\frac{5}{6}$. This time, if you try to subtract the fractions, you get

$$\frac{1}{6} - \frac{5}{6} = -\frac{4}{6}$$

Obviously, you don't want to end up with a negative number in your answer. You can handle this problem by borrowing from the column to the left. This idea is similar to the borrowing that you use in regular subtraction, with one key difference.

When borrowing in mixed-number subtraction:

1. **Borrow 1 from the whole-number portion and add it to the fractional portion, turning the fraction into a mixed number.**

   To find $11\frac{1}{6} - 2\frac{5}{6}$, borrow 1 from the 11 and add it to $\frac{1}{6}$, making it the mixed number $1\frac{1}{6}$:

   $$11\frac{1}{6} = 10 + 1\frac{1}{6}$$

2. **Change this new mixed number into an improper fraction.**

   Here's what you get when you change $1\frac{1}{6}$ into an improper fraction:

   $$10 + 1\frac{1}{6} = 10\frac{7}{6}$$

   The result is $10\frac{7}{6}$. This answer is a weird cross between a mixed number and an improper fraction, but it's what you need to handle the job.

3. **Use the result in your subtraction.**

   $$\begin{array}{r} 10\frac{7}{6} \\ -2\frac{5}{6} \\ \hline 8\frac{2}{6} \end{array}$$

   In this case, you have to reduce the fractional part of the answer:

   $$8\frac{2}{6} = 8\frac{1}{3}$$

Subtracting mixed numbers when the denominators are different

Subtracting mixed numbers when the denominators are different is just about the hairiest thing you're ever going to have to do in pre-algebra. Fortunately, though, if you work through this chapter, you acquire all the skills you need.

Suppose you want to subtract $15\frac{4}{11}-12\frac{3}{7}$. Because the denominators are different, subtracting the fractions becomes more difficult. But you have another question to think about: In this problem, do you need to borrow? If $\frac{4}{11}$ is greater than $\frac{3}{7}$, you don't have to borrow. But if $\frac{4}{11}$ is less than $\frac{3}{7}$, you do. (For more on borrowing in mixed-number subtraction, see the preceding section.)

In the section 'Understanding Cross-Multiplication', I show you how to test two fractions to see which is greater by cross-multiplying:

$$4\times7=28$$
$$3\times11=33$$

Because 28 is less than 33, $\frac{4}{11}$ is less than $\frac{3}{7}$, so you do have to borrow. I get the borrowing out of the way first:

$$15\frac{4}{11}=4+1\frac{4}{11}=14\frac{15}{11}$$

Now the problem looks like this:

$$14\frac{15}{11}-12\frac{3}{7}$$

The first step, subtracting the fractions, is the most time-consuming, so as I show you earlier in 'Subtracting fractions with different denominators', you can take care of that on the side:

$$\frac{15}{11}-\frac{3}{7}=\frac{(15\times7)-(3\times11)}{11\times7}=\frac{105-33}{77}=\frac{72}{77}$$

The good news is that this fraction can't be reduced (72 and 77 have no common factors: $72=2\times2\times2\times3\times3$ and $77=7\times11$). So the hard part of the problem is done, and the rest follows easily:

$$14\frac{15}{11}$$

$$-12\frac{3}{7}$$

$$\overline{\quad 2\frac{72}{77}\quad}$$

This problem is about as difficult as a mixed-number subtraction problem gets. Take a look at it step by step. Better yet, copy the problem and then close the book and try to work through the steps on your own. If you get stuck, that's okay: Better now than on an exam!

Multiplying and dividing mixed numbers

I can't give you a direct method for multiplying and dividing mixed numbers. The only way is to convert the mixed numbers to improper fractions and multiply or divide as usual. Here's how to multiply or divide mixed numbers:

1. **Convert all mixed numbers to improper fractions.**

   Refer to 'Converting a mixed number to an improper fraction' for details.

   For example, suppose you want to multiply $1\frac{3}{5} \times 2\frac{1}{3}$. First convert $1\frac{3}{5}$ and $2\frac{1}{3}$ to improper fractions:

   $$1\frac{3}{5} = \frac{5 \times 1 + 3}{5} = \frac{8}{5}$$
   $$2\frac{1}{3} = \frac{3 \times 2 + 1}{3} = \frac{7}{3}$$

2. **Multiply these improper fractions.**

   I show you this process earlier in this chapter, in 'Multiplying and Dividing Fractions'.

   $$\frac{8}{5} \times \frac{7}{3} = \frac{8 \times 7}{5 \times 3} = \frac{56}{15}$$

3. **If the answer is an improper fraction, convert it back to a mixed number.**

Refer to 'Converting an improper fraction to a mixed number'.

$$\frac{56}{15} = 56 \div 15 = 3r11 = 3\frac{11}{15}$$

In this case, the answer is already in lowest terms, so you don't have to reduce it.

As a second example, suppose you want to divide $3\frac{2}{3}$ by $1\frac{4}{7}$.

1. **Convert $3\frac{2}{3}$ and $1\frac{4}{7}$ to improper fractions:**

$$3\frac{2}{3} = \frac{3 \times 3 + 2}{3} = \frac{11}{3}$$
$$1\frac{4}{7} = \frac{7 \times 1 + 4}{7} = \frac{11}{7}$$

2. **Divide these improper fractions.**

   Divide fractions by multiplying the first fraction by the reciprocal of the second (see the earlier 'Multiplying and Dividing Fractions' section):

$$\frac{11}{3} \div \frac{11}{7} = \frac{11}{3} \times \frac{7}{11}$$

   In this case, before you multiply, you can cancel out factors of 11 in the numerator and denominator:

$$\frac{1\cancel{11}}{3} \div \frac{7}{\cancel{11}1} = \frac{1 \times 7}{3 \times 1} \times \frac{7}{3}$$

3. **Convert the answer to a mixed number.**

$$\frac{7}{3} = 7 \div 3 = 2r1 = 2\frac{1}{3}$$

Fathoming Fractions on Your Calculator

One of the most useful tools in the real world for dealing with fractions is your calculator.

You may not be allowed to use a calculator in an exam — always check beforehand — but you can definitely use a calculator when you practise maths at home.

If you have a scientific calculator, it can probably handle fractions for you. Even calculators that don't handle fractions in the obvious sense are useful — you can do the same sums using decimals, which I tell you all about in Chapter 7.

In this section I run you through the ins and outs of using a calculator with fractions. You may want to turn to Chapter 7 as well, where I cover using a calculator with decimals.

Using the fraction button

Whoever decided to put a fraction button on calculators will be given a knighthood when I rule the world. The fraction button has made a whole area of maths much more accessible and useful and I blow a giant raspberry in the face of anyone who grumbles about dumbing down.

On my calculator the fraction button is towards the top left, underneath 'Abs'. The picture on the button looks like a filled white box on top of a line, on top of an empty white box. If your calculator doesn't have a fraction button, don't worry — just skip straight to the section 'Doing fractions with decimals' in Chapter 7.

No matter how many times you press 'Abs', the button won't help you get a six-pack. Equally, 'tan' does nothing at all to make you look like you've been somewhere nice on holiday (in fact, 'Abs' and 'tan' are abbreviations for 'absolute value' and 'tangent', functions used in more advanced maths, which you don't need to worry about for now, phew).

You use the fractions button a little differently from the more everyday buttons on your calculator. Here, I walk you through how to do a sum like $\frac{3}{5} \times \frac{7}{8}$:

1. **To enter a fraction, press the fraction button.**

   The calculator shows a couple of stacked boxes in the display. The top box may contain a flashing line.

2. **Type the top number of the fraction.**

   In this example, you press 3.

3. **Press the round button.**

   The flashing line moves into the lower box.

4. **Type the bottom number of the fraction.**

   In this example, you press 5.

5. **Press the right side of the round button to escape from the box.**

6. **Carry on with the rest of the sum.**

   In this example you press the × button and enter $\frac{7}{8}$ using the fraction button like you did for Steps 1–5.

7. **Press the = button.**

   The calculator shows you the answer: $\frac{21}{40}$

If you need to turn your answer into a decimal, press the button marked with two arrows (it looks a little like this < >). On my calculator, this button is just above the enter key.

If you need to type in something like $1\frac{3}{4}$ into the calculator, it's pretty similar — the only difference is you press 'shift' before the fraction button:

1. **Press 'shift' (in the very top left) then the fraction button.**

   You see three boxes — a big one on the left and two smaller ones stacked as before (see Figure 6-5). The big box is for the number in front, and the smaller ones for the fraction, just like before.

2. **Fill in the first box with the whole number.**

   In this example, this is 1.

3. **Press right on the round button and fill in the top.**

   Three in this example.

4. **Press down on the round button and fill in the bottom.**

   Four in this example.

5. **Press right on the round button to escape from the boxes.**

   Now carry on with the rest of the sum.

Figure 6-5:
Typing
fractions
into a
calculator.

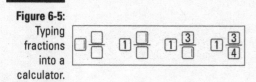

Don't worry if you make a mistake. Just press the 'AC' or 'C' button to clear everything away and start again. Or, if you feel brave, use the arrow keys and delete button to try to fix the mess.

Chapter 7

What's the Point? Dealing with Decimals

In This Chapter

▶ Understanding the decimal basics

▶ Using rounding and estimating when working with decimals

▶ Looking at decimal and fraction conversions

▶ Applying decimals to the Big Four operations

---

*B*ecause early humans used their fingers for counting, the number system is based on the number 10. So numbers come in ones, tens, hundreds, thousands, and so on. A *decimal* — with its handy decimal point — allows people to work with numbers smaller than 1: Tenths, hundredths, thousandths, and the like.

Here's some lovely news: Decimals are much easier to work with than fractions (which I discuss in Chapter 6). Decimals look and feel more like whole numbers than fractions do, so when you're working with decimals, you don't have to worry about reducing and increasing terms, improper fractions, mixed numbers, and a lot of other stuff.

Performing the main four operations — addition, subtraction, multiplication and division — on decimals is very similar to performing them on whole numbers (which I cover in Part I of this book). The numerals 0 through 9 work just like they usually do. As long as you get the decimal point in the right place, you're home free.

In this chapter, I show you all about working with decimals, including rounding and estimating. I also show you how to convert fractions to decimals and decimals to fractions. Finally, I give you a peek into the strange world of repeating decimals.

Understanding Basic Decimal Stuff

The good news about decimals is that they look a lot more like whole numbers than fractions do. So a lot of what you find out about whole numbers in Chapters 2 and 3 applies to decimals as well. In this section, I introduce you to decimals, starting with place value.

When you understand place value of decimals, a lot falls into place. Then I discuss trailing zeros and what happens when you move the decimal point either to the left or to the right.

Counting dollars and decimals

You use decimals all the time when you count money. And a great way to begin thinking about decimals is as dollars and cents. For example, you know that $0.50 is half of a dollar, so this information tells you:

$$0.5 = \frac{1}{2}$$

Notice that, in the decimal 0.5, I drop the zero at the end. This practice is common with decimals.

You also know that $0.25 is a quarter — that is, one-fourth of a dollar — so:

$$0.25 = \frac{1}{4}$$

Similarly, you know that $0.75 is three quarters, or three-fourths, of a dollar, so:

$$0.75 = \frac{3}{4}$$

Taking this idea even further, you can use the denominations of coins — 50¢, 20¢, 10¢ and 5¢ — to make further connections between decimals and fractions.

A 5¢ coin is five-hundreds of a dollar, or $0.05. Notice that I keep the zeros in the decimal 0.05. You can drop zeros from the right end of a decimal, but you can't drop zeros that fall between the decimal point and another digit.

Decimals are just as good for cutting up cake as for cutting up money. Figure 7-1 gives you a look at the four cut-up cakes that I show you in

Chapter 6. This time, I give you the decimals that tell you how much cake you have. Fractions and decimals accomplish the same task: Allowing you to cut a whole object into pieces and talk about how much you have.

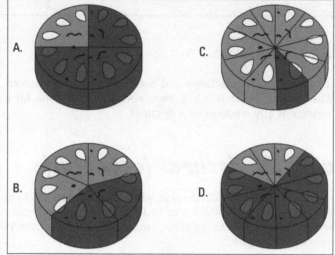

Figure 7-1:
Cakes cut and shaded into (A) 0.75, (B) 0.4, (C) 0.1, and (D) 0.7.

Identifying the place value of decimals

In Chapter 2, I mention the place value of whole numbers. Table 7-1 shows how the whole number 4,672 breaks down in terms of place value.

Table 7-1	Breaking Down 4,672 in Terms of Place Value		
Thousands	*Hundreds*	*Tens*	*Ones*
4	6	7	2

This number means 4,000 + 600 + 70 + 2.

With decimals, this idea is extended. First, a decimal point is placed to the right of the ones place in a whole number. Then more numbers are appended to the right of the decimal point.

For example, the decimal 4,672.389 breaks down as shown in Table 7-2.

Table 7-2				Breaking Down the Decimal 4,672.389			
Thousands	*Hundreds*	*Tens*	*Ones*	*Decimal Point*	*Tenths*	*Hundredths*	*Thousandths*
4	6	7	2	.	3	8	9

This decimal means $4,000 + 600 + 70 + 2 + \frac{3}{10} + \frac{8}{100} + \frac{9}{1,000}$.

The connection between fractions and decimals becomes obvious when you look at place value. Decimals really are a shorthand notation for fractions. You can represent any fraction as a decimal.

Knowing the decimal facts of life

When you understand how place value works in decimals (as I explain in the preceding section), a whole lot of facts about decimals begin to make sense. Two key ideas are trailing zeros and what happens when you move a decimal point left or right.

Understanding trailing zeros

You probably know that you can attach zeros to the beginning of a whole number without changing its value. For example, these three numbers are all equal in value:

27   027   0,000,027

The reason becomes clear when you know about place value of whole numbers. See Table 7-3.

Table 7-3		Example of Attaching Leading Zeros				
Millions	*Hundred Thousands*	*Ten Thousands*	*Thousands*	*Hundreds*	*Tens*	*Ones*
0	0	0	0	0	2	7

As you can see, 0,000,027 simply means $0 + 0 + 0 + 0 + 0 + 20 + 7$. No matter how many zeros you add to the beginning of a number, the number 27 doesn't change. Zeros attached to the beginning of a number in this way are called *leading* zeros.

In decimals, this idea of zeros that don't add value to a number can be extended to trailing zeros.

A trailing zero is any zero that appears to the right of both the decimal point and every digit other than zero. For example:

34.8   34.80   34.8000

All three of these numbers are the same. The reason becomes clear when you understand how place value works in decimals. See Table 7-4.

Table 7-4		Example of Attaching Trailing Zeros				
Tens	Ones	Decimal Point	Tenths	Hundredths	Thousandths	Ten Thousandths
3	4	.	8	0	0	0

In this example, 34.8000 means $40 + 4 + \frac{8}{10} + \frac{0}{100} + \frac{0}{1,000} + \frac{0}{10,000}$.

You can attach or remove as many trailing zeros as you want without changing the value of a number.

When you understand trailing zeros, you can see that every whole number can easily be changed to a decimal. Just attach a decimal point and a 0 to the end of it. For example:

$$4 = 4.0$$
$$20 = 20.0$$
$$971 = 971.0$$

Make sure that you don't attach or remove any non-leading or non-trailing zeros — it changes the value of the decimal. For example, look at this number:

0450.0070

In this number, you can remove the leading and trailing zeros without changing the value, as follows:

450.007

The remaining zeros, however, need to stay where they are as placeholders between the decimal point and digits other than zero. See Table 7-5.

I continue to discuss zeros as placeholders in the next section.

Table 7-5				Example of Zeros as Placeholders				
Thousands	Hundreds	Tens	Ones	Decimal Point	Tenths	Hundredths	Thou- sandths	Ten Thousandths
0	4	5	0	.	0	0	7	0

Moving the decimal point

When you're working with whole numbers, you can multiply any number by 10 just by adding a zero to the end of it. For example:

$$45,971 \times 10 = 459,710$$

To see why this answer is so, again think about the place value of digits and look at Table 7-6.

Table 7-6	Example, Decimal Points and Place Value of Digits					
Millions	Hundred Thousands	Ten Thousands	Thousands	Hundreds	Tens	Ones
		4	5	9	7	1
	4	5	9	7	1	0

Here's what these two numbers really mean:

$$45,971 = 40,000 + 5,000 + 900 + 70 + 1$$
$$459,710 = 400,000 + 50,000 + 9,000 + 700 + 10 + 0$$

As you can see, that little zero makes a big difference: It causes the rest of the numbers to shift one place.

This concept makes even more sense when you think about the decimal point. See Table 7-7.

Table 7-7		Example, Numbers Shifting One Place						
Hundred Thousands	Ten Thousands	Thousands	Hundreds	Tens	Ones	Decimal Point	Tenths	Hun- dredths
	4	5	9	7	1	.	0	0
4	5	9	7	1	0	.	0	0

In effect, adding a 0 to the end of a whole number moves the decimal point one place to the right. So for any decimal, when you move the decimal point one place to the right, you multiply that number by 10. This fact becomes clear when you start with a simple number like 7:

7.0

70.0

700.0

7,000.0

In this case, the net effect is that you moved the decimal point three places to the right, which is the same as multiplying 7 by 1,000.

Similarly, to divide any number by 10, move the decimal point one place to the left. For example:

7.0

0.7

0.07

0.007

This time, the net effect is that you moved the decimal point three places to the left, which is the same as dividing 7 by 1,000.

Are We Nearly There Yet? Rounding and Estimating

Rounding and estimating seem — on first glance — to be much less fundamental to maths than the main four operations you meet in Chapters 2 and 3. I would argue, however — and frequently do — that being able to estimate intelligently is at least as important a maths skill as knowing how to multiply and divide big numbers accurately.

In real life, you have computers for getting accurate answers. I genuinely can't think of a real-life situation where long division would be a useful skill (outside of a maths test). The important thing to me is to be able to ask 'Does that answer make sense, or have I made a mistake in what I've asked the computer to do?'

To answer that question, you need to have an idea of what the answer *ought* to be — which is where estimation comes in. Estimation is a simple process: Round off the numbers in your sum to something easy to work with, and then do the sum with those rough numbers. If I do my estimate and see that my computer's answer is off by a relatively huge amount, I know I've done something wrong and need to check things more carefully. If my answer is in the right neighbourhood, I can feel a bit more comfortable with it. (It doesn't mean I've *definitely* got it right, but it's a good indicator.)

In the following sections, I show you how to round off numbers, including those that use decimals, and then how to use rounded numbers to produce a solid estimate for your answer.

Rounding: What's nearest?

When I was a penniless student, trips to the supermarket were fraught. I had to buy enough food so I didn't starve, but I also had to make sure I didn't spend so much that I got kicked out of my flat for not paying my rent.

Because I thought I was terribly cool (for a maths student, anyway), I refused to walk around with a notepad, diligently adding up the exact cost of every tin of plain brand baked beans and loaf of generic, textureless bread product I threw in the basket. Instead, I started rounding. 'Those three tins together are 93¢ — that's about a dollar. That cardboard pizza is $1.17 — that's also about a dollar. That bottle of student special apple juice is $2.69 — let's call it three dollars.' Instead of juggling long and nasty numbers, I just counted the nearest dollars. For that hypothetical shopping bag, I'd have guessed $5 — not far away from the real value of $4.79, and certainly close enough to say 'I'm not spending too much.'

With rounding, instead of working with the full, ugly number, you pick a number that's near to the ugly one but much easier to work with.

A walk between two towns

Imagine you're running between two towns, Albury and Wodonga, which for this example I'm going to say are 10 kilometres apart — the same as 10,000 metres. After you run 1 kilometre, someone from Wodonga calls you and says, 'Are you nearly there yet?' You say, 'No, I'm still closer to Albury.' You reach the 4.95 kilometre mark and your phone goes again. 'No,' you say, 'I'm still closer to Albury — but not by much. I'm practically halfway.' At 5.05 kilometres, you've gone more than halfway and can say to your friend in Wodonga, 'I'm nearly there — I just passed halfway.'

This is how rounding works: You decide which of the two options you're closer to by looking at whether you're more or less than halfway between the two options.

If you're less than halfway to the next town — or number — you're closer to where you came from (and so you *round down*). If you're more than halfway, you're closer to where you're going (and so you *round up*).

Rounding on a ruler

You don't need to run between two towns to round off distance to an *appropriate degree of accuracy*. If you measure something with a ruler, you probably automatically do a little bit of rounding — the chances of a measurement landing absolutely precisely on a millimetre mark are pretty small, and in any case you may not need such a precise measurement.

Using a ruler, you look and make a judgement about whether the thing you're measuring is closer to one mark or the other. You don't waste time wondering whether the thing is 12.76 millimetres or 12.77 millimetres long — in most cases (where we're concerned, anyway) you can happily say the thing is 13 millimetres long.

You can use a ruler to get the hang of rounding decimals quite easily, at least for numbers up to 30. Here's what you do if you have to round something below 30 to the nearest whole number (I give you a non-ruler-based method later in this chapter, so don't worry if you don't have one to hand):

1. **Find the whole number you want on the ruler.**

   For example, if you want to round 15.43 to the nearest whole number, look on your ruler for 15.

2. **Go to the millimetre mark corresponding to the first digit after the decimal point in your number.**

   In our example, the first number after the decimal point is 4, so you look for the fourth millimetre mark.

3. **Ask whether you're to the left or right of the slightly bigger tick marking midway.**

   In our example, if you're on the 15 side, your answer is 15. If you're closer to 16, you round up to 16. (For the record, 15.43 rounds down to 15.)

I show the ruler-rounding process in detail in Figure 7-2.

All rounding is based on the idea of finding which measurement (at a given accuracy) your number is closest to.

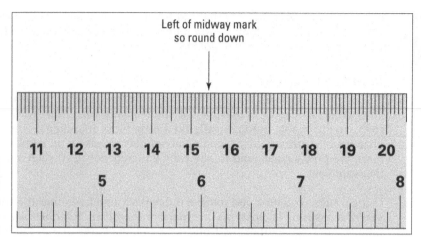

Figure 7-2:
Rounding
on a ruler.

Tie-breaks: What to do when you're midway

When I was about seven, my family went on a trip to Queensland. A sign marks the border between New South Wales and Queensland. Being a literal-minded elder daughter and vaguely aware that I was supposed to test boundaries, I stood with one foot on either side of the marker and asked what state I was in. I still believe I deserved a better answer than an eye-roll and a sigh.

In maths, though, we have an answer for rounding numbers that are exactly halfway: They go up. If you have to round $4.50 to the nearest dollar, you call it five dollars, even though the price is equally far from four dollars and five dollars.

Rounding decimals

Rounding decimals works almost exactly the same as rounding numbers. You'll use this skill when dividing decimals later in the chapter. Most commonly, you need to round a decimal either to a whole number or to one or two decimal places.

To round a decimal to a whole number, focus on the ones digit and the tenths digit. Round the decimal either up or down to the nearest whole number, dropping the decimal point:

$$7.1 \rightarrow 7 \quad 32.9 \rightarrow 33 \quad 184.3 \rightarrow 184$$

When the tenths digit is 5, round the decimal up:

$$83.5 \rightarrow 84 \quad 296.5 \rightarrow 297 \quad 1,788.5 \rightarrow 1,789$$

If the decimal has other decimal digits, just drop them:

$$18.\underline{4}7 \rightarrow 18 \quad 21.\underline{6}18 \rightarrow 22 \quad 3.\underline{1}415927 \rightarrow 3$$

Occasionally, a small change to the ones digit affects the other digits. (If you've ever seen the odometer in a car roll a bunch of 9s over to 0s, this example may remind you of that):

$$99.\underline{9} \rightarrow 100 \quad 999.\underline{5} \rightarrow 1,000 \quad 99,999.\underline{7}12 \rightarrow 100,000$$

The same basic idea applies to rounding a decimal to any number of places. For example, to round a decimal to one decimal place, focus on the first and second decimal places (that is, the tenths and hundredths places):

$$76.\underline{54}3 \rightarrow 76.5 \quad 100.\underline{68}22 \rightarrow 100.7 \quad 10.\underline{10}101 \rightarrow 10.1$$

To round a decimal to two decimal places, focus on the second and third decimal places (that is, the hundredths and thousandths places):

$$444.4\underline{44}4 \rightarrow 444.44 \quad 26.5\underline{55}55 \rightarrow 26.56 \quad 99.9\underline{97} \rightarrow 100.00$$

A common misconception

I was about ten the first time I ever realised that a teacher could possibly be wrong. My class was learning about rounding, and the teacher said, 'If you have to round something like 1.45 to the nearest whole number, you round it up to 1.5 and then to 2.'

No! No, no, no, no, no! And, furthermore, no.

The number 1.45 is categorically *not* as close to 2 as it is to 1. The number 1.45 is less than halfway to 2, and so you round it down to 1.

The only important number for deciding whether to round a whole number up or down is the one immediately after the dot. As mentioned in the preceding section, forget everything after that line: Those digits are dead to you.

That's about right: Estimating answers

Imagine you're in a shop and need to buy 80 Christmas cards at 99¢ ($0.99) each. (I know this example is unrealistic. Just roll with it for a minute.) How much will your cards cost?

Rather than get your calculator or your pen and paper, you can make a sensible guess — each card costs almost exactly a dollar, so your total haul is something pretty close to $80. (The exact answer, if you want to practise your arithmetic skills, is $79.20 — so not far off $80.)

Estimating answers like this is one of the most important skills in maths — having an idea of what you expect an answer to be can help you spot calculator mistakes very quickly.

One of the reasons I find estimating so important is that you have to think about what's going on. As an entrepreneur, I'd prefer to employ someone who thinks about problems but sometimes makes mistakes over someone who uses algorithms immaculately. (Everyone makes mistakes. Not everyone takes a moment to check whether the answer is reasonable.) In a multiple-choice exam, estimating is especially useful, because you can often throw out an option or two as completely implausible after a quick estimation.

In the next section, I show you how to come up with a decent estimate of a sum by rounding all of the numbers to the first digit (or *most significant figure*) when asked to, and give you an idea of how to use the technique even when you're not asked about it.

Rough and ready: Rounding to the first digit

The benefit of rounding to the first digit is that you end up with a much easier sum to work with than if you did it the long way. Think about this: Would you rather work out $1,234 \times 5,678 \div 60,210$, or $1,000 \times 6,000 \div 60,000$? I know which I find easier — the second one comes out to 100, just using my head. The exact answer is a little over 116, using a calculator — on paper, that question would take *me* several minutes, and I'm good at this stuff.

The trick is to round everything to the biggest number you can get away with. In the preceding example, 1,234 to the nearest thousand is 1,000; 5,678 to the nearest thousand is 6,000; and 60,210 to the nearest ten thousand is 60,000. Then you simply split off the zeros, just like in this example:

> A sales rep drives 936 kilometres in a month. Her car travels around 10 kilometres on one litre of petrol. Petrol costs $1.33 per litre. She estimates her monthly fuel cost by rounding her distance travelled to the nearest 100 kilometres and the cost of petrol to the nearest 10¢.
>
> What is her estimate?

1. **Do the rounding that the question suggests.**

   Round her distance to 900 kilometres and the cost of petrol to $1.30 (or 130¢).

2. Work out the amount of fuel needed.

900 kilometres divided by 10 kilometres per litre gives 90 litres of petrol.

3. To work out the cost, do 90 × 130¢.

For the moment, put the zeros at the end to one side, but take a note that you have two of them. That leaves you with 9 × 13.

4. Do this sum using your favourite times method.

The answer is 117. Adding the two zeros back on gives 11,700¢.

5. Turn the figure back into dollars.

Your final answer is $117.

Take the following steps to round a sum to the first digit:

1. Take each number in the sum in turn and decide what's the biggest number you can get away with rounding to.

Hint: Try the first number in the sum that's not a zero.

2. Round each number, being careful to round up or down as appropriate.

3. Work out the sum with the rounded numbers.

4. Write down your answer.

Remember your answer is only an estimate. The real answer could be significantly bigger or smaller, especially if you round a number that is close to halfway, or if you round all the numbers in the same direction (all up or all down). The idea isn't to get an exact answer (for that, you can just use a calculator) but to get an answer that's in the right ballpark.

As a general rule, I expect the answer to be between double and half of the estimate most of the time, and practically never more than ten times bigger or less than a tenth of the size — although this varies depending on the calculation and the roughness of the rounding.

Rounding in the middle of the sum

Sometimes, halfway through a sum, you wind up with a horrible mess of a number. Maybe you add things together and end up with something that isn't so nice any more. Maybe you times or divide and get an ugly answer.

Don't panic! My swift and brutal solution to your problem is simply to round off again.

Make sure you follow the same steps as before — remember, you're looking for a rough ballpark answer rather than getting a bang-on result.

Careful with that calculator!

Calculators are marvellous machines. Even since I was at school, which wasn't *that* long ago, calculators have become more and more sophisticated — and I'm pretty sure that the scientific calculators on the market today are more powerful than the best computers I had access to in the 1990s.

As far as the calculations in this book go, you don't need a crazy fancy calculator — one that doesn't have much more than the numbers, the operations (add, take away, times, divide) and a decimal point should serve you perfectly well. But if you hope to do more maths after reading this book, you may want to invest in a good scientific calculator. My personal favourite is the TI-30XB (the one with a big round button near the top-right). It's even available in green, if you think black and grey are too boring!

Whatever kind of calculator you have, it's certain to be better at doing sums than you

are. I don't mean that as a put-down — after all, calculators are better at pretty much *any* kind of sum than *I* am — but a teensy-weensy problem exists with all calculators.

The problem with learning to juggle is that the balls always go where you throw them. Likewise, calculators do *exactly* what you tell them. Your calculator has no idea whether you've asked it to do the right thing.

This is one of the reasons I recommend coming up with a rough answer on paper, even if you use a calculator: Your estimate can save you from coming up with embarrassingly wrong answers.

In real life, do a rough version of every sum on paper before you ask your calculator or computer, just to get a ballpark figure for the answer.

Checking your answers

One of the main uses of estimating and rounding is to check that the answers you get from more accurate methods — say, working out sums on paper or using a calculator — make some kind of sense.

Estimating and rounding can't tell you for sure that you have the right answer — if it could do that, doing the full sum would be pointless — but the various methods I show you in this chapter give you an idea of whether your accurate answer is reasonable.

The first, and probably most reliable, port of call for estimating an answer is to think about your real-life experience and guess what range of answers you expect to get. For example, to answer a question about a car journey between two towns 50 kilometres apart, try thinking about the last time you went on a journey of about 50 kilometres. How long did your journey take?

Depending on the roads, maybe 45 minutes to an hour? Here's how I may react to some different answers:

- ✔ **My guess and my answer disagree significantly:** If I work out an answer of 12 minutes or 8 hours, I may scratch my head and say, 'That can't *possibly* be right!' and do the sum all over again.

- ✔ **My guess is a little off of my answer:** If I get an answer of 40 minutes or 2.5 hours, I may say, 'Hmm, that's not quite what I expected, but it's not completely implausible — let me check my numbers just to be sure.'

- ✔ **My guess is pretty good:** If I get an answer somewhere around an hour, I may pat myself on the back and say, 'That seems about right — I can run with that.'

This is pretty much the standard way of checking your answers, whatever method you pick to come up with a ballpark number. You can decide whether your answer is just plain wrong, a little iffy or perfectly plausible — and do the appropriate thing (start over, check it over or celebrate).

Linking Decimals to Fractions

In this chapter, I talk about the number directly after the dot as 'how many tenths', the number after that as 'how many hundredths' and so on. Decimals are just another way of writing fractions in a simple way. You may want to have a look at Chapter 6 before you wade through this section if you're not comfortable with fractions. The number 75.43 means seven tens, five units, four tenths and three hundredths — or $70 + 5 + \frac{4}{10} + \frac{3}{100}$. Each new decimal place gives you another fraction with an extra zero on the bottom — the next one here would be something over 1,000, then something over 10,000, and so on.

In practice, we don't work out decimals like that. Instead, you know that $\frac{4}{10}$ is the same as $\frac{40}{100}$, so $\frac{4}{10} + \frac{3}{100}$ is the same as $\frac{40}{100} + \frac{3}{100}$, or $\frac{43}{100}$. I describe this nice easy way to turn decimals into fractions in detail in this section.

Turning a fraction into a decimal is a bit more of a hassle. You first turn the bar of the fraction into a divide sign. So to work out $\frac{3}{5}$ as a decimal, you work out $3 \div 5$ — which is 0.6. I show you how to do this later in this section.

Also in this section I include a table of decimal/fraction conversions with some notes on remembering them easily.

Converting decimals to fractions

Converting decimals to fractions is as easy as counting. Well ... maybe not quite as easy as counting, but counting is a significant part of the sum you do. Here's what you do:

1. **Ignore anything to the left of the decimal point.**

    When you convert a decimal to a fraction, the answer is either a fraction (in which case your number has no digits to the left of the decimal point) or a whole number followed by a fraction, such as $2\frac{1}{2}$ — the number to the left of the decimal point is simply the whole number.

2. **Count the number of digits to the right of the decimal point.**

    The bottom of the fraction is 1 followed by this many zeros.

3. **Work out the top of the fraction.**

    Write down all of the digits to the right of the decimal point. You can leave off any zeros at the beginning, but not zeros in the middle or at the end.

4. **Write down the top and bottom of the fraction.**

    Cancel down if possible (I explain cancelling in detail in Chapter 6).

5. **On a new line, write the whole number, if there's one, from Step 1, followed by the cancelled-down fraction.**

    You're done!

For example, here's what you do to convert 1.75 into a fraction:

1. **Leave the 1 alone.**

2. **You count two digits to the right of the decimal point.**

    So the bottom of the fraction is 100.

3. **The top of the fraction is 75.**

4. **The fraction is** $\frac{75}{100}$.

   You can cancel down to $\frac{15}{20}$ and then $\frac{3}{4}$

5. **Bring back the 1 from earlier and write it in front of the fraction.**

   Your answer is $1\frac{3}{4}$.

Converting fractions to decimals

A fraction is really a divide sum — you can think of the bar in a fraction as a divide sign. So if you want to convert a fraction to a decimal, you just divide the top number by the bottom number — have a look at Chapter 3 on dividing if you could use a refresher.

When you divide decimals, you have to put a dot at the end of the number you're dividing, the one that goes 'under the bus stop' when you write it out. You then add the right number of zeros afterwards. Remember: Sticking zeros after the decimal point is like adding no 1 or 10¢ pieces— you don't actually change the number but you write a number that can then split up evenly if you want.

Follow these steps if you want to convert a fraction into a decimal number:

1. **If your fraction has a whole number in front, ignore that number for the moment.**

   You bring the whole number back in at the end.

2. **Draw a 'bus stop', as I explain in Chapter 3 on dividing.**

3. **Under the bus stop, write the number you want to divide, followed by a decimal point and as many zeros as you think you need.**

   Three zeros are probably plenty, but leave space at the end of the bus stop in case you need more — and there's no harm in having too many zeros!

4. **Put a dot above the bus stop, directly above the decimal point in the number below.**

5. **In front of the bus stop, write the number you want to divide by.**

6. **Divide as usual.**

   Completely ignore the decimal point.

7. **If you get to the end of the number with a remainder left over, add a zero to the end.**

   Carry on until you have no remainder.

8. **If you had a whole number in Step 1, add the whole number back in just before the decimal point.**

   For example, if your answer so far is 0.75 and you ignored a 1 in Step 1, your final answer is 1.75.

In Figure 7-3 I show you how to convert $4\frac{3}{8}$ into a decimal.

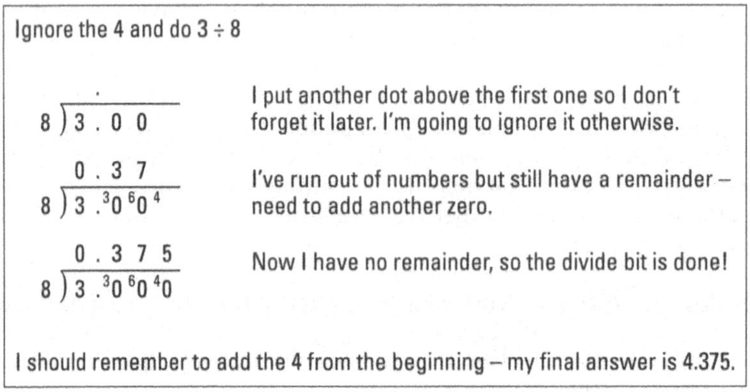

Figure 7-3: A worked example of converting a fraction into a decimal number.

Ignore the 4 and do $3 \div 8$

$$8 \,)\overline{3 \,.\, 0 \,\,\, 0}$$

I put another dot above the first one so I don't forget it later. I'm going to ignore it otherwise.

$$\begin{array}{r} 0\,.\,3\,7 \\ 8\,)\overline{3\,.\,^30\,^60\,^4} \end{array}$$

I've run out of numbers but still have a remainder – need to add another zero.

$$\begin{array}{r} 0\,.\,3\,7\,5 \\ 8\,)\overline{3\,.\,^30\,^60\,^40} \end{array}$$

Now I have no remainder, so the divide bit is done!

I should remember to add the 4 from the beginning – my final answer is 4.375.

Remembering some common fractions and decimals

Certain fractions and decimals come up over and over again, so I list them in Table 7-8. If you get bored of working them out each time, try learning the numbers in the table.

Table 7-8	Common Fractions and Decimals	
Decimal	**Fraction**	**Comment**
0.01	$\frac{1}{100}$	\$0.01 is one cent — and 100¢ is \$1.
0.05	$\frac{1}{20}$	Twenty 5¢ pieces make \$1.

Decimal	Fraction	Comment
0.1 (or 0.10)	$\frac{1}{10}$	Ten 10¢ pieces make $1.
0.2 (or 0.20)	$\frac{1}{5}$	Five 20¢ pieces make $1.
0.25	$\frac{1}{4}$	In the US, a quarter is 25¢.
0.5 (or 0.50)	$\frac{1}{2}$	Two 50¢ pieces make $1.
0.75	$\frac{3}{4}$	Three times as big as a quarter.

Doing fractions with decimals

If your calculator doesn't have a fractions button, or you don't like the thought of using this button, you can work out your fraction sums using decimals. Instead of using the fraction button, you need to turn your fractions into divide sums. Here's an example for the sum $\frac{1}{2} + \frac{9}{10}$:

1. **Type the top number of the first fraction, then the divide key, and then the bottom number.**

   For this example, you do 1 ÷ 2.

2. **Carry on with the sum in the normal way.**

   In this example, type the + sign.

3. **Treat the second fraction as you did in Step 1.**

   In this example, type 9 ÷ 10.

4. **Press the = key.**

   Your calculator should say 1.4. If your calculator gives the answer as a fraction — in this example, $1\frac{2}{5}$ — press the < > button in the middle towards the right to convert the fraction to a decimal.

A recurring theme

I start this section with a divide sum: What is 1 ÷ 3? (If you find this difficult, look first at Chapter 3, where I give the details of division.) For example:

> I have $1 and want to split it between three people. I split the dollar into ten 10¢ pieces and give everyone three 10¢ pieces. But I have a 10¢ piece left over. Now imagine Australia still had 1¢ coins (taken out of circulation in 1992 so, I know, this is like imagining ancient history.) I change the 10¢ piece into ten 1¢ pieces, and I give everyone three 1¢ pieces. But I have a cent left over. Because I'm in charge, I decide a tenth of a cent exists, and I change my cent into ten tenth-of-a-cent coins. Again, everyone gets three ... and again, I have one left over. No matter how finely I divide the coins, everyone always gets three coins and I have one left over. I show what I mean in Figure 7-4.

Figure 7-4:
1 ÷ 3:
A recurring decimal.

$$
3 \overline{)\, 1 \,.\,{}^10\,{}^10\,{}^10\,{}^10\,{}^10} \quad 0\,.\,3\;3\;3\;3\;3\;...
$$

This pattern repeats forever. We call the number a *recurring decimal* because the number three recurs over and over and over and ...

Every fraction with a whole number on the top and bottom can be written either as a terminating decimal or as a recurring decimal. Sometimes the recurring pattern is longer than one digit — for example, $\frac{1}{11} = 0.0909...$ Sometimes the pattern doesn't start straightaway — for example, $\frac{1}{6} = 0.16666...$ Eventually the number either falls into a pattern or stops — in which case the number is a *terminating decimal*.

Don't worry, I explain terminating and repeating decimals in the following sections.

The last stop: Terminating decimals

Sometimes when you divide the numerator of a fraction by the denominator, the division eventually works out evenly. The result is a *terminating decimal*.

For example, suppose you want to change the fraction $\frac{2}{5}$ to a decimal. Here's your first step:

$$5\overline{)2}$$

One glance at this problem and it looks like you're doomed from the start because 5 doesn't go into 2. But watch what happens when I add a few trailing zeros. Notice that I also place another decimal point in the answer just above the first decimal point. This step is important — you can read more about it in 'Dividing decimals':

$$5\overline{)2.000}^{\,.}$$

Now you can divide because, although 5 doesn't go into 2, 5 does go into 20 four times:

$$
\begin{array}{r}
0.4 \\
5\overline{)2.000} \\
\underline{20} \\
0
\end{array}
$$

You're done! As it turns out, you needed only one trailing zero, so you can ignore the rest:

$$\frac{2}{5} = 0.4$$

Because the division worked out evenly, the answer is an example of a *terminating decimal*.

As another example, suppose you want to find out how to represent $\frac{7}{16}$ as a decimal. As earlier, I attach three trailing zeros:

$$
\begin{array}{r}
0.437 \\
16\overline{)7.000} \\
\underline{64} \\
60 \\
\underline{48} \\
120 \\
\underline{112} \\
8
\end{array}
$$

This time, three trailing zeros aren't enough to get my answer, so I attach a few more and continue:

```
        0.4375
 16)7.000000
    64
    ──
     60
     48
     ──
    120
    112
    ───
      80
      80
      ──
       0
```

At last, the division works out evenly, so again the answer is a terminating decimal. Therefore, $\frac{7}{16} = 0.4375$.

The endless ride: Repeating decimals

Sometimes when you try to convert a fraction to a decimal, the division *never* works out evenly. The result is a *repeating decimal* — a decimal that cycles through the same number pattern forever.

You may recognise these pesky little critters from your calculator, when an apparently simple division problem produces a long string of numbers.

For example, to change $\frac{2}{3}$ to a decimal, begin by dividing 2 by 3. As in the last section, start by adding three trailing zeros, and see where it leads:

```
      0.666
 3)2.000
   18
   ──
    20
    18
    ──
     20
     18
     ──
      2
```

At this point, you still haven't found an exact answer. But you may notice that a repeating pattern has developed in the division. No matter how many trailing zeros you attach to the number 2, the same pattern continues forever. This answer, 0.666 ..., is an example of a repeating decimal. You can write $\frac{2}{3}$ as

$$\frac{2}{3} = 0.\overline{6}$$

The bar over the 6 means that, in this decimal, the number 6 repeats forever. You can represent many simple fractions as repeating decimals. In fact, *every* fraction can be represented either as a repeating decimal or as a terminating decimal — that is, as an ordinary decimal that ends.

Now suppose you want to find the decimal representation of $\frac{5}{11}$. Here's how this problem plays out:

$$
\begin{array}{r}
0.4545 \\
11\overline{)5.0000} \\
\underline{44} \\
60 \\
\underline{55} \\
50 \\
\underline{44} \\
60 \\
\underline{55} \\
5
\end{array}
$$

This time, the pattern repeats every other number — 4, then 5, then 4 again, and then 5 again, forever. Attaching more trailing zeros to the original decimal only strings out this pattern indefinitely. So you can write

$$\frac{5}{11} = 0.\overline{45}$$

This time, the bar is over both the 4 and the 5, telling you that these two numbers alternate forever.

Repeating decimals are an oddity, but they aren't hard to work with. In fact, as soon as you can show that a decimal division is repeating, you've found your answer. Just remember to place the bar only over the numbers that keep on repeating.

Recurring decimals are particularly problematic on a calculator that doesn't deal comfortably with fractions. If you work out the sum $\frac{1}{2}+\frac{1}{3}=\frac{5}{6}$ and want to your answer on a calculator, figuring out what to type in is difficult — try following these steps to see what I mean:

1. **Work out the first number on the calculator.**

   In this example, do 1 ÷ 2 and write down the answer (0.5). If the answer's a recurring decimal, just write the first few digits until you see a pattern.

2. **Do the same for the second number.**

   In this example, work out 1 ÷ 3 and write down 0.333 (no need to go overboard with the 3s).

3. **Type the sum into the calculator with decimals.**

   For this example, do 0.5 + 0.333 and write down 0.833.

4. **Calculate the answer you worked out by hand.**

   $5 \div 6 = 0.8333\ldots$

5. **If the numbers are pretty much identical, be happy you have the answer right.**

   Don't worry too much about the last decimal place of what you write down, but any differences before that might be a clue that something is wrong.

Performing the Main Four Operations with Decimals

Everything you already know about adding, subtracting, multiplying, and dividing whole numbers (see Chapters 2 and 3) carries over when you work with decimals. In fact, each case really only has one key difference: How to handle that pesky little decimal point. In this section, I show you how to perform the main four maths operations with decimals.

The most common use of adding and subtracting decimals is working with money. In Chapter 9, you find that multiplying and dividing by decimals is also useful for calculating percentages.

Adding decimals

Adding decimals is almost as easy as adding whole numbers. As long as you set up the problem correctly, you're in good shape. To add decimals, follow these steps:

1. **Arrange the numbers in a column and line up the decimal points vertically. Grid paper can be especially useful if you are finding it difficult to line up the digits and the decimal point.**

2. **Add as usual, column by column, from right to left.**

3. **Place the decimal point in the answer in line with the other decimal points in the problem.**

For example, suppose you want to add the numbers 14.5 and 1.89. Line up the decimal points neatly, as follows:

$$
\begin{array}{r}
14.5 \\
+\,1.89 \\
\hline
\end{array}
$$

Begin adding from the right-most column. Treat the blank space after 14.5 as a 0 — you can write this in as a trailing 0 (see earlier in this chapter to see why adding zeros to the end of a decimal doesn't change its value). Adding this column gives you $0 + 9 = 9$:

$$
\begin{array}{r}
14.50 \\
+\,1.89 \\
\hline
9
\end{array}
$$

Continuing to the left, $5 + 8 = 13$, so put down the 3 and carry the 1:

$$
\begin{array}{r}
1 \\
14.50 \\
+\,1.89 \\
\hline
39
\end{array}
$$

Complete the problem column by column and, at the end, put the decimal point directly below the others in the problem:

$$
\begin{array}{r}
14.50 \\
+\ \ 1.89 \\
\hline
16.39
\end{array}
$$

When adding more than one decimal, the same rules apply. For example, suppose you want to add 15.1 + 0.005 + 800 + 1.2345. The most important idea is lining up the decimal points correctly:

$$
\begin{array}{r}
15.1 \\
0.005 \\
800.0 \\
+\ 1.2345 \\
\hline
\end{array}
$$

To avoid mistakes, be especially neat when adding a lot of decimals.

Because the number 800 isn't a decimal, I place a decimal point and a 0 at the end of it, to be clear about how to line it up. If you like, you can make sure all numbers have the same number of decimal places (in this case, four) by adding trailing zeros. When you properly set up the problem, the addition is no more difficult than in any other addition problem:

$$
\begin{array}{r}
15.1000 \\
0.0050 \\
800.0000 \\
+1.2345 \\
\hline
816.3395
\end{array}
$$

Subtracting decimals

Subtracting decimals uses the same trick as adding them (which I talk about in the preceding section). Here's how you subtract decimals:

1. **Arrange the numbers in a column and line up the decimal points. There is no shame in using grid paper for this process either.**

2. **Subtract as usual, column by column from right to left.**

3. **When you're done, place the decimal point in the answer in line with the other decimal points in the problem.**

For example, suppose you want to figure out 144.87 – 0.321. First, line up the decimal points:

$$
\begin{array}{r}
144.870 \\
-0.321 \\
\hline
\end{array}
$$

In this case, I add a zero at the end of the first decimal. This placeholder reminds you that, in the right-most column, you need to borrow to get the answer to 0 – 1:

$$
\begin{array}{r}
\mathbf{6} \\
144.8\cancel{7}\ 10 \\
-\ 0.32\ \ \ 1 \\
\hline
4\ 9
\end{array}
$$

The rest of the problem is straightforward. Just finish the subtraction and drop the decimal point straight down:

$$
\begin{array}{r}
\mathbf{6} \\
144.8\cancel{7}\ 10 \\
-\ 0.32\ \ \ 1 \\
\hline
144.54\ \ 9
\end{array}
$$

So 144.87 – 0.321 = 144.549.

As with addition, the decimal point in the answer goes directly below where it appears in the problem.

Multiplying decimals

Multiplying decimals is different from adding and subtracting them, in that you don't have to worry about lining up the decimal points (see the preceding sections). In fact, the only difference between multiplying whole numbers and decimals comes at the end.

Here's how to multiply decimals:

1. **Perform the multiplication as you do for whole numbers.**

2. **When you're done, count the number of digits to the right of the decimal point in each factor, and add the result.**

3. **Place the decimal point in your answer so that your answer has the same number of digits after the decimal point.**

This process sounds tricky, but multiplying decimals can actually be simpler than adding or subtracting them. Suppose, for instance, that you want to multiply 23.5 by 0.16. The first step is to pretend that you're multiplying numbers without decimal points:

$$
\begin{array}{r}
23.5 \\
\times\,0.16 \\
\hline
1410 \\
2350 \\
\hline
3760 \\
\end{array}
$$

This answer isn't complete, though, because you still need to find out where the decimal point goes in the answer. To do this, notice that 23.5 has one digit after the decimal point and that 0.16 has two digits after the decimal point. Because $1 + 2 = 3$, place the decimal point in the answer so that it has three digits after the decimal point. (You can put your pencil at the 0 at the end of 3760 and move the decimal point three places to the left.)

$$
\begin{array}{ll}
23.5 & \text{1 digit after the decimal point} \\
\underline{\times 0.16} & \text{2 digit after the decimal point} \\
1410 & \\
2350 & \\
\hline
3760 & 1 + 2 = 3 \text{ digits after the decimal point}
\end{array}
$$

Even though the last digit in the answer is a 0, you still need to count this as a digit when placing the decimal point. When the decimal point is in place, you can drop trailing zeros (flip to 'Understanding Basic Decimal Stuff,' earlier in this chapter, to see why the zeros at the end of a decimal don't change the value of the number).

So the answer is 3.760, which is equal to 3.76.

Dividing decimals

Long division has never been a crowd pleaser. Dividing decimals is almost the same as dividing whole numbers, which is why a lot of people don't particularly like dividing decimals, either.

But at least you can take comfort in the fact that, when you know how to do long division (which I cover in Chapter 3), figuring out how to divide decimals is easy. The main difference comes at the beginning, before you start dividing.

Here's how to divide decimals:

1. **Turn the divisor (the number you're dividing by) into a whole number by moving the decimal point all the way to the right; at the same time, move the decimal point in the dividend (the number you're dividing) the same number of places to the right.**

   For example, suppose you want to divide 10.274 by 0.11. Write the problem as usual:

   $$0.11\overline{)10.274}$$

   Turn 0.11 into a whole number by moving the decimal point in 0.11 two places to the right, giving you 11. At the same time, move the decimal point in 10.274 two places to the right, giving you 1,027.4:

   $$11.\overline{)1027.4}$$

2. **Place a decimal point in the quotient (the answer) directly above where the decimal point now appears in the dividend.**

   Here's what this step looks like:

   $$11.\overline{)1027.4}$$

3. **Divide as usual, being careful to line up the quotient properly so that the decimal point falls into place.**

   To start out, notice that 11 is too large to go into either 1 or 10. However, 11 does go into 102 (nine times). So write the first digit of the quotient just above the 2 and continue:

   $$
   \begin{array}{r}
   9. \\
   11.\overline{)1027.4} \\
   \underline{99} \\
   37
   \end{array}
   $$

   I paused after bringing down the next number, 7. This time, 11 goes into 37 three times. The important point is to place the next digit in the answer just above the 7:

   $$
   \begin{array}{r}
   93. \\
   11.\overline{)1027.4} \\
   \underline{99} \\
   37 \\
   \underline{33} \\
   44
   \end{array}
   $$

I paused after bringing down the next number, 4. Now, 11 goes into 44 four times. Again, be careful to place the next digit in the quotient just above the 4, and complete the division:

$$
\begin{array}{r}
93.4 \\
11\overline{)1027.4} \\
\underline{99} \\
37 \\
\underline{33} \\
44 \\
\underline{44} \\
0
\end{array}
$$

So the answer is 93.4. As you can see, as long as you're careful when placing the decimal point and the digits, the correct answer appears with the decimal point in the right position.

Dealing with more zeros in the dividend

Sometimes you have to add one or more trailing zeros to the dividend. As I discuss earlier in this chapter, you can add as many trailing zeros as you like to a decimal without changing its value. For example, suppose you want to divide 67.8 by 0.333:

$$0.333\overline{)67.8}$$

Follow these steps:

1. **Change 0.333 into a whole number by moving the decimal point three places to the right; at the same time, move the decimal point in 67.8 three places to the right:**

   $$333.\overline{)67800.}$$

   In this case, when you move the decimal point in 67.8, you run out of room, so you have to add a couple zeros to the dividend. This step is perfectly valid, and you need to do this whenever the divisor has more decimal places than the dividend.

2. **Place the decimal point in the quotient directly above where it appears in the dividend:**

   $$333.\overline{)67800.}$$

3. **Divide as usual, being careful to correctly line up the numbers in the quotient. This time, 333 doesn't go into 6 or 67, but it does go into 678 (two times). So place the first digit of the quotient directly above the 8:**

$$
\begin{array}{r}
2 . \\
333.\overline{)67800.} \\
\underline{666} \\
120
\end{array}
$$

I've jumped forward in the division to the place where I bring down the first 0. At this point, 333 doesn't go into 120, so you need to put a 0 above the first 0 in 67,800 and bring down the second 0. Now, 333 does go into 1,200, so place the next digit in the answer (3) over the second 0:

$$
\begin{array}{r}
203. \\
333.\overline{)67800.} \\
\underline{666} \\
1200 \\
\underline{999} \\
201
\end{array}
$$

This time, the division doesn't work out evenly. If this were a problem with whole numbers, you'd finish by writing down a remainder of 201. (For more on remainders in division, see Chapter 3.) But decimals are a different story. The next section explains why, with decimals, the show must go on.

Completing decimal division

When you're dividing whole numbers, you can complete the problem simply by writing down the remainder. But remainders are never allowed in decimal division.

A common way to complete a problem in decimal division is to round off the answer. In most cases, you're instructed to round your answer to the nearest whole number or to one or two decimal places (see earlier in this chapter to find out how to round off decimals).

To complete a decimal division problem by rounding it off, you need to add at least one trailing zero to the dividend:

✔ To round a decimal to a whole number, add one trailing zero.

✔ To round a decimal to one decimal place, add two trailing zeros.

✔ To round a decimal to two decimal places, add three trailing zeros.

Here's what the problem looks like with a trailing zero attached:

$$
\begin{array}{r}
203. \\
333.\overline{)67800.0} \\
\underline{666} \\
1200 \\
\underline{999} \\
2010
\end{array}
$$

Attaching a trailing zero doesn't change a decimal, but it does allow you to bring down one more number, changing 201 into 2,010. Now you can divide 333 into 2,010:

$$
\begin{array}{r}
203.6 \\
333.\overline{)67800.0} \\
\underline{666} \\
1200 \\
\underline{999} \\
2010 \\
\underline{1998} \\
12
\end{array}
$$

At this point, you can round the answer to the nearest whole number, 204.

Chapter 8

It's All Relative: Ratios, Proportions and Speed

In This Chapter

▶ Finding the sum with the Table of Joy

▶ Thinking rationally about ratios

▶ Perfecting proportions

▶ Whipping through time and speed sums

Ratio and proportion are both about the relative size of things. If I say I'm going to split something with you 50:50, I'm using a ratio to describe how big your share is in comparison with mine — in this case, the two shares are the same. If we split something 60:40, one of us has a bigger share than the other — the ratio tells us how much bigger.

Proportion is similar to ratio, only it generally says something like 'you've got twice as much as I have' or 'I need three times as many of all the ingredients.'

The difference between proportion and ratio is really all in the way you write them: Ratios have a colon between two (or more) numbers, and proportion says directly, 'This is so many times bigger or smaller.'

Since proportion and ratio are so similar, I tackle them both the same way, using a tool called the Table of Joy, which I lay out for you in this chapter. The Table of Joy is an insanely useful tool. I use it in all sorts of chapters in this book to help you work out percentages, draw pie charts and any number of other things.

Don't worry if the Table of Joy isn't your thing. I also show you another way of dealing with ratios and proportions.

I end this chapter with some information on working through speed sums.

Getting to Know the Table of Joy

The Table of Joy is an incredibly useful method for working out any kind of problem involving proportions — that is to say, if you double one of the numbers, the other automatically doubles. For example, the price of most things is proportional to how much you buy; two cans of beans cost twice as much as one can of beans does. In the same way, twelve cans of beans cost twice as much as six cans.

Among other things, the Table of Joy in its basic form can be used for the following:

- **Currency conversion:** If you need the exchange rate, or want to know how many dollars you get for a number of euros, turn to the Table of Joy.

- **Percentages:** Whether you want to find one number as a percentage of another, the percentage increase or decrease, or an amount with or without tax . . . the Table of Joy is your friend.

- **Pie charts:** If you want to know the angle, the value of a slice or the total value of a pie chart, you can use an easy sum . . . the Table of Joy reminds you of that sum.

- **Proportion:** If you have two linked values where doubling or tripling one automatically triples the other (if I drive three times as far, I use three times as much petrol), the values are *proportional*. And the Table of Joy deals with that.

- **Ratios:** Whenever you see a colon, crack your knuckles and say, 'Here's a Table of Joy question!'

- **Scaled maps and drawings:** How far is that in real life? How far is that on the map? What's the scale? Ask the Table of Joy and it will answer you truly.

- **Speed–distance–time calculations:** Given any two of these three, you can work out the other using the Table of Joy.

- **Unit conversion:** Apart from temperatures, which are a bit squiffy, you can use the Table of Joy to do just about any unit conversion in this book.

Glancing through an old numeracy test, I reckon you can use the Table of Joy in the answers of somewhere between a third and a half of the questions. I can't stress too much how useful this little baby is, both for numeracy and for further studies.

The story of the Table of Joy

The Table of Joy is based on a way of working out similar sums called the Rule of Three, but I find this name is less obvious and less delightful than the Table of Joy. For a long while, the Table of Joy was just called The Table. Then one of my students started using it and suddenly started answering dozens of questions correctly that she hadn't had a clue about before. She decided it ought to be called the 'Table of Doom'. Then she thought for a moment and changed her mind. 'Not doom! That makes it sound like a bad thing. It should be the Table of Joy.'

Good name, I thought, *Good name.*

Seeing how the Table of Joy works

The Table of Joy — as its name suggests — is a table. You use the table to lay out the information you already have so you know precisely which sum you need to work out. The table doesn't solve the sum for you — you still need to do that yourself — but the table takes all the guesswork out of deciding what to times and divide by what.

To create a Table of Joy, you draw a three-by-three grid like you play noughts and crosses on, label the rows and columns, decide where to put three numbers that you either have already or can easily work out, and then do a sum that has the same structure each time.

One of the many beauties of the Table of Joy is that it doesn't matter which way around you label the rows and columns, as long as you put the numbers in a sensible place. The sum is exactly the same if you swap both of the rows with the columns or if you swap the two columns or the two rows over. You can't swap a row with a column, though.

Follow these five steps when using the Table of Joy to solve a problem:

1. **Draw a fairly big noughts-and-crosses grid.**

   It needs to be big enough so you can write labels in the rows and columns.

2. **Label the rows and columns with the names of relevant information from the question.**

3. **Fill in the numbers relevant to each row and column, and a question mark for the square representing the answer you want.**

4. **Circle the number in the same column as the question mark and the number in the same row as the question mark.**

   Write these numbers with a times sign between them. Then write a divide sign followed by the remaining number.

5. **Work out the answer!**

The main trick of using the Table of Joy is working out what labels to use and which number to put where.

In Figure 8-1 I show a Table of Joy in various stages of completion, solving the following question:

> Larry and Curly split the loot in the ratio 3:7. Curly walks away with $350. How much loot does Larry receive?

	Larry	Curly
Ratio		
Loot		

Figure 8-1: The Table of Joy being used to answer a very tricky question.

	Larry	Curly
Ratio	3	7
Loot		350

$$\frac{350 \times 3}{7} = 150$$

Understanding what goes where

Labelling the rows and columns is a very important part of the Table of Joy. This labelling may seem like a chore, but it really helps you to keep track of which number goes where.

The way I normally do my labelling — and I invented the Table of Joy, so I get to choose — is to write the things I'm counting or measuring across the top. Down the side, I put the different pieces of information I have or want.

For the example in Figure 8-1, the things I am counting are Larry's money and Curly's money. Down the side, I write the ratio and a question mark, because I want to know the total amount of money.

Labelling in this way makes the meaning of each number much more obvious. If you've just got a noughts-and-crosses grid, figuring out where to put Curly's part of the ratio is really hard — but with the label 'Curly' at the top and 'ratio' at the side, things are more obvious.

Getting Rational: Understanding Ratios

A ratio describes how many times bigger one share of something is than another share. If you say, 'We'll split the money 50:50', you mean that, however much money there is, you get half and I get half. If we agree on a 2:1 split, you get twice as much as I do.

The ratio tells you about the *relative* sizes of the shares. You can't tell from the ratio whether we split $3 or $300 million, only that you received twice as much as I did. (You're welcome to it. It's only pretend money.)

You meet ratios when you mix things — for example, cake mixture or concrete — and when you try to divide things between several people. The traditional examples for splitting things up are money, people and lollies. I have no idea why lollies are so important in the scheme of things.

You also see ratios in the scale on maps. I talk more about that, and maps in general, in Chapter 12.

One for you, two for me: Sharing

Picture the cinema cliché of bad guys sitting around a table and splitting up their ill-gotten gains: 'One for you, two for me. One for you, two for me ...' These chaps are dividing their money in a ratio of 1:2. For every dollar the other person gets, the first person gets two.

If they start with three dollars, the other guy would get one dollar and the first would get two. If they start with 30 dollars, the split would be 10 and 20. The key thing is that however much money is in the pile to begin with, the first guy gets twice as much as the other.

Cancelling ratios

Exam questions often ask you to 'reduce a ratio to its simplest form'. The reason for this is to make the numbers as small as possible — it's much easier to see the relative size of two things if their ratio is written as 1:4 than, say, 90:360. It also makes the Table of Joy sums easier.

Reducing a ratio to its simplest form is very similar to *cancelling down* a fraction to its simplest form, which I cover in scary detail in Chapter 6 — fractions and ratios are very closely related. It's okay, though, you don't need to be a fractions expert to work with ratios!

Here's the recipe for cancelling ratios:

1. **Find a number that you can divide both sides of the ratio by so you still end up with a whole number.** Sometimes no such number is possible — if that's the case, the ratio is already in its simplest form.

2. **Divide each side of the ratio by that number.**

3. **Go back to Step 1 until you can't find any more numbers to divide by.**

4. **Write down the numbers in the same order as in the original ratio, with the colon between them.**

In maths tests, more often than not you can cancel ratios all the way until one of the sides of the ratio is 1. Sometimes, though, the question asks you to cancel until one of the sides of the ratio is 1, even if the other side isn't a whole number. (You may see the question 'Write the ratio in the form n:1' or 'Use the form 1:n.') To do this, divide the bigger number by the smaller number and write down the ratio in the right order — the bigger number should always be on the same side as the bigger number in the original ratio.

For example, you can cancel 60:40 to 3:2 (in whole numbers) or 1.5:1 (in the form n:1).

Applying the Table of Joy

A typical ratio question might tell you that someone splits their time between Project A and Project B in a ratio of 5:3. If he spends 15 hours this week on Project B, how long does he spend on Project A?

In this question, you have three key pieces of information: The two sides of the ratio (5 and 3) and the time for Project B (15). You can put these numbers into the Table of Joy. Before I outline the idea in detail, see if you can figure out what goes where.

Here's what you do (I also show the steps in Figure 8-2):

1. **Draw a noughts-and-crosses grid.**

   Leave plenty of space for the labels.

2. **Figure out what the two sides of the ratio represent.**

   In this example, the two sides of the ratio represent Project A and Project B. These labels go in the top row.

3. **On the left, write 'ratio' in one row and whatever you want to measure in the other.**

   In this case, write 'time'.

4. **Fill in the ratio in the middle row (remember to keep it the right way around) and put the time you know in the correct column.**

   Here, the time goes in the column marked 'Project B'. Put a question mark in the remaining square.

5. **Write out the Table of Joy sum.**

   Take the number in the same column as the question mark, times by the number in the same row as the question mark, divide by the number opposite. For this example, you do $5 \times 15 \div 3$.

6. **Work out the sum.**

   In this example, the answer is 25.

Figure 8-2: Using the Table of Joy to solve a ratio problem.		Project A	Project B	
	Ratio	5	3	$\dfrac{5 \times 15}{3} = 25$
	Hours	?	15	

You'd be a little bit lucky to get a question as simple as the preceding one in an exam. More often than not, you have to work with the total and one side of the ratio.

The good news is this isn't any more difficult — you simply need an extra layer of thought before you do the Table of Joy sum.

Take a moment to read the question and decide whether you're interested in the two parts or a part and a total. The preceding example looks at the two-parts version.

By contrast, with the part-and-a-total version, you replace the missing part of the ratio with the total of the ratio — just add the numbers either side of the colon.

After that, you follow exactly the same process, but change one of the column labels to 'total' and the numbers in that column as appropriate. I give an example in Figure 8-3 to answer the following question:

> Alice and Bob share 12 biscuits in the ratio 3:1. How many does Alice eat?

Figure 8-3:
Ratios, totals and the Table of Joy.

	Alice	Total
Ratio	3	4
Biscuits	?	12

$$\frac{3 \times 12}{4} = 9$$

Working with parts

If you don't like the Table of Joy, the more traditional way of doing ratios is to think about the value of a share. The ratio 2:7 means that for every two shares in the first group, seven shares go in the other. If you divide some biscuits in the ratio 2:7 and the first group gets 50, each share is worth 25 biscuits. From there, you can say that the other group has seven shares, or $7 \times 25 = 175$ biscuits, and nine shares altogether: $9 \times 25 = 225$.

Here's the recipe for working out ratios using the traditional method:

1. **Work out how many shares the number you have represents.**

   You need to add up the parts if you know the total.

2. **Divide the number you know by the answer in Step 1.**

   This is the value of each share.

3. **Times your answer to Step 2 by the number of shares you're interested in.**

   This is your answer.

The method I describe in the preceding steps has fewer steps than the Table of Joy method, but the Table of Joy makes obvious which sum to do. You're the boss, so use whichever method works best for you.

Managing multiple ratios

Sometimes you have three or even more numbers in a ratio. You might see a drink made of orange juice, apple juice and pineapple juice mixed in the ratio 3:1:1 — which means that for every three measures of orange juice, you add one measure of apple juice and one measure of pineapple juice.

To deal with multiple ratios, you use the same method as for ratios with only two numbers. You can work with pairs of numbers from the ratio or a number and the total using the Table of Joy, or you can work out the value of a share as before. Here's an example question:

> You want to make a litre of drink containing orange juice, apple juice and pineapple juice in the ratio 3:1:1. How much of each juice do you need?

To answer this question using the share method, follow these steps:

1. **A litre equals 1,000 millilitres and the ratio adds up to five, so each share is worth 1,000 ÷ 5 = 200ml.**

2. **Three shares of orange juice is 3 × 200 = 600ml.**

3. **One share of apple juice is 1 × 200 = 200ml.**

4. **One share of pineapple juice is 1 × 200 = 200ml.**

In Figure 8-4 I show you how to reach the same conclusion with the Table of Joy.

Figure 8-4:
A multiple ratio. Top: The sum for orange juice. Bottom: The sum for apple juice. The sum for pineapple juice is the same as the one for apple juice.

	Juice	Mixture
Ratio	3	5
Total	?	1000

$$\frac{3 \times 1000}{5} = 600$$

	Juice	Mixture
Ratio	1	5
Total	?	1000

$$\frac{1 \times 1000}{5} = 200$$

Getting a Sense of Proportion

Two quantities are *proportional* if, whenever you double one, the other also doubles. For example, speed and distance are proportional: If you drive for an hour at 60 kilometres per hour, you travel twice as far as you do if you drive for an hour at 30 kilometres per hour. An example that often comes up in maths tests concerns the amount of each ingredient you need for a recipe. The recipe is proportional to the number of people the dish feeds. If you double all of the ingredients, you can feed twice as many people with the end result.

Proportion doesn't stick to doubling. If you know two quantities are proportional, you can multiply them both by the same number and end up with the appropriate relationship. For example, if you drive at 20 kilometres per hour, you get a third as far as if you drive at 60. Likewise, if you multiply your recipe ingredients by seven, you can feed seven times as many people.

The reason the Table of Joy works in so many topics is that quite a lot of maths — particularly the maths covered art school — is based on proportional quantities, and that's exactly what the Table of Joy handles best.

In maths tests, proportion questions generally involve taking two proportional values and *scaling* them — finding out what happens to one of them when the other changes. The good news is you can use the Table of Joy to find the answer. The other good news is that the Table of Joy isn't the only way to answer these questions — although I think the other options are trickier.

Typical proportion questions in maths tests involve adjusting a recipe so you can feed more people, or enlarging the measurements of a shape.

Defining proportion

Having a sense of proportion is supposed to be a good thing. Artists spend years studying so they can draw the proportions of the human body correctly. But what exactly is proportion?

A decent definition of proportion is this:

> The proportion between two values is how many times bigger one is than the other.

To explain that two things are proportional, you would normally say something like 'miles and kilometres are proportional in the ratio 1:1.6' or '1 mile is the same as 1.6 kilometres'. The number of miles is a fixed multiple of the number of kilometres, so the two quantities are proportional.

Perfecting proportions with the Table of Joy

Here's how you answer a proportions question using the Table of Joy:

1. **Draw a noughts-and-crosses grid.**

   Leave plenty of space for labels.

2. **Label the columns to reflect what's changing.**

   For example, use 'small' and 'large', or 'before' and 'after'.

3. **Label the rows with the information you're interested in.**

   For example, you may use 'people' and 'grams' if you're doing a recipe, or 'short side' and 'long side' if you're working on a shape.

4. **Fill in the numbers you already know in the appropriately labelled cells.**

   Put a question mark in the empty cell.

5. **Write down the Table of Joy sum.**

   Times the number in the same column as the question mark by the number in the same row as the question mark, and divide by the one opposite.

6. **Work out the sum.**

   That's your answer.

In Figure 8-5 I show a worked example for the following question:

   One mile is about 1.6 kilometres. How many kilometres is 20 miles?

Figure 8-5: A proportions example.

	miles	km
conversion	1	1.6
distance	20	?

$$\frac{20 \times 1.6}{1} = 32$$

So 20 miles is equivalent to 32 kilometres. Another way to work out proportions is to use the 'value of a share' approach that I use for ratios in the section 'Working with parts', earlier in this chapter. (In fact, ratios and proportions are so similar that treating them as different things is almost fraud.)

For example, with a recipe, you work out how much of an ingredient you need for one person and then times that amount by the number of people you want to feed. Here's what to do:

1. **Divide the amount of ingredients you're interested in by the number of people the recipe is for.**

2. **Times this by the new number of people you want to feed.**

You probably think this two-step process looks simpler than the six-step Table-of-Joy process I describe earlier. But try the two-step process with the example in Figure 8-5 ... you get a pretty unpleasant fraction when you do the divide in Step 1, something the Table of Joy avoids.

Applying proportion

One of the reasons maths is such an important subject (and, to me, such a beautiful one) is that the same methods often apply across a broad range of subjects. You can apply proportion in dozens upon dozens of real-life situations (and, of course, many different questions in an exam). Here are some examples of times when you may need to apply proportion:

- **Capacities:** If you know how many glasses a bottle of water fills, how many glasses would seven bottles fill?

- **Coverage:** If a tin of paint covers $4m^2$ of wall, how many tins do you need to paint a room with wall space of $48m^2$?

- **Fuel usage and cost:** If your Mum's car uses one litre of petrol to travel 11 kilometres, how far can she travel on a full 45-litre tank?

- **Prices:** What is the total cost or the cost per item? How many items can you buy with a certain amount of money?

- **Scaling recipes:** If you have a recipe for four people, how much food do you need to feed ten people?

- **Typing speeds:** If you can type a page of drivel ... I mean, descriptive prose, at 50 words per minute and work solidly for an hour, how much prose do you have at the end of your hour?

- **Umpteen others:** Anything where doubling one value doubles the other can lead to a question where a proportion sum is appropriate.

Scaling recipes

One kind of proportion question seems to come up more often than any other in maths tests, and it involves scaling recipes. Imagine you have a recipe that serves a certain number of people, but you need to cook for a bigger or smaller party. The amount of each ingredient you need is proportional to the number of people it serves, so you need to adjust the quantities to account for your head count.

A typical maths exam question looks something like this:

Here are the ingredients for a recipe for a cake that serves four people:

100g butter

100g self-raising flour

150g caster sugar

2 eggs

You want to make a cake that serves ten people. How much caster sugar do you need?

You can solve this question using the Table of Joy. If you follow the instructions in the section 'Perfecting proportions with the Table of Joy', you get a table and sum that look like that in Figure 8-6.

	recipe	real life	
people	4	10	$\dfrac{150 \times 10}{4} = 375$
sugar	150	?	

Figure 8-6: Solving a recipe problem with the Table of Joy.

If you're comfortable with decimals (which I cover in Chapter 7), you can work out that one portion would be 37.5 grams, so ten portions would require 375 grams.

Here's another example, now you're in the swing of things:

I just bought a 10 kilogram bag of cement, which has this recipe on the side of it: 'To make 100 kilograms of concrete, mix 10 kilograms of cement with 75 kilograms of aggregate, and 15 litres of water.'

Since this bag of concrete exists only in my imagination, I suggest you don't follow the recipe. Frankly, it's a toss-up as to whether this concrete recipe will give you something more or less edible than the cake recipe from earlier, and whether the cake or the concrete would be harder.

Unfortunately, I don't need 100 kilograms of concrete. I need 20 kilograms for the equally imaginary swimming pool I want to build in my dream mansion (which is, of course, only a dream).

I don't want to make 100 kilograms of cement, because I don't want to throw most of it away (even imaginary concrete is hard to get rid of). Instead, I want to scale the recipe down. Looking at the aggregate (the other ingredients work just the same way), I use the Table of Joy, as in Figure 8-7.

Figure 8-7:
Solving the concrete problem with the Table of Joy.

	aggregate	concrete
recipe	75	100
pool	?	20

$$\frac{75 \times 20}{100} = 15$$

I need (75 × 20 ÷ 100) kilograms of aggregate, which works out to 15 kilograms. In the same way, I find that I need 2 kilograms of cement and 3 litres of water.

Another way of doing this sum is to work out the *scale factor* — how many times more concrete am I making? In this case, I'm making a fifth as much concrete as the recipe is for, so I need to find a fifth of each ingredient.

A fifth of 75 is 15 — so I need 15 kilograms of cement, just like before. You can check the other amounts too, if you like.

This method has two possible problems: The scale factor may not be obvious, and you may end up with an especially ugly fraction sum.

Speeding Along

Speed is a measure of how far you travel in a certain time, and it comes in a variety of units. Most Australian cars measure speed in kilometres per hour (kmph or km/h). In the UK, you generally see speed written as miles per hour (mph). And scientists (just to be awkward) use metres per second (m/s). (A lecturer friend of mine insists that the imperial system using miles per hour is ridiculous and asks his students to work out speeds in furlongs per fortnight!)

As covered earlier in this chapter, speeds can be proportional. So the speed 60 kilometres per hour means that if you drive for an hour at that speed, you travel 60 kilometres. In half an hour you travel 30 kilometres. And in 2 hours you cover 120 kilometres.

To work out speed sums, I again use the Table of Joy. Figure 8-8 shows the steps I use to work out what speed I have to travel at if I want to go 90 kilometres in three hours, following these steps:

1. **Draw a big noughts-and-crosses grid.**

2. **In the top-middle square, write 'Distance'. In the top-right square, write 'Time'.**

3. **In the middle-left square, write 'Speed'. In the bottom-left square, write 'Journey'.**

4. **In the middle-right square, write the number 1.**

5. **If you know the journey time, write that time in the bottom-right square (under 'Time' and next to 'Journey').**

   In this example, in Figure 8-8, you write 3. In other questions, you might have a time that's not a whole number of hours. If so, convert the time into decimals — so 1 hour and 30 minutes is 1.5 hours.

6. **If you know the distance of the journey (here, 90 kilometres), write the distance in the bottom-middle square (under 'Distance' and next to 'Journey').**

7. **If you know the speed, write the speed in the middle-middle square (next to 'Speed').**

8. **Write a question mark in the space that's left.**

9. **Write out the Table of Joy sum: Times the question mark's neighbours together and divide by the other number.**

   In this case, it's $90 \times 1 \div 3$.

10. **Work out the answer.**

    For this example, that's 30 kilometres per hour.

Figure 8-8:
Using the
Table of
Joy to work
out at what
speed you
need to
travel to
cover 90
kilometres
in three
hours.

	Distance	Time
Speed	?	1
Journey	90	3

$$\frac{90 \times 1}{3} = 30$$

Chapter 9

Perfect Percentages, 100% of the Time

In This Chapter

▶ Understanding what percentages are

▶ Converting percentages back and forth between decimals and fractions

▶ Solving both simple and difficult percentage problems

▶ Using equations to solve three different types of percentage problems

*L*ike whole numbers and decimals, percentages are a way to talk about parts of a whole. The term *per cent* means 'out of 100'.' So if you have 50 per cent of something, you have 50 out of 100. If you have 25 per cent of it, you have 25 out of 100. Of course, if you have 100 per cent of anything, you have all of it.

In this chapter, I show you how to work with percentages. Because percentages resemble decimals, I first show you how to convert numbers back and forth between percentages and decimals. No worries — this switch is easy to do. Next, I show you how to convert back and forth between percentages and fractions — also not too bad. When you understand how conversions work, I show you the three basic types of percent problems, plus a method that makes the problems simple.

Perusing Some Percentages You Already Know

'Per cent' literally means 'for 100' but, in practice, it means closer to 'out of 100'. For example, suppose that a school has exactly 100 children — 50 girls and 50 boys. You can say that '50 out of 100' children are girls — or you can shorten it to simply '50 per cent.' Even shorter than that, you can use the symbol %, which means per cent.

Saying that 50% of the students are girls is the same as saying that $\frac{1}{2} \times$ base length $\times$ height(width) of them are girls. Or if you prefer decimals, it's the same thing as saying that 0.5 of all the students are girls. This example shows you that percentages, like fractions and decimals, are just another way of talking about parts of the whole. In this case, the whole is the total number of children in the school.

You don't literally have to have 100 of something to use a percentage. You probably won't ever really cut a cake into 100 pieces, but that doesn't matter. The values are the same. Whether you're talking about cake, a dollar, or a group of children, 50% is still half, 25% is still one-quarter, 75% is still three-quarters, and so on.

Any percentage smaller than 100% means less than the whole — the smaller the percentage, the less you have. You probably know this fact well from the school grading system. If you get 100%, you get a perfect score. And 85% is usually A work, 75% is a B, 60% is a C, and, well, you know the rest.

Of course, 0% means '0 out of 100' — any way you slice it, you have nothing.

You can also hardly avoid seeing percentages at the bank and in the shops. Banks give interest rates on savings accounts, loans and mortgages as percentages. Your parents may have set up a savings account for you, for example, with an interest rate of 3%. What this (roughly) means is that every year, the bank looks at your balance, works out 3% (or $\frac{3}{100}$) of that balance, and adds that much money to your account. Loans work the other way around. If your parents have a loan on which they pay 6% interest, each year the bank looks at how much they owe, works out 6% of that sum, and says 'You owe us this much more now'.'

Modern banks don't work quite like this. Instead they do a calculation every day and update your account each month, but the difference in the amount you accrue or pay is negligible.

You also see percentages in the shops, often in the sales. You may see signs screaming '30% off!' (normally with 'up to' in very small print). This means the shop has taken the original price, worked out 30% ($\frac{30}{100}$ or $\frac{3}{10}$) of that amount, and then taken that much money off the original price.

Dealing with Percentages Greater than 100%

100% means '100 out of 100' — in other words, everything. So when I say I have 100% confidence in you, I mean that I have complete confidence in you.

What about percentages more than 100%? Well, sometimes percentages like these don't make sense. For example, you can't spend more than 100% of your time playing basketball, no matter how much you love the sport; 100% is all the time you have, and there ain't no more.

But a lot of times, percentages larger than 100% are perfectly reasonable. For example, suppose I own a hot dog wagon and sell the following:

10 hot dogs in the morning

30 hot dogs in the afternoon

The number of hot dogs I sell in the afternoon is 300% of the number I sold in the morning. It's three times as many.

Here's another way of looking at this: I sell 20 more hot dogs in the afternoon than in the morning, so this is a 200% increase in the afternoon — 20 is twice as many as 10.

Spend a little time thinking about this example until it makes sense. You visit some of these ideas again in Chapter 10, when I show you how to do word problems involving percentages.

Comparing Percentages, Decimals and Fractions

To solve many percentage problems, you need to change the percentage to either a decimal or a fraction. Ten per cent is the same thing as $\frac{1}{10}$, and 25 per cent equals 0.25. You may well wonder why we use so many different ways of saying the same thing. This isn't an easy question to answer. The best answer I have is that in different contexts you need to communicate in different ways — just like you use one language to persuade your two-year old cousin to stop playing with his noisy toys and another language to persuade your aunty not to bring her son's noisy toys next time.

For example, saying 'Prices went up by 5%' is easier than saying 'Prices increased by a factor of 1.05' or 'Prices went up by a twentieth'. Having said that, we can use decimals, fractions and percentages to express the same thing. In this section, I show you how to convert percentages into decimals and fractions, and vice versa.

Percentages and decimals

Converting a percentage to a decimal is easy — just remember 'per cent' means the same as 'hundredths' or 'divided by 100'. Here's what you do to convert 25% to a decimal:

1. **Write down the number of per cent.**

   In this example, you write 25.

2. **If the number doesn't have a decimal point already, put one at the end.**

   Now you have '25.'.

3. **If the number is less than 100, put a zero at the beginning.**

   In this example, you have '025.'.

4. **If the number is less than 10, put another zero at the beginning.**

   Twenty-five is bigger than 10, so you can miss this step out.

5. **Move the decimal point two places to the left.**

   In this example, you get 0.25.

6. **If the number has zeros at the end, ignore them.**

As another example, 10% becomes 010. and then 0.10. You ignore the zero at the end and write '10% = 0.1'.

Converting a percentage to a decimal is almost exactly the same as converting a price in cents into dollars: 25¢ is the same as $0.25. The only difference is you don't ignore a zero at the end in money sums, so you write 10¢ as $0.10 rather than $0.1.

To convert a decimal into a percentage, you work in the opposite way. Here are the steps using 0.4 as an example:

1. **Write down the decimal.**

   In this example, you write 0.4.

2. **If you have only one digit after the dot, write a 0 on the end.**

   You write 0.40.

3. **Move the decimal point two places to the right.**

   You now have 040.

4. **If you have any zeros at the beginning of the number, before the decimal point, ignore them.**

   You write 40.

5. **Write a % at the end. If the decimal point is at the end of the number, you can ignore it, too.**

   Your answer is 40%.

Percentages and fractions

Converting a percentage to a fraction is as easy as cancelling. Here's my easy recipe:

1. **Write down the percentage.**

   In place of the % sign, write '/100'. You now have a fraction — for example, $25\% = \frac{25}{100}$.

2. **Find a number you can divide the top and the bottom by.**

   Good numbers to look for are 2, 5 and 10. If you can't find any number to divide both the top and the bottom by, you're done. In this example, you can divide the top and bottom by 5.

3. **Divide the top and bottom by the number in Step 2.**

   In this case you'd get $\frac{5}{20}$.

4. **Repeat Steps 2 and 3 until you're done.**

   You can divide the top and bottom numbers by 5 to get $\frac{1}{4}$. So $25\% = \frac{1}{4}$.

Once in a while, you may start out with a percentage that's a decimal, such as 99.9%. The rule is still the same, but now you have a decimal in the numerator (top number), which most people don't like to see. To get rid of it, move the decimal point one place to the right in both the numerator and the denominator:

$$99.9\% = \frac{99.9}{100} = \frac{999}{1,000}$$

Thus, 99.9% converts to the fraction $\frac{999}{1,000}$.

Going from a fraction to a percentage is a little harder, but the Table of Joy is a good friend to you here. Get the low-down on the Table of Joy in Chapter 8 if you don't know how to use it. Here's my fractions-to-percentages recipe using the Table of Joy:

1. **Draw a noughts-and-crosses grid.**

2. **Label the middle column 'fraction' and the right column 'per cent'.**

3. **Label the middle row 'top' and the bottom row 'bottom'.**

4. **Fill in the top and bottom of the fraction in the middle column.**

5. **Write 100 in the bottom-right square (remember 'per cent' means 'over 100').**

   Put a question mark above the square containing 100. You need to find the number in the question-mark square.

6. **Do the Table of Joy sum.**

   Times the question mark's neighbours together (the top of the fraction times 100) and divide by the opposite number (the bottom of the fraction). The number that comes out is your answer.

Have a look at Figure 9-1, where I show the Table of Joy in action converting a fraction to a percentage.

Figure 9-1:
Converting a fraction into a percentage with the Table of Joy.

	fraction	per cent	
top	1		$\frac{1 \times 100}{4} = 25$
bottom	4	100	

Going up and going down

You may have heard percentages used in the context of increases and decreases — for example, 'Wages went up by 3 per cent' or 'The dollar has lost 25 per cent of its value against the US dollar since our last overseas trip.' (Well, maybe you've heard something like this.) Increases and decreases add an extra step of complication to your percentage sums, but things are still straightforward if you keep your concentration.

Working out the difference first

At this point in your life, your parents probably handle most of the household finances. But imagine a time (in hopefully the not-to-distant future) when you'll be paying your bills yourself! If your electricity company plans to increase bills by 5% or your internet company is giving you a 10% discount, you may want to figure out what your new bill will be. In both instances, you do roughly the same thing:

1. **Work out the appropriate percentage of the whole bill.**

   For example, if your electricity bill was previously $40 and will increase by 5%, work out 5% of $40 = $2. Alternatively, if you pay $25 per month for internet and the company is giving you a 10% discount, you work out 10% of $25 = $2.50.

2. **Decide whether the change will make your answer bigger or smaller.**

   An increase means your number goes up. A decrease means your number goes down.

3. **If you have an increase, add your answer from Step 1 to the original amount.**

   For example, for your water bill you add $2 + $40 = $42.

4. **If you have a decrease, take away your answer from Step 1 from the original amount.**

   For example, for your internet bill, you do $25 — $2.50 = $22.50.

Working out the full percentages

Another way to deal with increases and decreases is to use the full-percentages method. Many students in my class at school got a bit flummoxed at this point. By which I mean, I remember finding this hard and yelling, 'But I don't understand!' I was 13. It was sunny. I wanted to be outside playing basketball.

This method needs a bit of patience and thinking. The basic idea is to ask 'What percentage of the original number do I need?' and then calculate that percentage. You work out the difference like you did in the last section, but in a different order.

Here's what you do:

1. **Start from 100%.**

   Always always always.

2. **Decide whether you need to go up or down, and then add or take away that percentage.**

   For example, if you have a 5% rise, you end up with 105%. If you have a 7% drop, you end up with $100 - 7 = 93\%$.

3. **Work out that percentage of the original number.**

   For the examples in the previous section, you need to find 105% of $40 for the electricity bill, so you do $1.05 \times \$40$. For the internet bill, you need 90% of $25, or $0.9 \times \$25$.

As well as the steps in the preceding list, I can give you a sneaky way to increase and decrease amounts by percentages, starting with increasing amounts.

Pretend that you are a shopkeeper and you buy your goods at a wholesale rate. You need to add a percentage of that value to the goods to make sure that you earn a profit. For this example, say the wholesale price was $49.95 and you want to increase it by 15 per cent. Here's a way to do so:

1. **Add the 15% to 100%.**

   Remember that you always start with 100%.

2. **Change this value to a decimal by dividing by 100.**

   Remember that you can do that by moving the decimal point to the left two places (because there are two zeros in 100), and that the decimal point is at the end of the number.

   In this example, 115.0% becomes 1.15.

3. **Multiply the wholesale price by the decimal to increase it by 15 per cent.**

   This gives you the store (retail) price, which in this case will be $57.44 (correct to two decimal places).

And here's an example that looks at decreasing amounts. Again pretend that you are a shopkeeper. In this case, you have not been able to sell certain items for a long time, so you decide to have a sale and to subtract a certain percentage off the retail value of the goods. (In some instances, this discount will eat away at your profit, and may mean you a loss. The perils of a retail business!) For this example, say the store (retail) price was $74.45 and you want to decrease it by 20 per cent.

1. **Subtract the 20% from 100%.**

   Remember that you always start with 100%.

2. **Change this value to a decimal by dividing 80 by 100.**

   Remember that you can do that by moving the decimal point to the left two places (because there are two zeros in 100), and that the decimal point is at the end of the number.

   In this example, 80.0% becomes 0.8.

3. **Multiply the store price by the decimal.**

   This gives you the sale price, which in this instance is $59.56.

Changing prices

The last big arena for percentages is the shops. In the January sales, you can't move for signs saying '40% off everything' and 'Save 50%' on this, that or the other.

In the exam, you may need to work out the sale price of an item, or the new price after an increase, or even the percentage increase if you know the prices before and after. The first two of these sums are very similar. Here's an example:

> My local stationer is offering 70% off calendars. The one I'm interested in, 'Beautiful Patterns of the Fractal World', was selling for $9.00 before Christmas. How much will it cost me now?

I show you the Table-of-Joy version in Figure 9-2. To find the discount you do $9 \times 70 = $630, and then divide that by 100 to get $6.30. Then you take that away from the original $9.00 to get $2.70 — which happens to be the exact amount of change I have in my pocket. Oh, happy days.

	money	percent		
discount		70	$\dfrac{9 \times 70}{100} = 6.30$	$9.00 - 6.30 = 2.70$
total	9	100		

Figure 9-2: Calendar discount with the Table of Joy.

You could also do this sum directly by working out 30% of the original price, which is what remains after you take off 70%. That saves you a step of working but doesn't always give you a nice Table-of-Joy sum.

Working out a discount is also straightforward. Here's another example:

> A nice coat is reduced from $80 to $56. What percentage is the reduction?

Start by working out the price reduction: $80 – $56 = $24. Then set up a Table of Joy, as in Figure 9-3, and work out 24 × 100 = 2,400. Next, 2,400 ÷ 80 = 30, so you have a 30% reduction.

Figure 9-3:
Coat
discount
with the
Table of Joy.

	money	percent
discount	24	
total	80	100

$$\frac{24 \times 100}{80} = 30$$

Solving Percentage Problems

When you know the connection between percentages and fractions, which I discuss earlier in 'Comparing Percentages, Decimals and Fractions', you can solve a lot of percentage problems with a few simple tricks. Other problems, however, require a bit more work. In this section, I show you how to tell an easy percentage problem from a tough one, and I give you the tools to solve all of them.

Figuring out simple percentage problems

A lot of percentage problems turn out to be easy when you give them a little thought. In many cases, just remember the connection between percentages and fractions, and you're halfway home:

✔ **Finding 100% of a number:** Remember that 100% means the whole thing, so 100% of any number is simply the number itself:

> 100% of 5 is 5.
>
> 100% of 91 is 91.
>
> 100% of 732 is 732.

✔ **Finding 50% of a number:** Remember that 50% means half, so to find 50% of a number, just divide it by 2:

50% of 20 is 10.

50% of 88 is 44.

50% of 7 is $\dfrac{7}{2}$ (or $3\dfrac{1}{2}$ or 3.5).

✔ **Finding 25% of a number:** Remember that 25% equals $\frac{1}{4}$, so to find 25% of a number, divide it by 4:

25% of 40 = 10

25% of 88 = 22

25% of 15 $= \dfrac{15}{4} = 3\dfrac{3}{4} = 3.75$

✔ **Finding 20% of a number:** Because 20% equals $\frac{1}{5}$, you can find 20% of a number by dividing it by 5. But I can show you an easier way: Remember that 20% is 2 times 10%, so to find 20% of a number, move the decimal point one place to the left and double the result:

20% of 80 $= 8 \times 2 = 16$

20% of 300 $= 30 \times 2 = 60$

20% of 41 $= 4.1 \times 2 = 8.2$

✔ **Finding 10% of a number:** Finding 10% of any number is the same as finding $\frac{1}{10}$ of that number. To do this, just move the decimal point one place to the left:

10% of 30 = 3

10% of 41 = 4.1

10% of 7 = 0.7

✔ **Finding 200%, 300%, and so on of a number:** Working with percentages that are multiples of 100 is easy. Just drop the two 0s and multiply by the number that's left:

200% of 7 $= 2 \times 7 = 14$

300% of 10 $= 3 \times 10 = 30$

1,000% of 45 $= 10 \times 45 = 450$

(Refer to the earlier 'Dealing with Percentages Greater than 100%' section for details on what having more than 100% really means.)

Turning the problem around

Here's a trick that makes certain tough-looking percentage problems so easy that you can do them in your head. Simply move the per cent sign from one number to the other and flip the order of the numbers.

Suppose someone asks you to figure out the following:

88% of 50

Finding 88% of anything isn't an activity anybody looks forward to. But an easy way of solving the problem is to switch it around:

88% of 50 = 50% of 88

This move is perfectly valid, and it makes the problem a lot easier. It works because the word *of* really means multiplication, and you can multiply either backward or forward and get the same answer. As I discuss in the preceding section, 50% of 88 is simply half of 88:

88% of 50 = 50% of 88 = 44

As another example, suppose you want to find

7% of 200

Again, finding 7% is tricky, but finding 200% is simple, so switch the problem around:

7% of 200 = 200% of 7

In the preceding section, I tell you that, to find 200% of any number, you just multiply that number by 2:

7% of 200 = 200% of 7 = $2 \times 7 = 14$

Deciphering more difficult percentage problems

You can solve a lot of percentage problems using the tricks I show you earlier in this chapter. For more difficult problems, you may want to switch to a calculator. If you don't have a calculator at hand, solve percentage problems by turning them into decimal multiplication, as follows:

1. **Change the word *of* to a multiplication sign and the per cent to a decimal (as I show you earlier in this chapter).**

   Suppose you want to find 35% of 80. Here's how you start:

   $$35\% \text{ of } 80 = 0.35 \times 80$$

2. **Solve the problem using decimal multiplication (refer to Chapter 7).**

   Here's what the example looks like:

   $$
   \begin{array}{r}
   0.35 \\
   \times\ \ 80 \\
   \hline
   28.00
   \end{array}
   $$

   So 35% of 80 is 28.

Putting All the Percentage Problems Together

In the preceding section, I give you a few ways to find any percentage of any number. This type of percentage problem is the most common, which is why it gets top billing.

But percentages crop up in a wide range of business applications, such as banking, real estate, payroll and taxes. (I show you some real-world applications when I discuss word problems in Chapter 10.) And depending on the situation, two other common types of percentage problems may present themselves.

In this section, I show you these two additional types of percentage problems and how they relate to the type you now know how to solve. I also give you a simple tool to make quick work of all three types.

Identifying the three types of percent problems

Earlier in this chapter, I show you how to solve problems that look like this:

50% of 2 is ?

The answer, of course, is 1. (Refer to 'Solving Percentage Problems' for details on how to get this answer.) Given two pieces of information — the percentage and the number to start with — you can figure out what number you end up with.

Now suppose instead that I leave out the percentage but give you the starting and ending numbers:

? % of 2 is 1

You can still fill in the blank without too much trouble. Similarly, suppose that I leave out the starting number but give the percentage and the ending number:

50% of ? is 1

Again, you can fill in the blank.

If you get this basic idea, you're ready to solve percentage problems. When you boil them down, nearly all percentage problems are like one of the three types I show in Table 9-1.

Table 9-1	The Three Main Types of Percentage Problems	
Problem Type	*What to Find*	*Example*
Type #1	The ending number	50% of 2 is *what?*
Type #2	The percentage	*What* percentage of 2 is 1?
Type #3	The starting number	50% of *what* is 1?

In each case, the problem gives you two of the three pieces of information, and your job is to figure out the remaining piece. In the next section, I give you a simple tool to help you solve all three of these types of percentage problems.

Solving percentage problems with equations

Here's how to solve any percentage problem:

1. **Change the word *of* to a multiplication sign and the per cent to a decimal (as I show you earlier in this chapter).**

   This step is the same as for more straightforward percentage problems. For example, consider this problem:

   60% of what is 75?

   Begin by changing as follows:

60%	of	what	is	75
0.6	×			75

2. **Turn the word *is* to an equals sign and the word *what* into the letter *n*.**

   Here's what this step looks like:

60%	of	what	is	75
0.6	×	*n*	=	75

   This equation looks more normal, as follows:

   $$0.6 \times n = 75$$

3. **Find the value of *n*.**

   Technically, the last step involves a little bit of algebra, but I know you can handle it. (For a complete explanation of algebra, see Part IV of this book.) In the equation, *n* is being multiplied by 0.6. You want to 'undo' this operation by *dividing* by 0.6 on both sides of the equation:

   $$0.6 \times n \div 0.6 = 75 \div 0.6$$

   Almost magically, the left side of the equation becomes a lot easier to work with because multiplication and division by the same number cancel each other out:

   $$n = 75 \div 0.6$$

Remember that n is the answer to the problem. If your teacher lets you use a calculator, this last step is easy; if not, you can calculate it using some decimal division, as I show you in Chapter 7:

$n = 125$

Either way, the answer is 125 — so 60% of 125 is 75.

As another example, suppose you're faced with this percentage problem:

What per cent of 250 is 375?

To begin, change the *of* into a multiplication sign and the per cent into a decimal.

What	per cent	of	250	is	375
	× 0.01	×	250		375

Notice here that, because I don't know the per cent, I change the term *per cent* to × 0.01. Next, change *is* to an equals sign and *what* to the letter n:

What	per cent	of	250	is	375
n	× 0.01	×	250	=	375

Consolidate the equation and then multiply:

$n \times 2.5 = 375$

Now divide both sides by 2.5:

$n = 375 \div 2.5 = 150$

Therefore, the answer is 150 — so 150% of 250 is 375.

Here's one more problem: 49 is what per cent of 140? Begin, as always, by translating the problem into words:

49	is	what	per cent	of	140
49	=	n	× 0.01	×	140

Simplify the equation:

$49 = n \times 1.4$

Now divide both sides by 1.4:

$49 \div 1.4 = n \times 1.4 \div 1.4$

Again, multiplication and division by the same number allows you to cancel on the left side of the equation and complete the problem:

$49 \div 1.4 = n$

$35 = n$

Therefore, the answer is 35, so 49 is 35% of 140.

Chapter 10

Word Problems with Fractions, Decimals and Percentages

In This Chapter

▶ Adding and subtracting fractions, decimals, and percentages in word problems

▶ Translating the word *of* as multiplication

▶ Changing percentages to decimals in word problems

▶ Tackling business problems involving percentage increases and decreases

In Chapter 4, I show you how to solve word problems (also known as story problems) by setting up word problems that use the main four operations (adding, subtracting, multiplying, and dividing). In this chapter, I show you how to extend these skills to solve word problems with fractions, decimals, and percentages.

First, I show you how to solve relatively easy problems, in which all you need to do is add or subtract fractions, decimals, or percentages. Next, I show you how to solve problems that require you to multiply fractions. Such problems are easy to spot because they almost always contain the word *of*. After that, you discover how to solve percentage problems by setting up a word problem and changing the per cent to a decimal. Finally, I show you how to handle problems of percentage increases and decreases. These problems are often practical money problems in which you figure out information about raises and salaries, costs and discounts, or amounts before and after tax.

Adding and Subtracting Parts of the Whole in Word Problems

Certain word problems involving fractions, decimals, and percentages are really just problems in adding and subtracting. You may add fractions, decimals or percentages in a variety of real-world settings that rely on weights and measures — such as cooking and carpentry.

To solve these problems, you can use the skills that you pick up in Chapters 6 (for adding and subtracting fractions), 7 (for adding and subtracting decimals), and 8 (for adding and subtracting percentages).

Sharing a pizza: Fractions

You may have to add or subtract fractions in problems that involve splitting up part of a whole. For example, consider the following:

Joan ate $\frac{1}{6}$ of a pizza, Tony ate $\frac{1}{4}$, and Sylvia ate $\frac{1}{3}$. What fraction of the pizza was left when they were finished?

In this problem, just jot down the information that's given as word problems:

Joan $=\frac{1}{6}$ Tony $=\frac{1}{4}$ Sylvia $=\frac{1}{3}$

These fractions are part of one total pizza. To solve the problem, you need to find out how much all three people ate, so form the following word problems:

all three = Joan + Tony + Sylvia

Now you can substitute as follows:

$$\text{all three} = \frac{1}{6} + \frac{1}{4} + \frac{1}{3}$$

Chapter 6 gives you several ways to add these fractions. Here's one way:

$$\text{all three} = \frac{2}{12} + \frac{3}{12} + \frac{4}{12} = \frac{9}{12} = \frac{3}{4}$$

However, the question asks what fraction of the pizza was left after they finished, so you have to subtract that amount from the whole:

$$1 - \frac{3}{4} = \frac{1}{4}$$

Thus, the three people left $\frac{1}{4}$ of a pizza.

Buying by the kilo: Decimals

You frequently work with decimals when dealing with money, measurements (see Chapter 12), and food sold by the kilo. The following problem requires you to add and subtract decimals, which I discuss in Chapter 7. Even though the decimals may look intimidating, this problem is fairly simple to set up:

> Antonia bought 4.53 kilograms of beef and 3.1 kilograms of lamb. Lance bought 5.24 kilograms of chicken and 0.7 kilograms of pork. Which of them bought more meat, and how much more?

To solve this problem, you first find out how much each person bought:

$$Antonia = 4.53 + 3.1 = 7.63$$
$$Lance = 5.24 + 0.7 = 5.94$$

You can already see that Antonia bought more than Lance. To find how much more, subtract:

$$7.63 - 5.94 = 1.69$$

So Antonia bought 1.69 kilograms more than Lance.

Splitting the vote: Percentages

When percentages represent answers in polls, votes in an election, or portions of a budget, the total often has to add up to 100%. In real life, you may see such info organised as a pie chart (which I discuss in Chapter 13). Solving problems about this kind of information often involves nothing more than adding and subtracting percentages.

Here's an example: In a recent state election, five candidates were on the ticket. Faber won 39% of the vote, Gustafson won 31%, Ivanovich won 18%, Dixon won 7%, Obermayer won 3%, and the remaining votes went to donkey votes. What percentage of voters cast a donkey vote?

The candidates were in a single election, so all the votes have to total 100%. The first step here is just to add up the five percentages. Then subtract that value from 100%:

$$39\% + 31\% + 18\% + 7\% + 3\% = 98\%$$
$$100\% - 98\% = 2\%$$

Because 98% of voters voted for one of the five candidates, the remaining 2% cast a donkey vote.

Problems about Multiplying Fractions

In word problems, the word *of* almost always means multiplication. So whenever you see the word *of* following a fraction, decimal, or per cent, you can usually replace it with a times sign.

When you think about it, *of* means multiplication even when you're not talking about fractions. For example, when you point to an item in a store and say, 'I'll take three of those,' in a sense you're saying, 'I'll take that one multiplied by three.'

The following examples give you practice turning word problems that include the word *of* into multiplication problems that you can solve with fraction multiplication.

Renegade grocery shopping: Buying less than they tell you to

When you understand that the word *of* means multiplication, you have a powerful tool for solving word problems. For instance, you can figure out how much you'll spend if you don't buy food in the quantities listed on the signs. Here's an example:

If zucchinis cost \$4 a kilogram, how much does $\frac{5}{8}$ of a kilogram cost?

Here's what you get if you simply change the *of* to a multiplication sign:

$$\frac{5}{8} \times 1 \text{ kilogram of zucchinis}$$

So you know how many zucchinis you're buying. However, you want to know the cost. Because the problem tells you that 1 kilogram = \$4, you can replace 1 kilogram of zucchinis with \$4:

$$= \frac{5}{8} \times \$4$$

Now you have an expression you can evaluate. Use the rules of multiplying fractions from Chapter 6 and solve:

$$= \frac{5 \times \$4}{8} = \$\frac{20}{8}$$

This fraction reduces to $\$\frac{5}{2}$. However, the answer looks weird because dollars are usually expressed in decimals, not fractions. So convert this fraction to a decimal using the rules I show you in Chapter 7:

$$\$\frac{5}{2} = \$2.5 = \$2.50$$

At this point, recognise that $\$2.5$ is more commonly written as $\$2.50$, and you have your answer.

Easy as pie: Working out what's left on your plate

Sometimes when you're sharing something such as a pie, not everyone gets to it at the same time. The eager pie-lovers snatch the first slice, not bothering to divide the pie into equal servings, and the people who were slower, more patient, or just not that hungry cut their own portions from what's left over. When someone takes a part of the leftovers, you can do a bit of multiplication to see how much of the whole pie that portion represents.

Consider the following example:

Jerry bought a pie and ate $\frac{1}{5}$ of it. Then his wife, Doreen, ate $\frac{1}{6}$ of what was left. How much of the total pie was left?

To solve this problem, begin by jotting down what the first sentence tells you:

$$\text{Jerry} = \frac{1}{5}$$

Doreen ate part of what was left, so write a word equation that tells you how much of the pie was left after Jerry was finished. He started with a whole pie, so subtract his portion from 1:

$$\text{pie left after Jerry} = 1 - \frac{1}{5} = \frac{4}{5}$$

Next, Doreen ate $\frac{1}{6}$ of this amount. Rewrite the word *of* as multiplication and solve as follows. This answer tells you how much of the whole pie Doreen ate:

$$\text{Doreen} = \frac{1}{6} \times \frac{4}{5} = \frac{4}{30}$$

To make the numbers a little smaller before you go on, notice that you can reduce the fraction:

$$\text{Doreen} = \frac{2}{15}$$

Now you know how much Jerry and Doreen both ate, so you can add these amounts together:

$$\text{Jerry} + \text{Doreen} = \frac{1}{5} + \frac{2}{15}$$

Solve this problem as I show you in Chapter 6:

$$= \frac{3}{15} + \frac{2}{15} = \frac{5}{15}$$

This fraction reduces to $\frac{1}{3}$. Now you know that Jerry and Doreen ate $\frac{1}{3}$ of the pie, but the problem asks you how much is left. So finish up with some subtraction and write the answer:

$$1 - \frac{1}{3} = \frac{2}{3}$$

The amount of pie left over was $\frac{2}{3}$.

Multiplying Decimals and Percentages in Word Problems

In the preceding section, I show you how the word *of* in a fraction word problem usually means multiplication. This idea is also true in word problems involving decimals and percentages. The method for solving these two types of problems is similar, so I lump them together in this section.

You can easily solve word problems involving percentages by changing the percentages into decimals (refer to Chapter 9 for details). Here are a few common percentages and their decimal equivalents:

$25\% = 0.25$ $50\% = 0.5$ $75\% = 0.75$ $99\% = 0.99$

To the end: Figuring out how much money is left

One common type of problem gives you a starting amount — and a bunch of other information — and then asks you to figure out how much you end up with. Here's an example:

> Maria's grandparents gave her $125 for her birthday. She put 40% of the money in the bank, spent 35% of what was left on a pair of shoes, and then spent the rest on a dress. How much did the dress cost?

Start at the beginning, forming a word problem to find out how much money Maria put in the bank:

money in bank = 40% of $125

To solve this word equation, change the per cent to a decimal and the word *of* to a multiplication sign; then multiply:

money in bank = 0.4 × $125 = $50

Pay special attention to whether you're calculating how much of something was used up or how much of something is left over. If you need to work with the portion that remains, you may have to subtract the amount used from the amount you started with.

Because Maria started with $125, she had $75 left to spend:

money left to spend

= money from grandparents – money in bank

= $125 – $50

= $75

The problem then says that she spent 35% of this amount on a pair of shoes. Again, change the per cent to a decimal and the word *of* to a multiplication sign:

shoes = 35% of $75 = 0.35 × $75 = $26.25

She spent the rest of the money on a dress, so

dress = $75 – $26.25 = $48.75

Therefore, Maria spent $48.75 on the dress.

Finding out how much you started with

Some problems give you the amount that you end up with and ask you to find out how much you started with. In general, these problems are harder because you're not used to thinking backward. Here's an example, and it's kind of a tough one, so fasten your seat belt:

> Maria received some birthday money from her aunt. She put her usual 40% in the bank and spent 75% of the rest on a purse. When she was done, she had $12 left to spend on dinner. How much did her aunt give her?

This problem is similar to the one in the preceding section, but you need to start at the end and work backward. Notice that the only dollar amount in the problem comes after the two percentage amounts. The problem tells you that she ends up with $12 after two transactions — putting money in the bank and buying a purse — and asks you to find out how much she started with.

To solve this problem, set up two word problems to describe the two transactions:

> money from aunt – money for bank = money after bank
>
> money after bank – money for purse = $12

Notice what these two word problems are saying. The first tells you that Maria took the money from her aunt, subtracted some money to put in the bank, and left the bank with a new amount of money, which I'm calling *money after bank*. The second word problem starts where the first leaves off. It tells you that Maria took the money left over from the bank, subtracted some money for a purse, and ended up with $12.

This second problems already has an amount of money filled in, so start here. To solve this problem, realise that Maria spent 75% of her money at that time on the purse — that is, 75% of the money she still had after the bank:

> money after bank – 75% of money after bank = $12

I'm going to make one small change to this equation so you can see what it's really saying:

> 100% of money after bank – 75% of money after bank = $12

Adding *100% of* doesn't change the problems because it really just means you're multiplying by 1. In fact, you can slip these two words in anywhere without changing what you mean, though you may sound ridiculous saying,

'Yesterday, I rode 100% of my bike home from school, walked 100% of my dog, and went with 100% of my mum to see 100% of a movie.'

In this particular case, however, these words help you to make a connection because 100% − 75% = 25%; here's an even better way to write this problems:

25% of money after bank = $12

Before moving on, make sure you understand the steps that have brought you here.

You know now that 25% of money after bank is $12, so the total amount of money after bank is 4 times this amount — that is, $48. Therefore, you can plug this number into the first equation:

money from aunt − money for bank = $48

Now you can use the same type of thinking to solve this equation (and it goes a lot more quickly this time!). First, Maria placed 40% of the money from her aunt in the bank:

money from aunt − 40% of money from aunt = $48

Again, rewrite this equation to make what it's saying clearer:

100% of money from aunt − 40% of money from aunt = $48

Now, because 100% − 40% = 60%, rewrite it again:

60% of money from aunt = $48

Thus, 0.6 × money from aunt = $48. Divide both sides of this equation by 0.6:

money from aunt = $48 ÷ 0.6 = $80

So this time Maria's aunt gave her $80 for her birthday.

Handling Percentage Increases and Decreases in Word Problems

Word problems that involve increasing or decreasing by a percentage add a final spin to percentage problems. Typical percentage-increase problems involve calculating the amount of a salary plus a raise, the cost of merchandise plus tax, or an amount of money plus interest or dividend. Typical percentage decrease problems involve the amount of a salary minus taxes or the cost of merchandise minus a discount.

To tell you the truth, you may have already solved problems of this kind earlier in the section 'Multiplying Decimals and Percentages in Word Problems'. But people often get thrown by the language of these problems — which, by the way, is the language of business — so I want to give you some practice in solving them (perhaps for situations you may face in the not-too-distance future).

Raking in the dough: Finding salary increases

A little street smarts should tell you that the words *salary increase* or *raise* mean more money, so get ready to do some addition. Here's an example:

> Alison's salary was $40,000 last year and, at the end of the year, she received a 5% raise. What will she earn this year?

To solve this problem, first realise that Alison got a raise. So whatever she makes this year will be more than she made last year. The key to setting up this type of problem is to think of the percentage increase as '100% of last year's salary plus 5% of last year's salary.' Here's the word equation:

> this year's salary = 100% of last year's salary + 5% of last year's salary

Now you can just add the percentages:

> this year's salary = 105% of last year's salary

Change the per cent to a decimal and the word *of* to a multiplication sign; then fill in the amount of last year's salary:

> this year's salary = 1.05 × $40,000

Now you're ready to multiply:

> this year's salary = $42,000

So Alison's new salary is $42,000.

Earning interest on top of interest

The word *interest* means more money. When you receive interest from the bank, you get more money. And when you pay interest on a loan, you pay more money. Sometimes people earn interest on the interest they earned earlier, which makes the dollar amounts grow even faster. Here's an example:

> Bethany placed $9,500 in a one-year cash deposit that paid 4% interest. The next year, she rolled this over into a bond that paid 6% per year. How much did Bethany earn on her investment in those two years?

This problem involves interest, so it's another problem in percentage increase — only this time, you have to deal with two transactions. Take them one at a time.

The first transaction is a percentage increase of 4% on $9,500. The following mathematical sentence makes sense:

> money after first year $= 100\%$ of initial deposit $+ 4\%$ of initial deposit
> $= 104\%$ of initial deposit

Now, substitute $9,500 for the initial deposit and calculate:

> $= 104\%$ of $9,500
> $= 1.04 \times \$9,500$
> $= \$9,880$

At this point, you're ready for the second transaction. This is a percentage increase of 6% on $9,880:

> final amount $= 106\%$ of $9,880
> $= 1.06 \times \$9,880$
> $= \$10,472.80$

Then subtract the initial deposit from the final amount:

> earnings $=$ final amount $-$ initial deposit
> $= \$10,472.80 - \$9,500$
> $= \$972.80$

So Bethany earned a tidy $972.80 on her investment.

Getting a deal: Calculating discounts

When you hear the words *discount* or *sale price*, think of subtraction. Here's an example:

> Greg has his eye on a television with a listed price of $2,100 (yes, it's massive). The salesman offers him a 30% discount if he buys it today. What will the television cost with the discount?

In this problem, you need to realise that the discount lowers the price of the television, so you have to subtract:

$$\text{Sale price} = 100\% \text{ of regular price} - 30\% \text{ of regular price}$$
$$= 70\% \text{ of regular price}$$
$$= 0.7 \times \$2,100$$
$$= \$1,470$$

Thus, the television costs $1,470 with the discount.

Part III
Picturing and Measuring: Shapes, Weights and Graphs

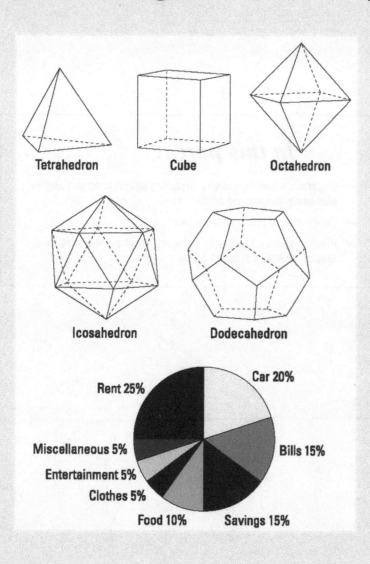

In this part . . .

✔ Understand basic geometry, including points, lines and angles, plus basic shapes and solids.

✔ Weigh and measure with the metric system.

✔ Present maths info visually, using bar graphs, pie charts, line graphs, and the Cartesian plane.

Chapter 11

Shaping Up

....

....

Most of this chapter is about shapes and what you can do with them. I remind you of some stuff you probably already know about shapes and what you can tell from just looking at them. I also take you through some of the words you need to be familiar with to deal confidently with shape questions.

Then I cover the joys of measuring angles (for example, to see how sharp a corner is) and get you to see how you can transform shapes. This leads on to the idea of symmetry — how you can transform a shape but end up with something that looks just the same. I also cover tessellation — making nice tile patterns with no gaps or overlaps — but to do this you need to understand how angles fit together.

I also run through the ideas of nets (unfolding a three-dimensional figure into a two-dimensional shape), and plans and elevations (what shapes look like from different angles — the top, the front and the side). Nets, plans and elevations aren't likely to come up in any numeracy test, but your teacher might ask you to investigate them at school.

You're Already in Good Shape

I reckon you're already familiar with all of the shapes you need to know about at this stage.

If you recognise squares, rectangles, triangles and circles, you're off to a good start. Add in cubes, cuboids (box shapes), spheres (ball shapes), cylinders and pyramids, and I think you're good on the 'recognising shapes' front. The shape of an object doesn't depend on its size or *orientation* — if you twist a square around, the shape is still a square, even if it looks like a diamond. Regardless of how big a shape is or which way around you draw it, a shape's properties and name stay the same.

You also need to know the difference between two-dimensional and three-dimensional shapes. The 'D' in a 3D movie stands for 'dimensions'. The dimensions make the movie seem as if everything isn't just flat on a screen but has depth. Similarly, in maths, two-dimensional objects are flat (you can draw them on paper) and three-dimensional figures come out of the page.

Sussing out shapes you know

You need to recognise the following *two-dimensional* — or flat — shapes, which I also show in Figure 11-1:

- ✔ **Square:** A shape with four equal-length straight sides arranged at right-angles to each other.

- ✔ **Rectangle:** A shape with four straight sides at right-angles to each other. The sides aren't necessarily all the same length, but sides opposite each other are always the same length.

- ✔ **Triangle:** A shape with three straight sides. As you progress with maths, most of the geometry you do is based on triangles.

- ✔ **Circle:** This is the only curved shape you really need to know about. The technical definition is 'a shape with all of the points a fixed distance from the centre', but you'll recognise a circle when you see one.

Figure 11-1:
A square,
a rectangle,
a triangle
and a circle.

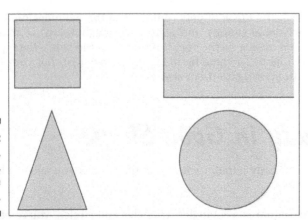

Three-dimensional figures are objects that don't lie flat. The following four three-dimensional figures, which I show in Figure 11-2, are closely linked to the four major two-dimensional shapes that I describe in the preceding list:

- ✔ **Cube:** The shape of a normal die. Each of a cube's sides is a square, and all of the edges are the same length.

- ✔ **Cuboid:** The shape of a shoebox. Each of its sides is a rectangle.

- ✔ **Pyramid:** The shape of . . . well, guess! It has a square on the bottom and four identical triangles around the side that come together and meet at the top.

- ✔ **Sphere:** The shape of a ball.

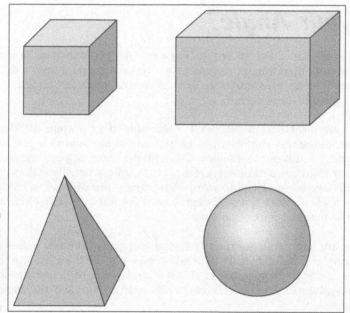

Figure 11-2:
A cube, a cuboid, a pyramid and a sphere.

Expanding your shapely vocabulary

In this chapter, I introduce some concepts that you may or may not have come across before. You may want to copy some of the definitions in this section into your notebook so you can work with them again later. Here are some extra words for your shape vocabulary:

- ✔ **Angle:** The sharpness of a corner, measured in degrees. If you turn all the way around to face the way you started, you move through 360 degrees.

- ✔ **Reflection:** Turning a shape over.

✔ **Regular:** A regular shape is one where all the sides are the same length and all the corners have the same angle. A square is a regular shape, but you can have regular shapes with any number of sides, as long as it's three or more.

✔ **Right angle:** A quarter-turn, or 90 degrees.

✔ **Rotation:** Twisting a shape around its centre.

✔ **Symmetry:** A *symmetrical* shape is one you can either fold precisely in half, or twist around its centre so you can't tell which way up it is.

✔ **Tessellation:** Putting shapes together to make a pattern, with no spaces between the shapes.

What's Your Angle?

Angle is another word for corner. For example, you may hear of footballers scoring from tight angles, meaning they've kicked a goal from a difficult spot. The word 'angle' also shows up in other words, such as 'triangle' — which simply means 'three corners'.

Angles are measured in degrees. For example, if a car spins 360 degrees, it spins all the way round, while the latitude of Melbourne is just under 38 degrees south of the equator. Confusingly, angle degrees are completely different from temperature degrees — the context usually makes clear which type of degrees you need to work with (except possibly when talking about pointy icicles!). Both types of degree are denoted by a little circle above and after the number, for example: 90°.

Angles are interesting for many reasons, but one of the key points is that their properties don't really depend on how big the lines leading to the corner are. For example, the angle on a bookend is the same whether it's a bookend for tiny books or huge books — in either case, the angle is 90 degrees.

Defining angles

When someone says an angle is a certain number of degrees, they're trying to tell you how sharp the corner is. A small angle means the corner is very sharp, while an angle of 180 degrees isn't much of an angle at all but instead is a straight line.

One degree is defined as 'one three-hundred-and-sixtieth of a circle', which isn't tremendously helpful (but then again, you may not find the technical definitions of metres and kilograms helpful either). I prefer to think of 90 degrees as a right angle — a sideways turn — and work from there.

Special angles

You need to know about the following special angles (which I show in Figure 11-3):

- ✔ **360 degrees** is a complete circle. If you turn around 360 degrees, you get back to where you started.

- ✔ **180 degrees** is half a circle. If you turn 180 degrees, you end up facing backwards.

- ✔ **90 degrees** is a quarter-circle, or a right-angle. If you turn 90 degrees, you end up facing to the left or the right of where you started. A right angle is usually represented with a small box drawn into the corner.

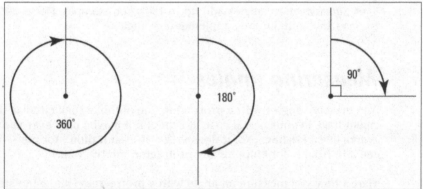

Figure 11-3:
Angles of 360, 180 and 90 degrees.

Other types of angle

You need to know the following angle-related words (I show examples in Figure 11-4):

- ✔ An *acute* angle is an angle smaller than a right angle — so less than 90 degrees. I like to think of 'acute little puppy' to remind me that it's a little angle.

- ✔ A *reflex* angle is an angle bigger than 180 degrees. You know when your doctor hits the outside of your knee with a hammer to test your reflexes? I think of that to remember what a reflex angle is: The outside of your knee is always more than 180 degrees.

- ✔ An *obtuse* angle is in between — so more than 90 degrees but fewer than 180. I don't have a good memory aid for obtuse angles — so let me know if you can think of one.

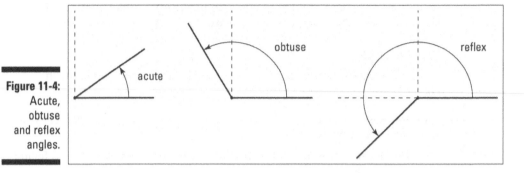

Figure 11-4:
Acute,
obtuse
and reflex
angles.

And here are a couple more important angle facts to remember:

- ✔ *Complementary* angles add up to 90°. For example, 42° + 48° = 90°, so 42° and 48° are complementary angles.

- ✔ *Supplementary* angles add up to 180°. For example, 150° + 30° = 180°, so 150° and 30° are supplementary angles.

Measuring angles

You measure angles with a protractor, one of those semi-circular things you might have in your pencil case at school but maybe only ever use to see if it works like a Frisbee. (No, it doesn't. Or at least it didn't for me — it just got me into trouble for chipping my protractor and the wall.)

Here's how you measure an angle with a protractor (I show the steps in Figure 11-5 to help you visualise the set-up):

1. **Put the cross-hair in the middle of your protractor over the corner where you want to measure the angle.**

2. **Turn the protractor so that one of the lines going into the angle is on the 'zero' line across the bottom of the protractor, to the left of the cross-hair.**

3. **Follow the other line to the edge of the protractor and read the number off the scale — that's the angle you're looking for.**

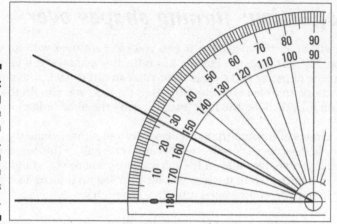

Figure 11-5:
Measuring
an angle
with a
protractor.
The angle in
this figure
measures
27 degrees.

Protractors are fiddly because they have two different scales running along the same edge and you can easily mix up which one is which. I recommend always using the outside scale — so make sure the zero you use is the zero on the outside track of the protractor.

After you measure an angle, look at the angle again and ask, 'Does my answer make sense?' If you have an angle that's obviously more than 90 degrees (an obtuse angle) but your protractor says the angle measures 15 degrees, you know something has gone wrong.

Playing with Symmetry

Symmetry is a description of how you can change a shape but leave it the same. For instance, you can take a checkers piece and flip it over, and the piece looks just the same — this is an example of reflective symmetry. If you take a rectangle and spin it through 180 degrees, the shape looks like the same rectangle — this is an example of rotational symmetry.

If you've ever tried to solve a double-sided jigsaw, you may know you can reasonably do three things to a jigsaw piece (if you don't count thumping the piece in a frustrated attempt to get it into a space). You can:

✔ Pick up the piece and move it around (the technical term for this is *translation* — you *translate* a shape when you move it).

✔ Turn it over (this is *reflection* — you *reflect* a shape when you turn it over).

✔ Turn it around (this is *rotation* — you *rotate* a shape when you twist it).

On reflection: Turning shapes over

A shape with *reflective symmetry* is one you can turn over without changing the shape. For instance, a rectangle has reflective symmetry: If you pick up a blank piece of paper and turn it over, you can put it back where it was before without anyone being any the wiser. (In fact, you can do that in two ways: Turn it over along the long edge or along the short edge.)

Squares, circles and some triangles also have reflective symmetry. The symmetry is described as reflective because one half of the shape mirrors the other. If you've ever played the mirror game where you stand facing the edge of a mirror so that when you lift your leg up it looks like you're standing in mid-air, you've used reflective symmetry.

A shape has reflective symmetry if you can draw a line on it somewhere so that one side of the line looks exactly like the other side of the line. Figure 11-6 shows some examples of reflective symmetry.

Figure 11-6:
Reflective
symmetry.
Top left: A
square has
four lines of
symmetry.
Top right:
A rectangle
has two
lines of
symmetry.
A circle has
an infinite
number
of lines of
symmetry
(any line
through
the middle
works). An
equilateral
triangle
(with all
sides the
same
length) has
three lines
of symmetry.

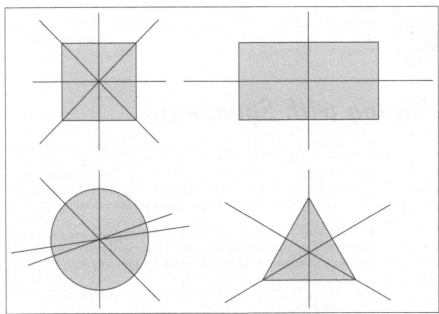

Doing the twist: Rotating shapes

If you do a normal jigsaw puzzle, the only way it makes sense to change a piece once it's the right way up is to turn it around so the bumps and spaces face another way, as I show in Figure 11-7.

Rotating means twisting the shape around its middle so the shape faces a different direction. The piece in Figure 11-7 looks different every time you turn it, but some pieces look the same however you turn them around (ignoring the picture) — they either have all four of the bumps on the edges pointing inwards or all four pointing outwards. These pieces have *rotational symmetry*, meaning you can twist them around their centre and not know which way was originally up.

In general, the order of rotational symmetry of a shape is how many ways you can twist it round to get the same shape before you get back to the beginning, as I show in Figure 11-8 — or how many different ways you can hold the paper and see exactly the same shape. A square has rotational symmetry of order four, because you can hold the paper the normal way up, upside down, facing to the left or facing to the right, and the square will look just the same. A rectangle has rotational symmetry of order two, because it looks the same the normal way up and upside-down — but if you turn the paper sideways, it looks different. A triangle, depending on the type, may have order three, order two or no rotational symmetry. And a circle ... that's a trick question: A circle has infinite rotational symmetry.

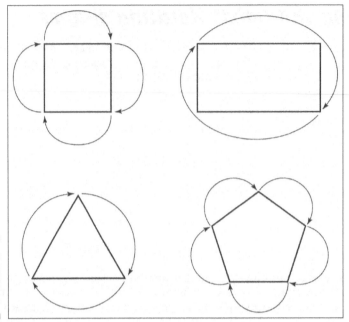

Figure 11-8:
Shapes and
rotational
symmetry.

Pretty patterns: Tessellation

Tessellation is a fancy word for fitting shapes together so no gaps appear between the shapes and none of the shapes overlap — as if you're solving a jigsaw puzzle, tiling a wall or paving a path. It may seem like not very much maths is involved in tessellation, but in fact it's all about the angles.

Sad fact for the day: Once upon a time, I was number 17 in the world at the Linux version of the game Tetris. I find it difficult to think of another achievement that's simultaneously so impressive and so pointless.

The idea of Tetris is to manoeuvre different-shaped blocks falling from above into a rectangular space — any time you complete a line all the way across without any gaps, the line disappears and the blocks above it shift down.

Tetris is all about tessellation: Fitting shapes together so no gaps appear. Some other places you see tessellation are in the work of Dutch artist M.C. Escher and in a great deal of Islamic art — for instance, at the Alhambra Palace in Spain.

You don't need to think of tessellation in quite the same depth as these artists — although it can be fun to do so. You only need to worry about fairly regular shapes.

Tessellation has one important rule: Wherever lines meet, the angles have to add up to 360 degrees.

Tetris works because the corners on all of the shapes are 90-degree angles, and when four of the shapes meet you end up with no spaces, as you can see in Figure 11-9. Not only 90-degree angles tessellate, though. To give just a few examples, you can also tile equilateral triangles (with 60-degree corners) and hexagons (six sides and 120-degree corners), also shown in figure 11-9.

The only kind of multiple-choice test question I can think of that would involve tessellation involves 'filling in the gap' — the test gives you two or three shapes that meet at a corner and you need to find the angle on the remaining shape.

This is a pretty simple process if you remember the important rule that I mention above:

1. **Write down the size of each angle touching the corner you're interested in.**

2. **Add up all the angles from Step 1.**

3. **You need to make 360 degrees in the corner, so work out 360 take away the angle you worked out in Step 2.**

   The answer is the size of the angle you need to put in the corner.

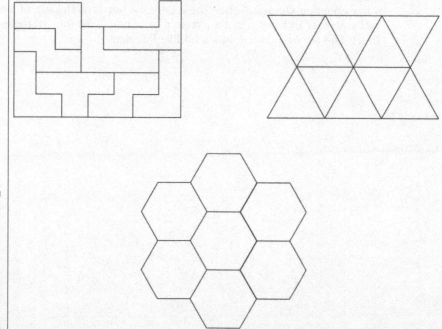

Figure 11-9:
Tessellation: Tetris blocks, triangles and hexagons tessellating.

Understanding Nets, Plans and Elevations, Oh My!

I've been told at least once that I'm the least artistic person on the planet, which rankles a bit: I *could* learn how to draw, I just haven't yet.

Maybe you have all of my missing artistic skills — I hope so, because in this section I'm asking you to investigate the following drawing-related ideas:

- ✔ **Net:** A picture of what a 3D shape looks like if you unfold it.
- ✔ **Plan:** A top-down view of a 3D shape.
- ✔ **Elevation:** A side-on view of a 3D shape from any side.

At this stage, you don't actually need to draw these things, although if you study maths further you may do. In this section, I just give you a few ideas about what you can do with nets, plans and elevations.

Folding under pressure: Nets

A *net* is a shape you can fold up, origami-style, to make a three-dimensional shape without any gaps. Nets are really hard to visualise, but you likely only need to know a few shapes at this stage. Figure 11-10 shows nets of a few common shapes. Notice the difference between the net of a cube (six squares) and the net of a pyramid (a square with four triangles next to it). The net of a cone looks a bit like Pacman.

Figure 11-10:
Nets of a few shapes. Top left: A cube. Top middle: A tetrahedron (a pyramid with a triangular base). Top right: A cone. Bottom left: A triangular prism (like a Toblerone). Bottom middle: A pyramid. Bottom right: A cylinder.

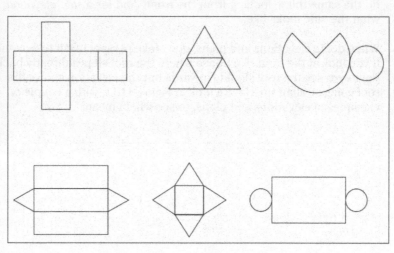

Looking at every angle: Plans and elevations

Architects like to show what the thing they're building looks like from the front, back and sides, and sometimes the top, in case you need to pick it out on Google Earth or locate it from an aircraft.

Being able to sketch what an object looks like from the front and sides — and conversely, to 'see' from those views what the object looks like in 3D — is unlikely to help you in an exam, but you may need to do it in an investigation in maths classes.

Understanding plans and elevations is also a useful step towards understanding 3D shapes for further study. Being able to visualise what's going on, and having a good sense of up, back and sideways can make the shape part of more advanced maths more accessible and engaging.

To draw a *plan* — a top view — you imagine what you'd see if you looked down on your shape. What shape is the top? Would you see any lines? How big is the top? Then you sketch what you see. For the *front elevation*, you do the same thing, looking from the front. And for a *side elevation*, you draw what the side looks like.

When doing elevations and plans, *don't* take perspective into account. If you look at the front of a house where the roof slopes directly back, your eyes see the roof sloping inwards but the elevation shows the roof going straight up. Have a look at Figure 11-11, with a couple of examples of elevations and plans, to see what I mean.

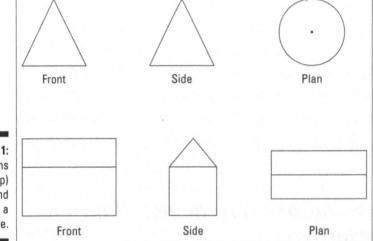

Figure 11-11: Elevations of (top) a cone and (bottom) a house.

Chapter 12

Considering Time, Weights, Temperature and Measurements

. . . .

In This Chapter

▶ Understanding time and dates

▶ Reading timetables and calculating with the clock

▶ Working out with weights

▶ Getting your head around temperatures, including negative temperatures

▶ Using measuring tools and understanding length, distance and perimeter

▶ Knowing all about area, volume and capacity

▶ Making sense of maps and plans

. . . .

*Y*ou've probably used clocks since you were in your first years at primary school. And you probably know quite a bit about weight already. For example, you know that moving a heavy object is harder than moving a light object. And you probably notice that you buy most food by weight and follow recipes according to weight — for example, '200 grams of the finest shiitake mushrooms known to humankind' or '1 kilogram of sugar' if you're following my mum's fudge recipe. You probably also know a bit about temperatures, and what a hot day temperature is versus a cold day.

In this chapter, I help you get to grips with basic times and dates. I show you how to put theory into practice by reading timetables, doing sums with time, and even calculating speeds. I also look at some of the obvious and not-so-obvious facets of the maths of weight. I show you how to use different types of weighing scale. I introduce the different units you use to weigh things, explain how to convert between different units, and offer some guidelines on how to estimate.

I also tell you about temperatures, including negative temperatures and look at some common measuring tools. I cover units of length, and measuring distance and perimeter, before moving on to area, volume and capacity.

To top all of that off, I end the chapter with some pointers for reading maps and plans.

Understanding the Vocabulary of Time

Time is almost the only area of basic maths where there's never been any serious attempt to use a decimal system. (Angles, arguably, are another area.) So instead of using tens, hundreds and so on, time uses irregular units:

- ✔ 60 seconds make a minute

- ✔ 60 minutes make an hour

- ✔ 24 hours make a day

- ✔ 7 days make a week

- ✔ 365 days (about 52 weeks) make a year — except a leap year, which has 366 days.

A *century* is 100 years. The word 'cent' usually means something to do with 100 — one dollar has 100 cents, and a metre has 100 centimetres. In cricket, a century is 100 runs.

A *millennium* is 1,000 years. The prefix 'mill-' is often used in words connected with 1,000. I don't think anyone's ever scored 1,000 runs in cricket, but I imagine it would be called a millennium if they did.

Fractions in time

Time uses a few fractions. If you're not sure about fractions, check out Chapter 6, where I ease you through the subject.

The main fractions you meet in time are quarter- and half-hours. Half an hour is 30 minutes — because 30 is half of 60. Quarter of an hour is 15 minutes, because 15 is a quarter of 60. Three-quarters of an hour is 45 minutes, because 45 is three-quarters of 60.

You can write 30 minutes as $\frac{1}{2}$ hour or 0.5 hours. Likewise, 15 minutes is $\frac{1}{4}$ hour or 0.25 hours, and 45 minutes is $\frac{3}{4}$ hour or 0.75 hours.

Be careful not to write '15 minutes = 0.15 hours'. That sum is not true, because there aren't 100 minutes in an hour. Fifteen minutes is a quarter of an hour and a quarter is 0.25. So you write: '15 minutes = 0.25 hours'.

Different date formats

To help with writing dates, each month has a number:

1 — January

2 — February

3 — March

4 — April

5 — May

6 — June

7 — July

8 — August

9 — September

10 — October

11 — November

12 — December

Different countries use slightly different formats for writing the date. As an example, I use Stephen Hawking's birthday — 8 January 1942. In Australia, the convention is to write the number of the day, followed by the number of the month, followed by the year. So, Stephen Hawking's birthday is 8/1/1942 or — when no doubt exists about the century — 8/1/42.

In the US, the convention is to write the day and the month the other way around — so 1/8/42.

A very, very brief history of time

Our crazy, mixed-up system of time units is due mainly to the Sumerians (who lived about 4,000 years ago), who used 60 instead of 10 as their base for numbers. You can blame the same people for a circle having 360 degrees.

As far as I can tell, nobody knows for sure why a day is divided into 24 hours.

The European calendar, with its odd variations from month to month, is a variation on the Roman calendar (you may have noticed that some of our months are still named after Latin numbers).

A day is how long it takes the planet to spin around its axis. A year is how long it takes the planet to go around the sun — a little short of 365.25 days. The 0.25 is why we have a leap year every four years. The 'little short' is why things are actually more complicated than that.

Comparing the 12-hour and 24-hour clocks

When telling the time in the normal way, using the *12-hour clock*, we split the day into two halves — am, from midnight to noon through the morning, and pm, from noon to midnight through the afternoon and evening.

The abbreviations am and pm stand for the Latin phrases *ante meridiem* and *post meridiem*, which mean 'before midday' and 'after midday', respectively. If you say, 'Let's talk at 9 o'clock tomorrow', the other person may not know which of the two 9 o'clocks you mean. Do you mean 9 am (9 in the morning) or 9 pm (9 in the evening)?

To overcome this problem, travel timetables and the military often use the *24-hour clock*. Most digital watches, computers and phones have an option to switch between 12- and 24-hour clocks.

Instead of going back to one after midday, the hours keep on going up to 24 in the 24-hour clock. In the 24-hour clock, the time is always given by four numbers — so we write 1 pm as 1300 and we write 4.30 am as 0430.

To say these out loud, you break the numbers into pairs and say 'hours' afterwards — 0430 is pronounced 'oh four thirty hours' and 1300 as 'thirteen hundred hours'.

Here's how to convert between the 12-hour and 24-hour clock:

1. **If your time is before 10 am, put a zero in front of the time. You're done.**

   For example, 6.57 am becomes 0657, and 9.00 am becomes 0900.

2. **If your time is between 10 am and 12.59 pm, don't do anything.**

   For example, 10.48 am becomes 1048, and 11.00 am becomes 1100.

3. **If your time is between 1 pm and midnight, add 12 to the hour.**

   For example, 1.02 pm becomes 1302, and 11.59 pm becomes 2359.

Going from the 24-hour to the 12-hour clock is easier. If the first pair of numbers is 13 or bigger, take away 12 to get the number of hours. Otherwise, you don't need to do anything.

So, 2300 is 11 pm, and 1100 is 11 am.

Almost everyone gets confused by midday and midnight sometimes. The convention is that midnight is called 12 am (either 0000 or 2400 in the 24-hour clock). Midday, on the other hand, is 12 pm or 1200. Personally, I like to make things clear by writing '12 midday' or '12 midnight' if any chance of confusion is possible.

Catching the Bus: Seeing How Timetables Work

Timetables are a ruthlessly efficient way to get as much information as possible into as small a space as possible. This is why almost everyone gets confused by them, and many stations have those electronic signs telling you the 1715 to Bendigo is on time when it's already 1733 and you've seen no sign of a train for three hours.

A traditional bus or train timetable looks something like that in Figure 12-1 — compact and a little tricky to read unless you can focus.

					FX	FO
Appleborough	1100	1130	1200	1230	1300	1310
Bellstown	1112	1142	1212	1242	1312	1322
Colinsville	1119	1149	1219	1249	1319	1329
Doddsmouth	1139	1209	1239	1309	1339	1349
East Hill	1153	1223	1253	1323	1353	1403

Figure 12-1: A traditional bus timetable.

Next time you need to understand a timetable, try following these steps (my example is for a bus timetable, but train timetables work just the same):

1. **Figure out in which direction you're travelling.** Some timetables list both directions — look for a timetable where your destination is listed below where you're travelling from.

2. **Find where you are and read across until you find a time that's after now (or around the time you want to travel).**

3. **Check any information at the top of the column to check the bus is running.**

You may see abbreviations such as 'FX' to say 'this bus doesn't run on Fridays' or 'WO' to say 'this bus only operates on Wednesdays'. If that bus isn't running, find the next one.

4. **Put a finger on where you're travelling from and another on the time you've picked.**

5. **Move each finger down one stop at a time until you reach the stop where you want to get off.**

   The time you're pointing at is when you ought to arrive at your destination.

You use a similar method to figure out when you need to leave if you want to arrive somewhere at a particular time. Look at the arrival times for your destination and find an appropriate one. Put your finger on it and move up the column until you're at your departure point to find the time you need to leave.

Doing Sums with Time

Sums with time can catch anybody out. I got so fed up with adjusting my clock the wrong way at the start or end of daylight savings and showing up two hours early or late for classes that for a while I stopped arranging to do anything on the days the clocks changed.

Any event has three main time-related properties: When it starts, how long it lasts and when it finishes. If you know any two of these properties, you can work out the third — for example, if something starts at 11 am and goes on for 30 minutes, then the event should finish at 11.30 am. But if time sums were always that easy, I wouldn't include a section about them in this book. Beware the nasty trap that comes up when you do sums with time that involve going into the next or previous hour.

For example, if it takes me 25 minutes to walk into town and I leave at 4.45 pm, when do I arrive? If I add 25 to 45, I end up with 70 — but 4.70 pm isn't a real time!

I have at least three ways to avoid this trap. One way is to think slightly backwards: Try to think of 25 minutes as '35 minutes less than an hour'. So, an hour later would be 5.45 pm, and 35 minutes before that would be 5.10 pm.

Another method is to split the 25 minutes into two parts — if I walk for 15 minutes, I get to 5 pm, but I'm still 10 minutes away from town. So I add on another 10 minutes and arrive at 5.10 pm. One other way is to accept that 4.70 pm doesn't exist as a time, but you know that 70 is 10 minutes more than an hour — so the time is four, plus an hour, plus 10 minutes, making 5.10 pm.

Whenever you do a sum with time, be ultra-paranoid about going past the hour. Messing up time sums is surprisingly easy.

When does something start?

If you know when something ends and how long it takes, you can figure out when the event starts.

If the number of minutes in the duration is less than the number of minutes in the time, follow these steps to work out when the event starts:

1. **Convert the end time into the 24-hour clock.**

   For example, if you know your train arrives at 10.50 pm, your end time is 2250.

2. **Take away the minutes in the duration from the minutes in the end time.**

   If your journey lasts for two and a half hours, take off 30 minutes, to get 2220.

3. **If you need to, take away the hours in the duration from the hours in the end time.**

   In this example, take off two hours, to get 2020.

4. **What's left is the answer.**

   The train sets off at 8.20 pm.

If the number of minutes in the duration is more than the number in the time, you need to follow this different approach:

1. **Take the number of minutes in the duration away from 60.**

   For example, I know my drive to Sydney takes an hour and 40 minutes and I want to arrive at 6 pm. I take 40 away from 60 to get 20.

2. **Add this number to the number of minutes in the end time. This is the number of minutes in the answer.**

   I have no minutes in the end time, so the number of minutes in my start time ought to be 20.

3. **Take away the number of hours in the duration from the number of hours in the end time — and then take away one more. This is the number of hours in the answer.**

   I take away the 1 hour in my travel time from 18 (6 pm = 1800) to get 17 and then take off another to get 16, which is the number of hours in my departure time.

   I need to set off at 1620, or 4.20 pm to get to Sydney for 6 pm.

When does something end?

If you know when something starts and how long it takes, you can figure out when it ends. Here's what you do:

1. **Convert the start time into the 24-hour clock.**

   For example, the time is 12.45 pm and I want to cook a lasagne in the oven for 45 minutes. My start time is 1245.

2. **Add the minutes in the duration to the minutes in the start time.**

   I add 45 minutes and get 1290.

3. **Add the hours in the duration to the hours in the start time.**

   I don't have any hours to add.

4. **If the number of minutes in your answer is 60 or more, add one to the number of hours and take 60 away from the minutes.**

   In this example, 90 is 30 more than 60, so I get 1330.

5. **What you have left is the answer.**

   My lunch is ready at 1330 — or 1.30 pm.

How long does something take?

If you know when something starts and when it ends, you can figure out how long the event lasts.

If the number of minutes in the start time is less than the number of minutes in the end time, follow these steps:

1. **Convert the end time into the 24-hour clock.**

2. **Convert the start time into the 24-hour clock.**

3. **Take away the minutes in the start time from the minutes in the end time.**

4. Take away the hours in the start time from the hours in the end time.

5. What's left is the duration.

If the number of minutes in the start time is more than the number of minutes in the end time, you need to follow this slightly different approach:

1. Take the number of minutes in the start time away from 60.

2. Add this number to the number of minutes in the end time. This is the number of minutes in the answer.

3. Take away the number of hours in the start time from the number of hours in the end time — and then take away one more. This is the number of hours in the answer.

Appreciating What You Already Know About Weights

At some point in your life, you have probably stepped on some bathroom scales. Pretty much anything you use to measure weight is called a scale (or a weighing scale). You can still see the earliest type of scale (a *balance*) in antique shops and in statues of Justice: A balance comprises two trays that balance on or hang from a pivoted beam. You place what you want to weigh on one tray and place a known weight on the other tray. When the beam is level, you have the same amount of weight in each tray. Antique scales normally come with various lumps of metal marked with the appropriate weight. Surprisingly, a well-designed balance is the most accurate tool we have for measuring the mass of an object.

A step up from the balance in ease of reading is the *analogue scale*, which is more like the scale in my bathroom or the scales you see in the veg section of the supermarket. These scales have only one surface, where you put the thing you want to weigh. A dial rotates to show the correct weight. By far the easiest scales to use are *digital scales* — some bathroom scales look like this, as do the things you put your suitcase on at the airport before the check-in person says your Dad has 1 kilogram too much luggage and charges him an extra $50. More pleasantly, the scales in my local coffee shop are digital. Digital scales have one surface to put things on. The weight appears as a number on the screen. I have no idea how they work. If you find out, tell me! I show several types of scale in Figure 12-2.

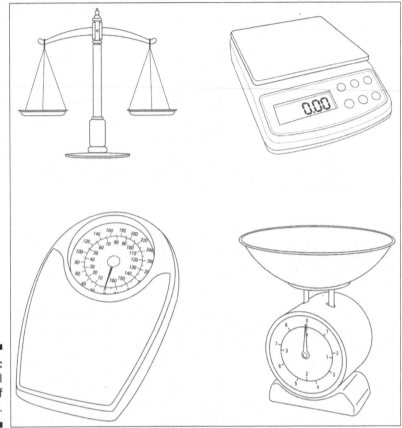

Figure 12-2:
Several
types of
scales.

Using digital scales

I used to own a cookbook called *How to Boil an Egg*. Maybe you're thinking, *How could anyone possibly get through adolescence without knowing that?* (Or maybe you're thinking, *Hey! I need that book*.) As it happened, I did know how to boil an egg, but I wasn't very good at it — and I'm still not. But I'm conscious that things that seem trivially easy to some people are quite hard for others. So, if using a digital scale is obvious to you, fine — skip to another section. I still want to help the people who are a bit puzzled by it.

A digital scale is a scale with an electronic display, a bit like a calculator. To weigh something, here's what you do:

1. **Check that the display reads zero before you start.**

   Those smarty-pants who skipped ahead may not realise you need to do this — so thanks for sticking around. If the display doesn't read zero, you might need to 'zero' the scale by pressing a button.

2. **Put what you're weighing on to the weighing surface — the plate or tray or bowl.**

3. **Read the number off the display.**

Don't forget to note the unit as well as the number (almost all digital scales in Australia measure in kilograms and grams). Make sure you notice the decimal point if there is one.

Using analogue scales

Analogue scales were common when I was growing up (I still think a bathroom's posh if it has a digital scale in it). Analogue scales contain an ingenious system of springs inside that measures how much weight you apply to the weighing surface, which rotates a dial marked with the appropriate weights until the number underneath the hairline on the display shows the weight you want to weigh.

As far as you need to know, analogue scales work by magic — I've always considered this to be the case and it's done me no harm at all. All you care about, unless you have a job as a scales technician (in which case, I expect you already know all there is to know about weighing things), is how to adjust and read an analogue scale. So, let me tell you:

1. **Make sure the scale is set to zero.**

   Without putting anything on the scale, look at the hairline and make sure it's over the zero mark on the dial. If not, twiddle the little twiddly thing at the front of the scale until the zero matches up with the line.

2. **Put the thing you want to weigh (possibly yourself) on the scale.**

3. **Look at the display and see what's underneath the hairline.**

   If the hairline lies over a tick marked with a number, that number is your measurement. If you're not on a tick, you need to estimate the weight.

   Count how many ticks there are between ticks with numbers by them, figure out how much weight each tick represents, and count how many ticks above (or below) a known point you are. You then times the number of ticks by the size of each tick, and add that to (or take it away from) the value given by the numbered tick.

Many scales have at least two sets of numbers on the dials — one for imperial measurements such as pounds and ounces, and one for metric measures such as kilograms and grams. Make sure you look at the right one.

Figure 12-3 shows some examples of reading a dial. The left scale shows about 73 kilograms and the right scale about 440 grams.

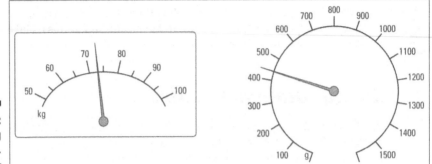

Figure 12-3:
Reading
a dial.

Measuring Weight Using the Metric System

Reading measurements off a scale is easy enough — but the different systems used on different scales can be confusing. My mum has a lovely antique set of scales in her kitchen, with weights marked in ounces, which was more or less useless any time I wanted to cook something at home because all of my recipe books called for a certain number of grams.

These days, the only time you'll likely hear pounds and ounces mentioned is after the birth of a baby. For some reason, most people continue to use imperial units for a baby's birth weight (and, if they don't, someone will invariably ask something like, 'What's that in the old money?')

Your maths tests and pretty much anything else you work on are almost certain to use metric — so I use metric too.

The base unit of mass is the kilogram — written 'kg' and sometimes called 'a kilo'. A kilogram is almost exactly the same mass as 1,000cm^3 of water. If you weigh a one-litre bottle of water, it should be just a smidge more than 1 kilogram, depending on how heavy the bottle itself is.

'Kilo' means thousand, so a kilogram is made up of 1,000 grams. A gram is a pretty light weight, maybe about the same as one of the small packets of sugar you might find on the table in a cafe.

Going the other way, a tonne is 1,000 kilograms, about the same weight as a small car, or (almost exactly) a cubic metre of water.

Converting Weights

In real life, you may need to convert between different weight systems — for example, American recipes (and old-fashioned Australian ones) generally use pounds or ounces for weights, and your scales may only show kilograms or grams. You may also need to convert between different units within the same system.

You have three main ways to convert weights: Using a conversion table, using a chart and using a formula — in roughly that order of difficulty. I cover using a table and using a chart in the following sections.

Using a table

Converting weights using a table is as easy as looking up numbers in a chart. You find the column showing the unit you have and look down that column until you find the weight you have. Then you find the other number in the same row, and write it down.

If your number isn't in the table, the first thing to do is check you're looking in the right column. (I mess that up all the time.)

If you're sure the number isn't there, you need to be a little smarter. Here are some things you can try:

✔ **Is your number about halfway between two other numbers, or some other fraction you can spot?**

Give an answer somewhere between the two corresponding numbers that makes sense.

✔ **Can you make up the weight you're looking for by adding other weights together?**

Try adding together the corresponding weights in the other column.

✔ **Does the table provide any other information that you can use?**

For example, is it double, triple or ten times as big as another weight that's listed?

✔ **Are you totally sure the number isn't in the table?**

Close your eyes, take a breath and look again.

Using a chart

A conversion chart can be really helpful when converting between different units. I like to photocopy these types of things and stick them on the wall near my desk, or on the back of the toilet door, or even on the outside of the shower glass. That way I can look at them a lot and start to remember them.

Figure 12-4 shows a mass conversion chart. *Note:* Tonnes are the largest units of mass while milligrams are the smallest units of mass in this chart. Larger and smaller units exist, but this is enough to consider for now.

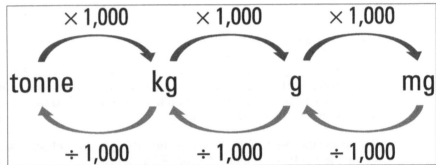

Figure 12-4:
A mass
conversion
chart.

Here some examples that show how you can use Figure 12-4 to convert units:

- ✔ Converting 1.5 tonnes to kilograms = 1.5 × 1,000 = 1,500 kilograms.
- ✔ Converting 3975 grams to kilograms = 3,975 ÷ 1,000 = 3.975 kilograms.
- ✔ Converting 5.65 tonnes to grams = 5.65 × 1,000 × 1,000 = 5,650,000 grams

Understanding Temperature

Temperature is simply a measure of how hot or cold something is. In Australia, we measure temperature in degrees Celsius, where 0˚C is just cold enough to freeze water and 100˚C is just hot enough to boil water. A kettle heats water up to 100˚C (so the water boils), and a freezer cools things down to below 0˚C (so they freeze).

A warm summer day is around 25–30˚C, and a typical temperature for baking a pizza is about 200˚C. As I found out in a soup-related disaster the other evening, a liquid at about 80˚C is more than hot enough to scald you quite badly, so be careful.

Thinking about thermometers

You measure temperature with a thermometer (*therm* means 'heat', and *meter* means 'measure'). You may encounter various types of thermometers.

The easiest to read is the digital thermometer, which displays the temperature as a number on a screen. The only dodgy thing to watch out for is a possible minus sign — check the following section for more on negative numbers.

Most other thermometers involve reading a scale of some sort. Most thermometers with scales have a straight-line scale, but some have circular scales. You work out the value of each tick or half-tick and read off the number. Flick back to the section 'Using analogue scales', earlier in this chapter, for more on reading a scale.

I give a couple of examples of thermometers showing 33°C in Figure 12-5.

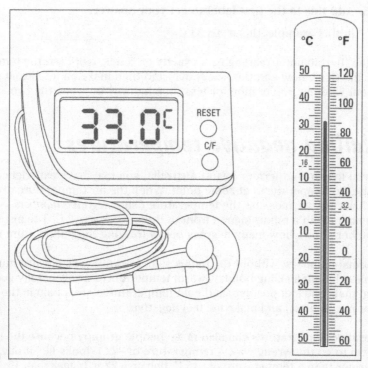

Figure 12-5:
33°C on two types of thermometer.

When you read a scale, make sure the ticks mean what you think they mean. Here's the tick tactic:

1. **Find two labelled ticks and note how many degrees apart the two ticks are.**

   For example, in the second of the thermometers in Figure 12-5, find 30 and 40. They are 40 − 30 = 10 degrees Celsius apart.

2. **Count the number of ticks between the two chosen points.**

   The example shown has ten ticks.

3. **Divide the degrees by the number of ticks.**

   In this example, 10 ÷ 10 = 1, so each tick is one degree.

4. **Count how many ticks above the first label the reading is and times this by how big each tick is.**

   This example has three ticks times by one degree each, which gives three degrees.

5. **Add this to the first label to get your answer.**

   In this example, this gives 33°C.

If the thermometer reading isn't exactly on a tick, work out the temperature for the tick below and the tick above, and then make an intelligent guess about whether you're more or less than halfway between the two.

Nailing negative temperatures

If you live in southern or inland Australia, you may have experienced sub-zero temperatures at some point. When the air temperature drops below zero, we measure the temperature using *negative numbers* — normal numbers with a minus sign in front of them, such as −2°C. The negative number shows how many degrees below freezing the temperature is.

Normal numbers, without the minus sign, are known as *positive* numbers. Unless I'm on a skiing holiday, warm temperatures are generally good news and make me feel positive, and cold temperatures are a pain in the neck (for me, at least) and make me feel negative.

Negative temperatures can also make people grumpy because the numbers seem to go the wrong way. A temperature of −22°C looks like it ought to be warmer than a temperature of −15°C, because 22 is bigger than 15. In fact, −22°C is 22 degrees colder than freezing, and −15°C is only 15 degrees colder than freezing, so −22°C wins in the 'wrap up extra snug' stakes.

For practical purposes, we care about negative temperatures in real life mainly for weather reports and for using the freezer.

Ordering negative temperatures

Putting temperatures in order, from coldest to hottest, or vice versa, is fairly straightforward, even when we have some negative numbers. Negative temperatures are *always* colder than positive (normal) temperatures, and the bigger the number after the minus sign, the colder the temperature is. Try following my recipe below, in conjunction with Figure 12-6, to put a group of temperatures in order:

1. **Circle all of the negative numbers so you don't mix them up with the positive numbers.**

2. **Find the most extreme circled number — the one furthest from zero.** This would be the biggest circled number if you ignored the minus sign. Label this number '1'.

3. **Find the biggest number you haven't labelled yet and put the next label ('2', '3', and so on) by it.**

   Repeat Step 3 until you've dealt with all the circled numbers.

4. **Find the smallest uncircled number and put the next label next to it.**

5. **Find the smallest uncircled number you haven't labelled yet and keep on labelling in this way until you run out of numbers to label.**

6. **Write down the temperatures in the order you've labelled them — they should now be in order from cold to hot.**

   To order them from hot to cold, simply reverse the list.)

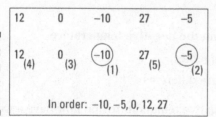

Figure 12-6: Ordering temperatures.

Finding the difference between negative temperatures

In this section, I get into the dreaded 'minus number' maths. I remember minus numbers being a real struggle in school, for myself and everyone else, until we started to think of minus numbers as points on the number line, like the one I show you in Chapter 2. Here are some places you might need to figure out the difference between temperatures:

- Comparing maximum and minimum air temperatures from a weather report.
- Deciding how much warmer it is in one place than another.
- Seeing how much warmer a defrosted freezer is than a working freezer.

You probably already know how to find the difference between two positive temperatures — you do a simple subtraction sum. For example, the difference between 24°C and 16°C is 24 − 16 = 8 degrees.

With two negative numbers, the drill is almost exactly the same: Ignore the minus signs and take one number away from the other. The difference between −9°C and −3°C is simply 9 − 3 = 6 degrees.

The numbers way

If you have one negative number and one positive number, things get interesting. The number in the negative temperature tells you how many degrees the temperature is below zero, while the positive number is how many degrees above zero the temperature is. To get from the negative number to the positive number, you have to _increase_ by how many negative degrees you have, and then _increase_ again by the number of positive degrees.

Instead of doing a subtraction sum, you end up doing an adding sum. So when the signs are opposite, you do the opposite of what you're asked!

Here's my recipe to find the difference between a positive and a negative temperature:

1. **Drop the minus sign from the negative temperature.**

2. **Add the two numbers together.**

   This gives the temperature difference.

If you started with a cold, negative temperature and now have a warm, positive temperature, the temperature's gone up.

And if you started with a warm, positive temperature and now have a cold, negative temperature, the temperature's gone down.

Your maths test may contain a question like, 'The temperature in the Sahara Desert drops from 45°C in the daytime to −10°C at night. What is the difference between those temperatures?'

Following the steps from my recipe, you drop the minus sign, to leave the numbers 45 and 10. Adding those up gives 55°, which is the difference between day and night in the desert.

The number-line way

You can look at differences between positive and negative temperatures using a number line. Have a look at Figure 12-7 and try following these steps to use the number line:

1. **Draw a line and mark a zero somewhere near the middle.**

   You only need to draw a rough-and-ready number line, so don't worry about measuring anything.

2. **Mark your two temperatures in the appropriate places.**

   Put positive numbers on the right and negative numbers on the left. Label the two numbers.

3. **Write down how far below zero the negative number is.**

   For instance, –10°C is 10 below 0. Write this description between the marks for the number and zero, as in Figure 12-7.

4. **Write how far above zero the positive number is.**

   For instance, 45°C is 45 above 0. Again, write this description between the marks for the number and zero, as in Figure 12-7.

5. **To get from the negative number to the positive one, you have to move right by the *total* of the numbers — so add up your two numbers.**

   This is your answer.

Figure 12-7:
The difference between day and night: Negative temperatures and the number line.

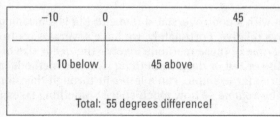

The difference between two temperatures is also called the *range*. Your maths test may include a question such as, 'What is the temperature range?'

Temperature ranges from a table

A particular favourite of examiners is to give you a table of temperatures and ask you to find the difference between the warmest and coldest temperatures. This adds an extra layer of complexity, but don't panic. Here's what you need to do:

1. **Find the warmest temperature — the biggest number without a minus sign. If they all have minus signs, pick the one closest to zero.**

   Circle this number or write it down.

2. **Find the coldest temperature — the number with a minus sign that's furthest from zero; if none of them have minus signs, pick the smallest number.**

   Circle this number or write it down.

3. **If both numbers are positive, or both are negative, take away the small number from the big number as normal.**

4. **If one number is positive and one number is negative, ignore the minus sign and add the two numbers.**

   Look back to 'The numbers way', earlier in this section, if that sounds a bit fishy.

Don't overcomplicate things! Always try to find the simplest way to do your temperature sums, and don't be afraid to draw out a number line to help you.

Working On Your Measurements

I start this section with a controversial statement: Big is a meaningless word. Size is always relative. Fortunately, we have several ways to measure bigness. Some of these methods involve the *linear* size of objects — how wide or tall or deep something is. Some methods involve *cross-sectional* area — for example, can a letter fit through this slot? Other methods involve the *volume* — how much space something takes up.

Sizing up the vocabulary you need

Most of the words you use to describe size are common English words. You probably know most of these words already, but I describe them here just in case: After all, sometimes the maths version of a word is a bit more strictly defined than the normal version:

- ✔ **Length:** How long an object is. We normally measure length with a ruler in centimetres, metres, feet or inches.

- ✔ **Perimeter:** How far around a shape is — that is, if you walked all the way around a shape, how far you would travel. We measure perimeter in units of length, such as centimetres, metres, feet or inches. You find the answer by adding up the length of all of a shape's sides.

- ✔ **Area:** How much paper or something similar you need to cover a surface. We use different formulas to work out area for different shapes. We measure area in centimetres squared (cm^2), metres squared (m^2) or any other unit of length squared.

- ✔ **Capacity:** How much stuff can fit in an object. We usually measure capacity in litres, but sometimes we use centimetres cubed (cm^3) or metres cubed (m^3).

- ✔ **Volume:** How much space an object takes up. We measure volume in centimetres cubed (cm^3) or metres cubed (m^3) or any other unit of length cubed.

Using a ruler properly

The most common measuring tools you come across are straight edges with distances marked on them — rulers and tape measures are obvious examples.

You may also see callipers (which look a bit like a pair of compasses), trundle wheels (which seem to have gone completely out of fashion) and those laser-type things workers in yellow jackets use. (I keep promising myself to ask if I can have a go the next time I see them out surveying.)

In this section, I give you a quick rundown on using a ruler. Apologies if you think working with a ruler is a basic skill, but you may be surprised to know that many perfectly intelligent people mess up making even the simplest measurements. For example, I once missed out on full marks in an exam because I mismeasured a circle. The shame has haunted me through my career, and I want to save you from that particular horror.

I've thoroughly revised the use of rulers, so I'm now in a position to tell you how to measure a distance:

1. **Decide which unit you want to use.**

   Many rulers have inches on one side and centimetres on the other side. Choose the side you need to work in.

2. **Find the zero on the side of the ruler you want to use.**

   The zero is normally very close to the left-hand end.

3. **Put the zero mark over the start of the thing you want to measure.**

   Line up the ruler so it goes to the other end of the thing you want to measure.

4. **Check the zero mark is still where you want it to be.**

   Read the number on the ruler where the thing you're measuring ends. The number is your length.

In Figure 12-8 I show a ruler in action. Try to contain your excitement.

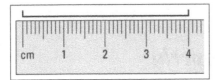

Figure 12-8: The line is 4 cm long.

A common problem in measuring — whether you use scales, a thermometer, a protractor, a graph or a dozen other things — is how to deal with a reading that falls between two marked numbers. In this section, I assume you're using a ruler, but my tips apply to any measuring device with a scale on it.

As I show in Figure 12-9, your ruler may have little marks between the numbered marks — or it may not.

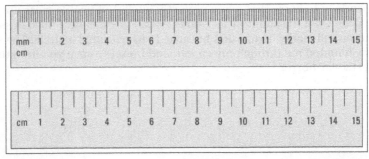

Figure 12-9: A ruler with little marks, and a ruler without.

The way you measure changes slightly depending on the kind of ruler you have: The ruler with the small marks allows you to be a little more accurate and to use a little less guesswork. Here's what you do when your measurement lies between two marked numbers and you have the little marks:

1. Count the number of little spaces between your marked numbers.

This number's normally ten, but some rulers are sneaky. Some rulers divide inches into sixteenths, which is almost perverse.

2. Take your main unit — however far apart your marked numbers are (usually 1 centimetre) — and divide it by the number in Step 1.

With a metric ruler, your answer is generally a nice decimal, but you may need a nastier fraction with a non-metric ruler.

3. Count how many little marks past a marked number your measurement is.

If you're between two little marks, I salute your eyesight and attention to detail! Just pick whichever is closer.

4. Work out how far above a marked number you are by multiplying your answers from Steps 2 and 3.

If your marks are 0.1 cm and you're six marks above the marked number, the number is 0.6 cm.

5. Add this to the marked number below.

Using the example from Step 4, if you're between 5 cm and 6 cm on the ruler, your answer is 5.6 cm.

Often the halfway mark between two centimetre marks is bigger than the other little marks. Try using the halfway mark to make sure you've counted correctly.

If you don't have little marks between the marked numbers, you need to use some intelligent guesswork. You make the following series of decisions:

1. Is your reading more or less than halfway between the two marks?

If more than, your answer ends in something bigger than '.5'. If less than, your answer ends in something smaller than '.5'. If your reading's just about exactly halfway, your measurement ends in '.5'.

2. Is your measurement closer to halfway, or closer to one of the marks?

Use this question to decide between '.6 and .7' and '.8 and .9' for the last digit if you're more than halfway, or between '.1 and .2' and '.3 or .4' if you're less than halfway.

3. **Make a choice between your two remaining options, largely based on gut feeling and eyesight.**

4. **Tack your decimal digit on to the lower number of the two marks.**

Using different units of length

A ruler often has a different scale on each of the two sides: One scale may go from 0 to 30 or 0 to 15 in spaces each measuring a centimetre — about the width of a finger — and the other scale may go from 0 to 12 or from 0 to 6 in inches — about the width of two fingers (all depending on the size of your fingers, obviously).

One hundred centimetres make a metre, as the name implies, and centimetres are part of the metric system — the same system that uses kilograms and grams for mass, which I talk about earlier in this chapter. The idea of the metric system is that converting between units is simply a matter of multiplying or dividing by 10, 100 or 1,000.

Figure 12-10 shows a conversion chart — one of the most useful tools you can use when converting between different units. *Note:* Kilometres are the largest units of length and millimetres are the smallest units of length in this chart. Larger and smaller units exist, but this is enough to consider for now.

You may notice that this chart is different from the conversion chart used for mass (refer to Figure 12-4). Each conversion factor is different. Personally I would stick this chart everywhere, because you'll likely use it the most.

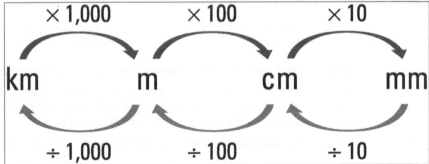

Figure 12-10:
A length
conversion
chart.

Starting off on the right foot

A *foot* was originally just that — about the size of a normal adult foot. A grown man's foot isn't a very practical thing to use if you want to measure something accurately, but describing someone as six feet tall would give you an idea of how tall the person was. At some point in the history of measuring things, somebody somewhere decided to standardise the foot. We now define one foot as 30.48 cm — which is why we use rulers that are 30 cm long.

Here some examples that show how you can use Figure 12-10 to convert units of length:

- Converting 2.75 kilometres to metres = 2.75 × 1,000 = 2,750 metres.

- Converting 5,842 millimetres to centimetres = 5842 ÷ 10 = 584.4 centimetres.

- Converting 9,875 millimetres to metres = 9,875 ÷ 10 ÷ 100 = 9,875 ÷ 1,000 = 9.875 metres.

Inches, on the other hand, are part of the more complex, traditional, imperial system. Twelve inches make a foot. Three feet make a yard. A furlong contains 220 yards. Eight furlongs make a mile ... maybe you see why using the metric system can be easier than using the imperial system.

One inch is about 2.5 centimetres long — or more precisely, 2.54 centimetres. A yard is 3 feet, or 36 inches or 91.44 centimetres, or a little less than a metre. A mile is 1,760 yards or a little over 1,600 metres. You may see furlongs (220 yards) used in horse racing, but pretty much nowhere else.

To convert from inches into centimetres, you just multiply by 2.54. But the tricky bit is working out how many inches you have to start with. Here's a step-by-step guide:

1. **Look at how many feet there are and times that number by 12.**

   Remember: 1 foot is 12 inches. For example, if you're 5 foot, 7 inches, do 5 × 12 = 60.

2. **Add on how many 'spare' inches you have.**

   In this example, you have seven 'spare' inches: 60 + 7 = 67.

3. **Times the result by 2.54.**

   For this example, 67 × 2.54 = 170.18 cm.

I shouldn't give the result that precisely: 5 feet, 7 inches is a pretty rough measure of height and I certainly can't justify an accuracy to the nearest hundredth of a centimetre. A more sensible answer is 'about 170 cm'.

Looking at Length, Distance and Perimeter

Length, distance and perimeter are all measures of length. They all behave in much the same way, and we measure all three in units of distance, such as metres, centimetres, kilometres or similar imperial units. The difference between the three is really one of language and application, rather than how they work.

How long is a piece of string?

The *length* of an object is how far apart the two ends of the object are. To find the length of a piece of string, you might put one end of the string on the zero mark of a ruler, pull the string straight and read off the ruler where the string ends.

A length is normally the answer to the question 'How long is [one thing]?'

How many miles to Babylon?

A *distance* is how far apart two things are. My house is 250 metres away from the railway station and New York is 4,500 kilometres away from Los Angeles.

A distance is the answer to the question 'How far apart are [two things]?'

The difference between length and distance is subtle and often barely exists. If the shortest distance between two towns is 10 kilometres, then the length of the straight road between the towns is also 10 kilometres. Generally, when you talk about the size of a single thing, you call it a length; when you talk about how far apart two things are, you call it a distance.

Going all the way round

Airports and military bases have *perimeter fences*, some of which are occasionally scaled by protesters and undercover police officers. These fences are so-called because they go all the way around the site — which is what the perimeter measures. (*Peri-* means 'around', as in 'periscope' — a contraption for looking around things.)

The *perimeter* of a thing is how far it is all the way round the thing. You find the perimeter of a rectangle by finding the length of each of the four sides and adding up the four lengths. You could also run a piece of string all the way round the rectangle and then measure the amount of string you use — but this is a fiddly way of doing an easy job.

A perimeter is the answer to the question 'How far is it round [a thing]?'

Summing up distance

Doing sums with distance is similar to doing sums with any other kind of measure. If you walk 10 metres and then another 20 metres, you walk a total of 30 metres — you just add up 10 + 20 as normal. If you walk 50 metres, realise you dropped your wallet 20 metres back, and turn around to fetch the wallet, you end up 30 metres from where you started — you just take away 50 − 20 = 30.

Lengths and distances add up as normal as long as you travel in the same straight line. If you walk 10 metres in one direction and then 10 metres in another, however, you could end up anywhere from 0 to 20 metres from where you started.

You can also times and divide distances by numbers. For example, if you have five 30 cm rulers and place them end to end, their total length is 5 × 30 = 150 cm. If you snap one ruler in half (don't try this at home, kids), each part is 30 ÷ 2 = 15 cm long.

Accessing All Areas

The *area* of a shape is how many squares of paper (of a given size) you need to cover the shape. Everything else being equal, the bigger the area of a meadow, the longer you need to mow the grass. We often measure smallish shapes, such as pieces of paper, in square centimetres (cm^2) or square millimetres (mm^2); medium-sized shapes, such as rooms and parks, in square metres (m^2); and huge shapes, such as countries, in square kilometres (km^2).

To understand what the 'square' in 'square centimetre' means, imagine a square where all of the sides are 1 cm long, as in Figure 12-11. The area of this square is defined as one square centimetre. We use a similar idea for square metres and square miles: If you draw a square (maybe in chalk in a car park) with sides measuring one metre each, the area is one square metre.

In Figure 12-11 I also show that you can think of the area of a shape as the number of little squares you need to cover the shape. In the next section, I help you work out areas without counting.

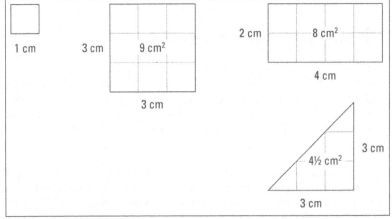

Figure 12-11:
A square centimetre, and the areas of some simple shapes.

Although 1 metre is the same as 100 centimetres, 1 square metre isn't the same as 100 square centimetres. If you draw a square metre and put a row of 100 square centimetres inside it, you cover only one edge of the square. You actually need another 99 rows of square centimetres to fill up the square. One square metre is actually (100 cm) × (100 cm) = 10,000 cm^2.

Recognising rectangles

In Figure 12-11, you can see just by counting that the rectangle in the middle — 2 cm tall and 4 cm wide — has an area of 8 cm^2. You may notice that if you have two rows, each with four boxes, you end up with 2 × 4 = 8 boxes. Equally, you may see this as four columns with two boxes each — both methods give you the same answer. These rules are true for all rectangles. If you have a box, 12 cm wide and 5 cm tall, its area is 12 cm × 5 cm = 60 cm². This even works if the lengths of the sides aren't whole numbers: You just times the numbers together and whatever comes out is the area.

Be very careful with units when you work out areas. Occasionally a test sneakily gives you the measurement of one side in centimetres and another side in millimetres. Before you do the sum, either convert the millimetres into centimetres or vice versa.

Joining things up: Compound rectangles

One of the most troublesome things you have to do with areas is find the total area of a shape made up of several rectangles. This may seem tricky, but after you see what's going on, things start to make sense.

The trick is to split up the shape into smaller rectangles for which you either know or can figure out the length of each side. This is a little bit more of an art than a science — but as with everything else in maths and life, the more you practise, the easier the method gets.

Take the following steps if you need to find the area of a shape that isn't a rectangle but is full of right angles:

1. **Try to find somewhere to draw a line that splits the shape into two, smaller rectangles.**

   If not, draw a line that splits off one rectangle and try to split the rest of the shape up into smaller rectangles. How many rectangles you have doesn't matter — but you're less likely to make mistakes if you use as few shapes as possible.

2. **Work out the sides of each rectangle you have left over.**

   You may need to do a bit of lateral thinking, but normally you just need to take something away from the total length of a side.

3. **Find the area of each rectangle by multiplying the sides together.**

   Write the answer in the middle of the rectangle so you don't forget it.

4. **Add up all of the areas you just worked out.**

   The answer is your total area.

In Figure 12-12 I show an example of this method. I start with a wibbly shape and neatly cut it into two rectangles with a sideways line near the top. I work out the height of the bigger rectangle, which is the only side I didn't know to start with. I find the areas of the two rectangles and add up these two areas to get a final answer.

On the bottom of Figure 12-12, I split up the rectangle in a different way, giving three separate shapes. Again, I work out the lengths of the sides, find the areas and add the areas to get a final answer. I end up with the same answer using both methods.

Figure 12-12:
Compound
rectangles
split
into smaller
parts.
It doesn't
matter
how you
split up the
rectangle —
you still get
the same
area.

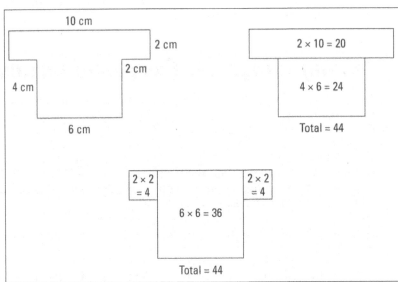

If you want to feel very proud of your estimation skills, start by thinking, *If I imagine a rectangle as tall as the total height of the shape, and as wide as the total width, what is the area of the shape?* Then say, 'My total area has to be smaller than that.' This estimate gives you a quick-and-dirty check on whether your eventual answer is correct, and in multiple-choice tests can help you eliminate one or two of the answers.

Trying out triangles

Your teacher may ask you to look at the area of triangles too, but don't stress. Triangles are closely linked to rectangles, which I cover in the preceding section.

Figure 12-13 shows a pretty standard rectangle. Its length is 5 metres and the width is 3 metres (no, the diagram is not to scale — if it were, I would need a much bigger book). You've probably already calculated the area of this rectangle in your head.

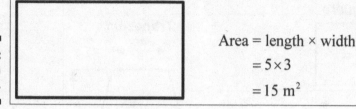

Figure 12-13:
Area of a
rectangle.

$$\text{Area} = \text{length} \times \text{width}$$
$$= 5 \times 3$$
$$= 15 \text{ m}^2$$

If you then divide the rectangle into two equal triangles by adding a line (see Figure 12-14), you can easily work out what the area of each triangle will be.

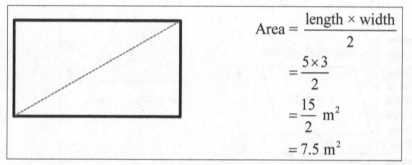

Figure 12-14:
Using the
area of the
rectangle
to find the
area of a
triangle.

$$\text{Area} = \frac{\text{length} \times \text{width}}{2}$$
$$= \frac{5 \times 3}{2}$$
$$= \frac{15}{2} \text{ m}^2$$
$$= 7.5 \text{ m}^2$$

That's right! Each triangle will be exactly half the area of the rectangle. That can help you to remember the formula used to calculate the area of triangles:

$$\text{Area of a triangle} = \frac{1}{2} \times \text{base length} \times \text{height(width)}$$

Working on other shapes

Now you have these two formulas under your belt (refer to the preceding section), you can move on to the formulas for other shapes — shown in Figure 12-15.

The easiest way a problem with a formula can be solved is to write down the formula and 'fill in what you know'. (I say this so often that my students often make fun of me. But they do remember what to do.)

Let's look at working out the area for the trickiest shape shown in Figure 12-16, the trapezoid. Figure 12-16 shows the measurements to work with in this example.

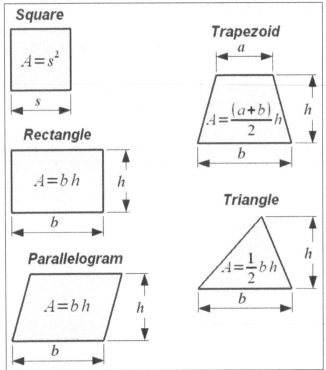

Figure 12-15: Using formulas to work out the area of other shapes.

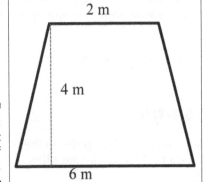

Figure 12-16: Working out the area of a trapezoid.

Here's how to work out the area of a common shape:

1. Identify the shape.

It is a trapezoid (or trapezium).

2. **Write the formula.**

In this example, Area $= \frac{(a+b)}{2} \times h$ or $\frac{1}{2} \times (a+b) \times h$.

You can use whichever one you're familiar with.

3. **Make a list of all of the things that you know, and add these to the formula.**

In this example, you know the following:

$a = 2$ m

$b = 6$ m

$h = 4$ m

4. **Fill in what you know.**

In this example, you get the following answer:

$$\text{Area} = \frac{(a+b)}{2} \times h$$
$$= \frac{(2+6)}{2} \times 4$$
$$= \frac{(8)}{2} \times 4$$
$$= 4 \times 4$$
$$= 16 \, \text{m}^2$$

This system has never failed me: Write the formula (or rule), fill in what you know and evaluate. Works every single time.

Compound shapes can be made up of shapes other than rectangles; all of the shapes covered in this section can be joined together in different ways. When working with composite shapes just remember to identify the two shapes in the diagram, calculate the area of each part and add them together to find the total.

Verifying Volume and Capacity

The *volume* of an object is how much space the object takes up — or, if you were to drop the object into a full tub of water, how much water would overflow. *Capacity* is how much space an object has inside — or, how much water you can fit inside the object. This distinction between volume and capacity is subtle — we can measure both in cm³, although confusingly we can also measure capacity in millilitres (ml), each of which is the same size as 1 cm³. A litre contains 1,000 millilitres, and a cubic metre contains 1,000 litres.

Incidentally, a cubic centimetre is the volume of a cube which has edges that are one centimetre long — about the size of a small die.

Working with cuboids

In a maths test, you may need to work out the volume of a *cuboid* or shoebox. You normally know the width, height and depth of the box. To work out the volume, you simply times the three numbers together.

A classic problem in numeracy exams involves working out how many small boxes fit into a bigger box. This kind of packing problem has real-life applications (how many DVDs can you fit into a box? Will this crate hold all the books you want to keep when you move house) and is quite straightforward. In an exam, you normally know the *orientation* — or which way round you need to pack the little boxes into the big box. Look at Figure 12-17 and follow these steps to work out how to fit little boxes into a bigger box:

1. **Work out how many boxes you can fit along the front of the box.**

   Divide the width of the big box by the width of one small box and write down the result. If you get a whole number answer, great! If not, round *down*, because even if your answer is 5.99, you can't squeeze a sixth little box into the crate.

2. **Work out how many boxes you can fit along the side of the box.**

   Divide the depth of the big box by the depth of the little box and write down the answer. Round down if you don't have a whole number.

3. **Work out how many boxes you can fit going up the box.**

   Divide the height of the big box by the height of the small box and write down the number. Round down if you need to.

4. **Times the three numbers together.**

   That's your answer!

Here's a typical question to follow as an example:

> A crate is 4 m wide, 12 m long and 3 m deep. You want to fill it with boxes that are 2 m wide, 3 m long and 1 m deep. How many boxes will fit in the crate?

1. **You can fit two boxes along the width of the crate.**

2. **You can fit four boxes along the length of the crate.**

3. You can fit three boxes along the depth of the crate.

4. **Times those numbers together.**

$$2 \times 4 \times 3 = 8 \times 3 = 24.$$

So you can fit 24 boxes into the crate.

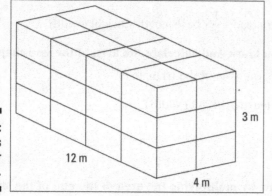

Figure 12-17:
Fitting boxes
in a bigger
box.

12 m

3 m

4 m

Working with all three-dimensional shapes

It would be awesome if all three-dimensional shapes were cuboids or rectangular in shape; unfortunately, that is not the case. But I can show you a foolproof way to calculate the volume of a three-dimensional object.

For example, say you want to find out the volume of the object shown in Figure 12-18.

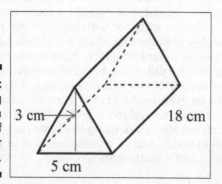

Figure 12-18:
Working
out the
volume of
a triangular
prism.

3 cm

18 cm

5 cm

Here's how to do it:

1. **Look at the shape at the end of the three-dimensional object.**

   In this example, the shape is a triangle.

2. **Write the formula you use to calculate the area for this shape.**

   Here you need the formula to calculate the area for a triangle.

   $$\text{Area of a triangle} = \frac{1}{2} \times \text{base length} \times \text{height (width)}$$

3. **Fill in what you know and calculate the area of the end shape.**

   In this example, the area of the triangle is

   $$= \frac{1}{2} \times \text{base length} \times \text{height (width)}$$
   $$= \frac{1}{2} \times 5 \times 3$$
   $$= 7.5 \text{ cm}^2$$

4. **Find the volume by multiplying the area of the end of the shape by the height of the shape.**

   In this example, this means the volume of the triangular prism $= 7.5 \times 18 = 135$ cm^3.

 When calculating volume, the measurement units are cubed. A way that I remember this is that the objects you're finding the area for are three-dimensional (three, cubed).

Reading Maps and Plans

Being able to read maps may be a less vital skill than it used to be: The rise of the GPS and satnav has almost eliminated the need for motorists to know the difference between a church with and without a steeple. But map-reading is still a useful ability to have, especially if you take part in outdoor activities such as hiking or mountain-biking: Your ability to work out which route to take can make the difference between people in your group loving or hating you; or even between living and dying. Nobody's going to ask you to draw maps or even read a map in great detail at this stage of your maths career. But you do need to be able to look at a map and understand what it says, to convert distances using the scale (this is the one that comes up most often in tests), and to understand how to see a plan simultaneously as a 'real' object and a mathematical shape.

A map is a geographically accurate picture of a piece of land, highlighting some features, such as roads, rivers, buildings, terrain and hills, but ignoring others, including things that move, small things and irrelevant things. Different types of map highlight different features — so a walking map tells you much more about the terrain than a driving map. Each feature on a map normally has its own symbol. Roads may be different-coloured lines, train stations may be marked TS, and towns may be marked with their names.

Scales and distance

One of the most important things to know about a map is its *scale*. This ratio tells you the relationship between distances depicted on the map and distances in reality.

If a map has a scale of 1:100,000, it means that 1 centimetre on the map represents 100,000 centimetres (the same as 1 kilometre) in real life. The scale allows you to say how big a real-life object is if you know how big its picture is on the map, as well as how big something should be on the map if you know its size in real life.

The most common map-based questions involve solving this type of problem. The test question may show you a map and ask you to do some measuring, or the question may just give you the scale and a distance (either on the map or in real life) and ask you to work out the other distance.

Scales questions are fiddly and often involve big numbers and conversions. Slipping up is very easy, so take extra care to work neatly so you can see what you're doing. Write down your units as well — mixing up kilometres and centimetres can give you wildly wrong results!

A scale looks like a ratio — two numbers with a colon in between. The map is always smaller than real life (you don't ever see a map of Scotland bigger than Scotland itself). The smaller number in the scale always refers to the map. For example, a scale of 1:10,000 means that 1 cm on the map represents 10,000 cm in real life — which is 100 m. You can do ratio calculations with scales using the Table of Joy, which I describe in Chapter 8, but unless you have a scale that's not 'one to some big number', the Table of Joy is slightly overkill. Instead — as long as you can keep your units straight — you can get by with multiplying or dividing. If you have a stranger scale, such as 2 cm to 5 km, you may do better using the Table of Joy.

Scales with a '1:'

The key to doing scales sums without the Table of Joy is to remember that multiplying by numbers bigger than one makes things bigger and dividing by numbers bigger than one makes things smaller. Here are the steps to do a sum involving a 'one to lots' scale, starting from a distance on the map:

1. **If you don't know the distance on the map, measure the distance on the map.**

   Write down the distance you measure, giving the right units — normally centimetres.

2. **Times the map distance by the scale.**

   Be very careful to use the right number of zeros. I always lose count of noughts!

3. **Convert your big number into more appropriate units.**

   If you're working in centimetres, divide by 100 to get metres. If you need an answer in kilometres, divide the number of metres by 1,000. The number is your answer.

Scales without a '1:'

Sometimes you see a scale that I describe, with a complete lack of affection, as 'silly' — say, something like '2 centimetres to 5 kilometres'. The only redeeming features of such monstrosities are that they tend to use whole numbers and you can use the Table of Joy on them easily.

Here's how to throw the Table of Joy at this kind of scale and get an answer without too much effort:

1. **Draw a Table of Joy noughts-and-crosses grid.**

   Leave plenty of space for labels.

2. **Label the columns 'map cm' and 'real-life km'.**

   Label the rows 'scale' and 'measured'.

3. **Fill in the scale row according to the scale on your map.**

   Fill in any other information you have: If you know a real-life distance, put it in the real-life column; if you have a map distance, put it in the map column.

4. **Put a question mark in the remaining cell and write down the Table-of-Joy sum.**

   Do the other number in the same row times the other number in the same column, divided by the number you haven't used yet.

5. **Work out the sum.**

   That's your answer.

Zeroing in ... and out again

If your number has lots of zeros — say, 1,000,000 — keeping track of your sums is really tricky. Plus copying long lists of zeros is so tedious.

Coming up with a strategy for dealing with lots of zeros makes sense. My favourite way to deal with many zeros is to forget about those noughts for a while. When I times numbers with lots of zeros, I write down how many zeros I have and do the sum as if the zeros didn't exist — then I throw them back in at the end.

If you deal with different units at the same time — kilometres, metres and centimetres, for example — first work on the number of zeros. Say you have five zeros on your number of centimetres: You know 100 centimetres make a metre, so your number of metres has two fewer zeros. To report your answer in metres, you need to use three rather than five zeros. You can go further too: You know 1,000 metres make a kilometre, so you can knock off another three zeros — which in this example means you end up with no zeros at all.

Chapter 13

Communicating Data with Graphs and Tables

Being able to read and understand tables and graphs is one of the most valuable real-life skills you can conceivably pick up from reading this book. In this chapter, I introduce you to most common types of graph. I help you read and understand bar charts, pie charts and line graphs, and show you which ones work best in different situations.

I also devote a fair chunk of this chapter to tables, which you may find easier than graphs — but beware, because even simple tables have pitfalls to watch out for. I also cover the *xy*-graph, and using this to obtain information.

A Spotter's Guide to Graphs and Charts

You use graphs and charts to communicate large amounts of data in a compact and organised way, normally using visual effects to show the big picture. For example, it's much easier to see that sales are growing from a graph that gradually rises than it is from a list of figures. In the same way, a pie chart could quickly show you where you're spending most of your money in a more obvious way than your tally of recent spending does.

Graphs and tables come in four basic varieties:

- ✔ A *number table* does exactly what it says on the tin. It's a table … with numbers in. A good example is the list of temperatures in cities around the world you sometimes see in the newspaper.

- ✔ A *bar chart* looks a little like a picture of a skyline, consisting of different heights of 'tower' lined up side-by-side. The heights of the towers represent the relative sizes of the categories they represent. Some graphs show the towers on their sides, but you can deal with those by tilting your head or turning the paper through 90°. (Incidentally, if you don't know what 90° means, head to Chapter 11, where I give the low-down on angles.) You could use a bar chart to show the typical fuel consumption of different types of car.

- ✔ A *pie chart* looks — you've guessed it — a bit like a pie. The chart is a circle with various-sized slices 'cut out' from the middle to the edge. The size of the slices shows the relative size of the categories. You often see a pie chart showing the results of an opinion poll.

- ✔ A *line graph* shows how a value changes, usually over time. Most line graphs look like a jagged line going across the page. How high the line is above a time marked on the axis tells you how high the value is. A dieter may use a line graph to track how their weight fluctuates as time goes by. A business may use a line graph to track its profits.

Nailing number tables

When my parents were at school, calculators weren't common — and those that existed were the size of a car. (Your mobile phone probably has more computing power than existed in the entire world 40 years ago.) Instead of working things out on a calculator, my parents looked up answers in a huge book full of numbers. They had to find the right page, and then find the right row and column, and copy the number down carefully — and assume that the printer hadn't made a mistake anywhere. Oh, and then do the sum.

Your task, thankfully, is less of an ordeal. At this stage in your maths career, you'll likely only use tables with a few rows and columns. You still have to find the right cell in the table and do the sum, but much less can go wrong than could have done for maths students of my parents' generation.

A number table normally has a *label row* at the top and a *label column* on the left, which give you information about each *cell* (square) in the table.

The Table of Joy, which I introduce in Chapter 8 and use in most chapters in this book, is a number table. It has a label row at the top and a label row on the left, and numbers in all the other cells. The labels tell you what each cell represents.

You use a number table if you want to look up a specific answer. You often use a table if you have numbers that depend on two other things. For instance, the price of a hotel room may depend on both the luxury of the room and what day of the week you want to stay — so you may represent hotel-room prices in a table.

Another example of a number table is a mileage chart showing the distance between pairs of cities. Each of the numbers in the table depends on two things — the two cities.

In comparison, a graph tends to show an overall picture of the data. For example, if you want to show the monthly average temperatures in several cities around the world, you may use a table ('I'm going to Sydney in April and want to look up what temperature to expect') but also a bar graph ('I want to see which of these cities is generally the warmest'). See the next section for more on graphs.

Bringing in the bar charts

Bar charts are made up of a series of rectangles — or *bars* — with each bar representing a different group. Each bar has the same width, but the heights vary to show the 'value' of each bar's group — for example, how many people are in the group, or how much money comes from the group, or how many goals the team scored.

Knowing when to use a bar chart

You use a bar chart to compare the values of several numbers at once. The numbers could be measurements, amounts of money, numbers of people or things, all in different groups or categories. The chart lets you see at a glance which group is the most or least important.

You can also figure out the actual value of each bar by drawing a horizontal line across to the scale and reading off the number.

You use bar charts and pie charts in similar situations — when you have several, separate values attached to separate categories. One situation where you definitely use a bar chart rather than a pie chart is when looking at the numbers as part of a whole doesn't make sense.

Bar charts are better than line graphs when your data are in several distinct groups rather than over something measurable like time.

Good examples of when to use a bar graph are to compare the house prices in several different regions of Australia, to show the personal best race times of several sprinters, or to compare the heights of different species of tree.

Single-bar charts

The simplest kind of bar chart is called, a little misleadingly, the single-bar chart. I say 'misleadingly' because any bar chart worth its salt has at least two bars in it — otherwise, it's not really comparing anything and you may as well just have written the number down. The word 'single' means that each category has only one number associated with it, so you get a single bar for each category.

Single-bar charts are by far the easiest type of bar chart to read and understand. To find out what a bar represents, here's what you do:

1. **Get a ruler (or anything with a straight edge) and lay it flat across the top of the bar, going sideways across the graph.**

2. **Make a small mark where the ruler crosses the vertical axis (the vertical numbered line).**

3. **If the mark lies on a value given on the scale, that's the value of the category represented by the bar.**

4. **If the mark lies between two values, make an estimate of the number.**

   Think about whether the number's halfway between the neighbouring values, or a little more or less.

I show an example of a single-bar chart in Figure 13-1.

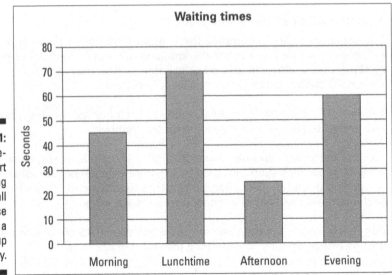

Figure 13-1:
A single-bar chart showing average call response times at a made-up company.

Multiple-bar charts

More complicated — and sadly, more common in exams — are multiple-bar charts. You use multiple-bar charts to compare two different values across categories. For example, to investigate exam pass rates of several schools, you may want to compare the results of boys and girls. You then have two distinct bars in each category, coded with shading, as in Figure 13-2.

Another example is using a multiple-bar chart to compare average summer and winter temperatures in several cities.

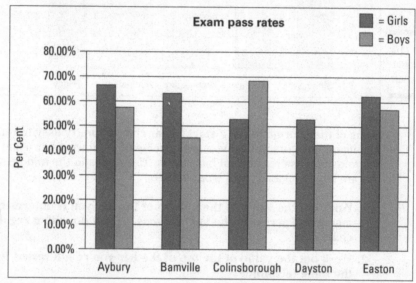

Figure 13-2:
A multiple-bar chart.

Reading a multiple-bar chart is very similar to reading a single-bar chart. The only difference is that you need to make sure you look at the correct bar. Before you start, check the *key* — the little box that tells you which colour or type of shading corresponds to which subcategory — and then look at the bar in the correct category with the right colour or shading.

Stacked-bar charts

I nearly forgot to mention stacked-bar charts, because I dislike them so much. The purpose of these monstrosities is to show the changes in both the totals and the composition of a value — for instance, not only how a company's income has changed but also how much of the income has come from each source. I give an example of a stacked-bar chart in Figure 13-3.

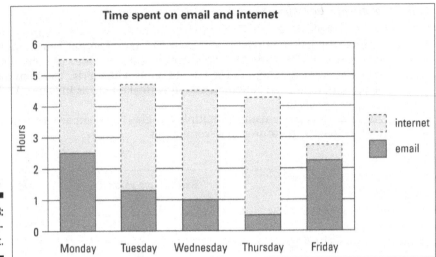

Some of the information in a stacked-bar chart is pretty easy to read — you can figure out the total value and the value of the lowest bar using the same methods you use for normal bar charts. The values in the middle and at the top are a bit trickier. Here's what you do:

1. **Work out the value of the bottom of the bar you're interested in by measuring across to the vertical axis, as you do with a regular bar chart.**

2. **Work out the value of the top of the bar you're interested in, using the same technique.**

3. **Take the answer in Step 1 away from the answer in Step 2.**

   The result is the value of the bar.

I don't like stacked-bar charts because they're a mess. Comparing two bars next to each other when their base has moved is really hard, so be careful. I'm not the world's biggest fan of multiple-bar charts either, but I think they're much clearer than stacked-bar charts.

Poking about in pie charts

Pie charts use angles to show the relative sizes of various categories. Pie charts are circular and are cut into 'slices'. The bigger the slice of pie, the bigger the group it represents. I give an example of a pie chart in Figure 13-4, showing you roughly how I spend my time during a typical day.

Deciding when to use a pie chart

You use a pie chart rather than a bar chart when you're not very interested in the actual numbers you want to represent but want to see how big the groups are compared with each other. A good example is if you want to give a presentation about the food types sold in your school canteen but don't want the audience to know precisely how many items of each food type are sold. You frequently see pie charts on election-night reports on TV to show the distribution of votes. In a very close election race, the slices representing the two front-runners are almost the same size.

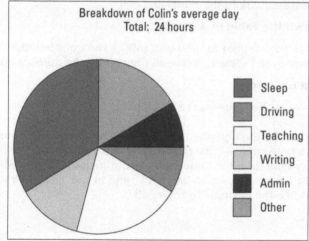

Figure 13-4:
A pie chart showing Colin's typical day.

Breakdown of Colin's average day
Total: 24 hours

- Sleep
- Driving
- Teaching
- Writing
- Admin
- Other

Handling angles, percentages and numbers

If you've read many other chapters in this book, you probably won't be surprised to find that you can work out the values associated with pie charts using the Table of Joy — and if you don't know what I mean, head to Chapter 8, where I explain the joy of the Table of Joy in great detail. A whole circle contains 360 degrees (as I describe in Chapter 11). In a pie chart, those 360 degrees correspond to the total of the values represented in the chart. When you work with a pie chart, you may need to figure out one of the following three things:

- ✔ The size of the angle in a slice.
- ✔ The value of a slice.
- ✔ The total of the values in all the slices.

To find one of these things, you need to know the other two. Here's how to use the Table of Joy to work with a pie chart:

1. **Draw out a noughts-and-crosses grid.**

   Leave yourself plenty of room in the grid for labels.

2. **Label the top row with 'value' and 'degrees' and the sides with 'slice' and 'circle'.**

3. **Write 360 in the 'circle/degrees' cell and the two other pieces of information you have in the appropriate places.**

   Put a question mark in the remaining cell.

4. **Write down the Table of Joy sum.**

   The sum is the number in the same row as the question mark times by the number in the same column, all divided by the number opposite.

5. **Work out the sum.**

   The answer is the value you're looking for.

To convert an angle into a percentage (or vice versa) you use a similar process. The whole circle — 360 degrees — corresponds to the whole of the data — 100 per cent. Use the same steps as outlined in the preceding steps, but change the 'value' column to 'per cent', and in the 'circle/per cent' cell write 100, just like the example in Figure 13-5.

Figure 13-5:
Converting percentages to pie-chart angles with the Table of Joy.

	Percent	Angle	
Circle	100	360	$\dfrac{30 \times 360}{100} = 108$
Slice	30	?	

Looking at line graphs

Line graphs are probably my favourite kind of graph. The idea of a line graph is to show how a value changes in response to another value — often, but not always, time.

In Figure 13-6 I give an example of a line graph showing the world population. Notice the zigzag on the vertical line — or *axis*, showing that the numbers don't start at zero. At first glance, it looks like the population has doubled, but in fact it's 'only' increased by about 20 per cent.

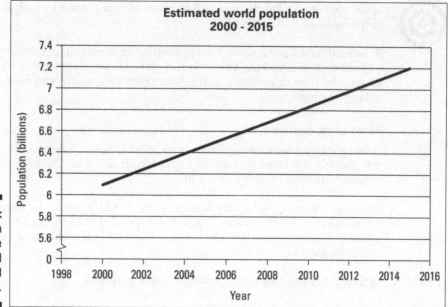

Figure 13-6:
A line graph showing the estimated world population.

Careful with those axes!

Graphs are supposed to make data easier to visualise and understand — and, to a large extent, they do. But obtaining precise data from a graph is still sometimes tricky.

Here's the process for reading a line graph when you know a value on the horizontal axis:

1. **Find the relevant value on the horizontal axis.**

   The value may be marked. If it's not, try to estimate where the value should be: Find the two values it sits between and decide which one it's closer to. Make a little mark on the axis there.

2. **Using a ruler, lightly draw a straight line in pencil directly up from the mark until it reaches the graph.**

3. **Now turn the ruler a quarter-turn and draw (still lightly in pencil) across from where your vertical line meets the graph, until you reach the vertical axis.**

4. **Where this line meets the vertical axis is your answer.**

   If the line is on a marked value, fantastic — that's your answer. If your line doesn't quite sit on a marked value, do a bit of inspired guesswork. Which values is your line between? Is it about halfway between them, or closer to one than the other?

Make your marks lightly in pencil because you may need to look at the graph again to find more values.

If, instead, you have a value for the vertical axis, you simply work the other way around: You find the value on the vertical axis, draw across to the graph, and then draw down to the horizontal axis, where you read off the value you need.

More than one line

Sometimes you have two or more lines to work with. You read the values off the graph in the same way as for a graph with one line. The only difficulty is making sure you use the correct line.

Before you start, look for the *key* or *legend* — a little area containing information about the graph. The key shows what the different colours or styles of line represent. Your mission is to pick the line that best suits what you're looking for.

I show a multiple-line graph with a key in Figure 13-7.

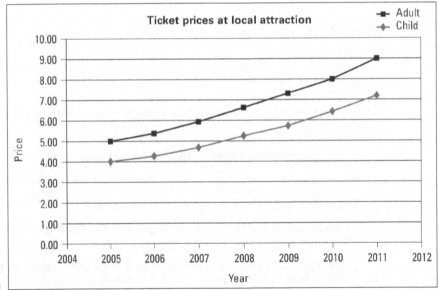

Figure 13-7: A multiple-line graph with a key.

Ch-ch-ch-changes

A line graph shows the change from one time period to the next really well. If the graph slopes up and to the right, the value is increasing. If the graph slopes down and to the right, the value is falling.

Try remembering that *upright* citizens are held in *high* regard, while *downright* dirty dogs are held in *low* esteem. Daft — but it works for me.

Here's how to work out by how much a value has risen or fallen between two time periods:

1. **Read the value for the first time period on the horizontal axis.**

   Use the same method as I explain in the section 'Careful with those axes!'

2. **Read the value for the second time period in the same way.**

3. **Take the smaller number away from the bigger number.**

4. **If the value has fallen, put a minus sign in front of the number.**

   The answer is how much your value has risen or fallen.

In a multiple-choice exam, read graph questions very carefully. Examiners are often sneaky and put in positive and negative versions of the same number. Make sure you get the sign right! For more on negative numbers, check out Chapter 4.

Reading Graphs, Tables and Charts

To interpret a good, properly drawn graph, you don't need special skills. What's going on should be obvious from the picture.

Unfortunately, most graphs you see aren't drawn properly. They're too busy, or not labelled clearly, or generally a mess. Here, I focus on how to gather information from graphs, tables and charts — which may not be that well laid out.

Picking the right data from a table

Many tables suffer from information overload. A big, complicated table, no matter how carefully produced and well set out, is intimidating and difficult to handle.

The more slowly and carefully you deal with tables, the better. Write down what you want to find out — even if that means copying out a test question. Writing like this forces you to slow down and think about what you need to know.

Finding the right row and the right column

When you know what you want to find, you can start looking for it. Sift through the labels at the top and at the side of the table to see which labels match what you're looking for. Then read down and across — the number you need is in that row and column.

I put a ruler along the right side of the column I'm interested in, so when I read across a row I know to stop when I reach the ruler.

Matching criteria

In a test, a common type of table question involves finding values that match a criterion — where the number is greater than or less than a given value. For instance, after reading a test question, you may know a business's sales for each month of the year and that the business needs to sell at least 100 widgets each month to make a profit. To find how many profitable months the business had over the year, you simply count how many of the entries in the 'widget sales' column are over 100.

Keeping up with keys and axes

Being able to read graphs depends critically on being able to understand the keys and the axes.

The *key* or *legend* to a graph is a set of information next to the graph that tells you what represents what — for instance, which colour in the graph represents which category, or which type of line means which set of data. The key is the first place you should look when you answer a test question on graphs, because the key tells you which part of the graph is important to you.

The *axes* are the horizontal and vertical lines at the bottom and side of the graph. I show you how to use axes in the section 'Bringing in the bar charts'. Axes are very important: Reading the numbers off an axis is the single most important step in answering graph questions.

Understanding graphs

Well-drawn graphs can be fantastically useful for communicating information on two levels:

- **Big picture:** You can see just by looking at a line graph whether a value is increasing, decreasing, staying the same or wobbling all over the place, much more easily than you can with a table. A bar chart or pie chart shows you which categories are the most important at a glance.

✔ **Detail:** With a little work, you can extract the numerical value of each category from a graph. This opens up a whole range of ways to interpret and describe the data in the graph.

The Cartesian Plane

When a graph uses the axes I talk about in the preceding section and in 'Bringing in the bar charts', this can also be called the Cartesian plane (also called the Cartesian coordinate system or just the plain-old *xy*-graph), shown in Figure 13-8. You see a lot of this graph when you study algebra, so getting familiar with it now is a good idea.

Figure 13-8:
An *xy*-graph includes horizontal and vertical axes, which cross at the origin (0, 0).

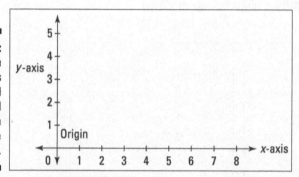

 A Cartesian plane is really just two number lines that cross at 0. These number lines relate to the *horizontal axis* (also called the *x-axis*) and the *vertical axis* (also called the *y-axis*). The place where these two axes (plural of axis) cross is called the *origin*.

Plotting points on the Cartesian plane

Plotting a point (finding and marking its location) on a graph isn't much harder than finding a point on a number line — after all, a graph is just two number lines put together. (Flip to Chapter 2 for more on using the number line.)

 Every point on a Cartesian plane (*xy*-graph) is represented by two numbers in parentheses, separated by a comma, called a set of *coordinates*. To plot any point, start at the origin, where the two axes cross. The first number tells you how far to go to the right (if positive) or left (if negative) along the horizontal axis. The second number tells you how far to go up (if positive) or down (if negative) along the vertical axis.

For example, here are the coordinates of four points called A, B, C and D:

$A = (2, 3)$	$B = (-4, 1)$	$C = (0, -5)$	$D = (6, 0)$

Figure 13-9 depicts a graph with these four points plotted. Start at the origin, $(0, 0)$. To plot point A, count 2 spaces to the right and 3 spaces up. To plot point B, count 4 spaces to the left (the negative direction) and then 1 space up. To plot point C, count 0 spaces left or right and then count 5 spaces down (the negative direction). And to plot point D, count 6 spaces to the right and then 0 spaces up or down.

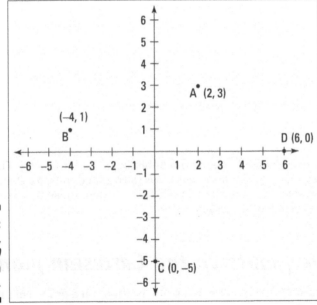

Figure 13-9:
Points A, B, C, and D plotted on an xy-graph.

Drawing lines on the Cartesian plane

When you understand how to plot points on a graph (refer to the preceding section), you can begin to plot lines and use them to show mathematical relationships.

The examples in this section focus on the number of dollars two people, Xenia and Yanni, are carrying. The horizontal axis represents Xenia's money, and the vertical axis represents Yanni's. For example, suppose you want to draw a line representing this statement:

Xenia has $1 more than Yanni.

Xenia	1	2	3	4	5
Yanni	0	1	2	3	4

Now you have five pairs of points that you can plot on your graph as (Xenia, Yanni): (1,0), (2,1), (3,2), (4,3), and (5,4). Next, draw a straight line through these points, as in Figure 13-10.

This line on the graph represents every possible pair of amounts for Xenia and Yanni because the arrows continue. For example, notice how the point (6,5) is on the line. This point represents the possibility that Xenia has $6 and Yanni has $5.

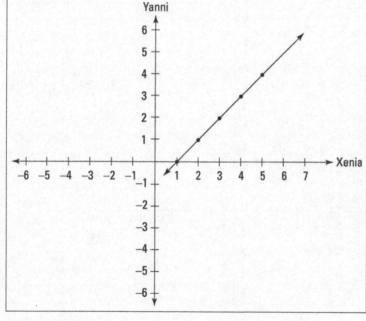

Figure 13-10:
All possible values of Xenia's and Yanni's money if Xenia has $1 more than Yanni.

Here's a slightly more complicated example:

Yanni has $3 more than twice the amount that Xenia has.

Xenia	1	2	3	4	5
Yanni	5	7	9	11	13

Again, start by making the same type of chart as in the preceding example. But this time, if Xenia has $1, then twice that amount is $2, so Yanni has $3 more than that, or $5. Continue in that way to fill in the chart, as follows:

Now plot these five points on the graph and draw a line through them, as in Figure 13-11.

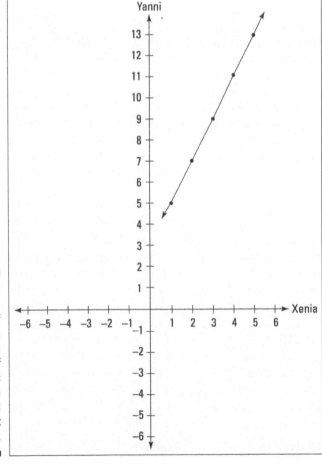

Figure 13-11: All possible values of Xenia's and Yanni's money if Yanni has $3 more than twice the amount Xenia has.

As in the other examples, this graph represents all possible values that Xenia and Yanni could have. For example, if Xenia has $7, Yanni has $17.

Part IV
The *x*-Files: Introduction to Algebra

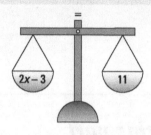

Expression	Number of Terms	Terms
$5x$	One	$5x$
$-5x + 2$	Two	$-5x$ and 2
$x^2y + \dfrac{z}{3} - xyz + 8$	Four	$x^2y, \dfrac{z}{3}, xyz$, and 8

Term	Coefficient	Variable
$-4x^3$	-4	x^3
x^2	1	x^2
$-x$	-1	x
-7	-7	None

In this part . . .

✔ Evaluate, simplify and factor algebraic expressions.

✔ Keep algebraic equations balanced and solve them by isolating the variable.

✔ Use algebra to solve word problems too difficult to solve with just arithmetic.

Chapter 14

Using the Alphabet for Maths

*Y*ou'll never forget your first love, your first car or your first x. Unfortunately, for some people, remembering their first x in algebra is similar to remembering their first love who stood them up at the end-of-school formal or their first car that broke down someplace in South Australia.

The most well-known fact about algebra is that it uses letters — like x — to represent numbers. So if you have a traumatic x-related tale, all I can say is that the future will be brighter than the past.

What good is algebra? That question is a common one, and it deserves a decent answer. Algebra is used for solving problems that are just too difficult for ordinary arithmetic. And because number crunching is so much a part of the modern world, algebra is everywhere (even if you don't see it): Architecture, engineering, medicine, statistics, computers, business, chemistry, physics, biology, and, of course, higher math. Anywhere numbers are useful, algebra is there.

In this chapter, I introduce (or reintroduce) you to that elusive little fellow, Mr x, in a way that's bound to make him seem a little friendlier. Then I show you how *algebraic expressions* are similar to and different from the arithmetic expressions that you're used to working with. (For a refresher on arithmetic expressions, see Chapters 2 and 3.)

Expressing Yourself with Algebraic Expressions

In this chapter, I introduce you to a new type of mathematical expression: The algebraic expression. An algebraic expression is any string of mathematical symbols that can be placed on one side of an equation and that includes at least one variable.

Here are a few examples of algebraic expressions:

$$2x + 3y$$

$$14p - 7 + 2c$$

$$8px^2 + 9abc^3$$

The difference between arithmetic and algebraic expressions is simply that an algebraic expression includes at least one variable.

In this section, I show you how to work with algebraic expressions. First, I show you how to separate an algebraic expression into one or more terms, and I walk through how to identify the coefficient and the variable part of each term.

Coming to algebraic terms

A *term* in an algebraic expression is any chunk of symbols set off from the rest of the expression by either addition or subtraction. As algebraic expressions get more complex, they begin to string themselves out in more terms. Here are some examples:

Expression	Number of Terms	Terms
$5x$	One	$5x$
$-5x + 2$	Two	$-5x$ and 2
$x^2y + \dfrac{z}{3} - xyz + 8$	Four	$x^2y, \dfrac{z}{3}, -xyz,$ and 8

No matter how complicated an algebraic expression gets, you can always separate it out into one or more terms.

When separating an algebraic expression into terms, group the plus or minus sign with the term that it immediately precedes.

When a term has a variable, it's called an *algebraic term*. When it doesn't have a variable, it's called a *constant*. For example, look at the following expression:

$$x^2y + \frac{z}{3} - xyz + 8$$

The first three terms are algebraic terms and the last term is a constant. As you can see, in algebra, *constant* is just a fancy word for *number*.

Terms are really useful to know about because you can follow rules to move them, combine them, and perform the Big Four operations on them. All these skills are important for solving equations, which I explain in the next chapter. But for now, this section explains a bit about terms and some of their traits.

Identifying the coefficient and variable

Every term in an algebraic expression has a coefficient. The *coefficient* is the signed numerical part of a term in an algebraic expression — that is, the number and the sign (+ or –) that goes with that term. For example, suppose you're working with the following algebraic expression:

$$-4x^8 + x^2 - x - y$$

The following table shows the four terms of this expression, with each term's coefficient:

Term	Coefficient	Variable
$-4x^3$	-4	x^3
x^2	1	x^2
$-x$	-1	x
-7	-7	none

Notice that the sign associated with the term is part of the coefficient. So the coefficient of $-4x^3$ is –4.

When a term appears to have no coefficient, the coefficient is actually 1. So the coefficient of x^2 is 1, and the coefficient of $-x$ is -1. And when a term is a constant (just a number), that number with its associated sign is the coefficient. So the coefficient of the term -7 is simply -7.

By the way, when the coefficient of any algebraic term is 0, the expression equals 0 no matter what the variable part looks like:

$$0x = 0 \qquad 0xyz = 0 \qquad 0x^3y^4z^{10} = 0$$

In contrast, the *variable part* of an expression is everything except the coefficient. The previous table shows the four terms of the same expression, with each term's variable part.

Making the commute: Rearranging your terms

When you understand how to separate an algebraic expression into terms, you can go one step further by rearranging the terms in any order you like. Each term moves as a unit, kind of like a group of students getting a bus to a school excursion — everyone in the bus stays together for the whole ride.

For example, suppose you begin with the expression $-5x + 2$. You can rearrange the two terms of this expression without changing its value. Notice that each term's sign stays with that term, although dropping the plus sign at the beginning of an expression is customary:

$$= 2 - 5x$$

Rearranging terms in this way doesn't affect the value of the expression because addition is *commutative* — that is, you can rearrange things that you're adding without changing the answer. (See Chapter 2 for more on the commutative property of addition.)

For example, suppose $x = 3$. Then the original expression and its rearrangement evaluate as follows:

$$
\begin{array}{ll}
-5x + 2 & 2 - 5x \\
= -5(3) + 2 & = 2 - 5(3) \\
= -15 + 2 & = 2 - 15 \\
= -13 & = -13
\end{array}
$$

Rearranging expressions in this way becomes handy later in this chapter, when you simplify algebraic expressions. As another example, suppose you have this expression:

$$4x - y + 6$$

You can rearrange it in a variety of ways:

$$= 6 + 4x - y$$
$$= -y + 4x + 6$$

Because the term $4x$ has no sign, it's positive, so you can write in a plus sign as needed when rearranging terms.

As long as each term's sign stays with that term, rearranging the terms in an expression has no effect on its value.

For example, suppose that $x = 2$ and $y = 3$. Here's how to evaluate the original expression and the two rearrangements:

$4x - y + 6$	$6 + 4x - y$	$-y + 4x + 6$
$= 4(2) - 3 + 6$	$= 6 + 4(2) - 3$	$= -3 + 4(2) + 6$
$= 8 - 3 + 6$	$= 6 + 8 - 3$	$= -3 + 8 + 6$
$= 5 + 6$	$= 14 - 3$	$= 5 + 6$
$= 11$	$= 11$	$= 11$

Identifying like terms

Like terms (or *similar terms*) are any two algebraic terms that have the same variable part — that is, both the letters and their exponents have to be exact matches. Here are some examples:

Variable Part	Examples of Like Terms		
x	$4x$	$12x$	$99.9x$
x^2	$6x^2$	$-20x^2$	$\frac{8}{3}x^2$
y	y	$1{,}000y$	3976
xy	$-7xy$	$800xy$	$\frac{22}{7}xy$
x^3y^3	$3x^3y^3$	$-111x^3y^3$	$3.14x^3y^3$

As you can see, in each example, the variable part in all three like terms is the same. Only the coefficient changes, and it can be any real number: Positive or negative, whole number, fraction, or decimal.

Considering algebraic terms and the main four equations

In this section, I get you up to speed on how to apply the main four equations to algebraic expressions. For now, just think of working with algebraic expressions as a set of tools that you're collecting, for use when you get on the job. You find how useful these tools are in Chapter 15, when you begin solving algebraic equations.

Adding terms

Add like terms by adding their coefficients and keeping the same variable part.

For example, suppose you have the expression $2x + 3x$. Remember that $2x$ is just shorthand for $x + x$, and $3x$ means simply $x + x + x$. So when you add them up, you get the following:

$$2x + 3x = x + x + x + x + x = 5x$$

As you can see, when the variable parts of two terms are the same, you add these terms by adding their coefficients: $2x + 3x = (2 + 3)x$. The idea here is roughly similar to the idea that 2 apples + 3 apples = 5 apples.

You cannot add non-like terms. Here are some cases in which the variables or their exponents are different:

$$2x + 3y$$
$$2yz + 3y$$
$$2x^2 + 3x$$

In these cases, you can't simplify the expression. You're faced with a situation that's similar to 2 apples + 3 oranges. Because the units (apples and oranges) are different, you can't combine terms.

Subtracting terms

Subtraction works much the same as addition. Subtract like terms by finding the difference between their coefficients and keeping the same variable part.

For example, suppose you have $3x - x$. Recall that $3x$ is simply shorthand for $x + x + x$. So doing this subtraction gives you the following:

$$x + x + x - x = 2x$$

No big surprises here. You simply find $(3 - 1)x$. This time, the idea roughly parallels the idea that $\$3 - \$1 = \$2$.

Here's another example:

$$2x - 5x$$

Again, no problem, as long as you know how to work with negative numbers (refer to Chapter 4 if you need details). Just find the difference between the coefficients:

$$= (2 - 5)x = -3x$$

In this case, recall that $\$2 - \$5 = -\$3$ (that is, a debt of $\$3$).

You cannot subtract non-like terms. For example, you can't subtract either of the following:

$$7x - 4y$$
$$7x^2y - 4xy^2$$

As with addition, you can't do subtraction with different variables. Think of this as trying to figure out $\$7 - 4$ euros. Because the units in this case (dollars versus euros) are different, you're stuck.

Multiplying terms

Unlike adding and subtracting, you can multiply non-like terms. Multiply any two terms by multiplying their coefficients and combining — that is, by collecting or gathering up — all the variables in each term into a single term, as I show you next.

For example, suppose you want to multiply $5x(3y)$. To get the coefficient, multiply 5×3. To get the algebraic part, combine the variables x and y:

$$= 5(3)xy = 15xy$$

Now suppose you want to multiply $2x(7x)$. Again, multiply the coefficients and collect the variables into a single term:

$$= 7(2)xx = 14xx$$

Remember that x^2 is shorthand for xx, so you can write the answer more efficiently:

$$= 14x^2$$

Here's another example. Multiply all three coefficients together and gather up the variables:

$$2x^2(3y)(4xy)$$
$$= 2(3)(4)x^2xyy$$
$$= 24x^3y^2$$

As you can see, the exponent 3 that's associated with x is just the count of how many xs appear in the problem. The same is true of the exponent 2 associated with y.

A fast way to multiply variables with exponents is to add the exponents together. For example:

$$(x^4y^3)(x^2y^5)(x^6y) = x^{12}y^9$$

In this example, I added the exponents of the xs $(4 + 2 + 6 = 12)$ to get the exponent of x in the expression. Similarly, I added the exponents of the ys $(3 + 5 + 1 = 9$ — don't forget that $y = y^1$!) to get the exponent of y in the expression.

Dividing terms

It's customary to represent division of algebraic expressions as a fraction instead of using the division sign $(\div)$. So division of algebraic terms really looks like reducing a fraction to lowest terms (refer to Chapter 6 for more on reducing).

To divide one algebraic term by another, follow these steps:

1. **Make a fraction of the two terms**.

   Suppose you want to divide $3xy$ by $12x^2$. Begin by turning the problem into a fraction:

   $$\frac{3xy}{12x^2}$$

2. **Cancel out factors in coefficients that are in both the numerator and the denominator.**

   In this case, you can cancel out a 3. Notice that when the coefficient in xy becomes 1, you can drop it:

   $$= \frac{xy}{4x^2}$$

3. **Cancel out any variable that's in both the numerator and the denominator.**

   You can break x^2 out as xx:

   $$= \frac{xy}{4xx}$$

   Now you can clearly cancel an x in both the numerator and the denominator:

   $$= \frac{y}{4x}$$

   As you can see, the resulting fraction is really a reduced form of the original.

As another example, suppose you want to divide $-6x^2yz^3$ by $-8x^2y^2z$. Begin by writing the division as a fraction:

$$\frac{-6x^2yz^3}{-8x^2y^2z}$$

First, reduce the coefficients. Notice that, because both coefficients were originally negative, you can cancel out both minus signs as well:

$$= \frac{3x^2yz^3}{4x^2y^2z}$$

Now you can begin cancelling variables. I do this in two steps, as before:

$$= \frac{3xxyzzz}{4xxyyz}$$

At this point, just cross out any occurrence of a variable that appears in both the numerator and the denominator:

$$= \frac{3zz}{4y}$$

$$= \frac{3z^2}{4y}$$

You can't cancel out variables or coefficients if either the numerator or the denominator has more than one term in it. This is a very common mistake in algebra, so don't let it happen to you!

Simplifying Algebraic Expressions

As algebraic expressions grow more complex, simplifying them can make them easier to work with. Simplifying an expression means (quite simply!) making it smaller and easier to manage. You see how important simplifying expressions becomes when you begin solving algebraic equations.

For now, think of this section as a kind of algebra toolkit. Here I show you *how* to use these tools. In Chapter 15, I show you *when* to use them.

Combining like terms

When two algebraic terms contain like terms (when their variables match), you can add or subtract them (see the earlier section 'Considering algebraic terms and the main four equations'). This feature comes in handy when you're trying to simplify an expression. For example, suppose you're working with the following expression:

$$4x - 3y + 2x + y - x + 2y$$

As it stands, this expression has six terms. But three terms have the variable x and the other three have the variable y. Begin by rearranging the expression so that all like terms are grouped together:

$$= 4x + 2x - x - 3y + y + 2y$$

Now you can add and subtract like terms. I do this in two steps, first for the x terms and then for the y terms:

$$= 5x - 3y + y + 2y$$
$$= 5x + 0y$$
$$= 5x$$

Notice that the x terms simplify to $5x$, and the y terms simplify to $0y$, which is 0, so the y terms drop out of the expression altogether.

Here's a somewhat more complicated example that has variables with exponents:

$$12x - xy - 3x^2 + 8y + 10xy + 3x^2 - 7x$$

This time, you have four different types of terms. As a first step, you can rearrange these terms so that groups of like terms are all together (I underline these four groups so you can see them clearly):

$$= 12x - 7x - xy + 10xy - 3x^2 + 3x^2 + 8y$$

Now combine each set of like terms:

$$= 5x + 9xy + 0x^2 + 8y$$

This time, the x^2 terms add up to 0, so they drop out of the expression altogether:

$$= 5x + 9xy + 8y$$

Removing brackets from an algebraic expression

Parentheses, or brackets, keep parts of an expression together as a single unit. In Chapter 3, I show you how to handle parentheses in an arithmetic expression. This skill is also useful with algebraic expressions. As you find when you begin solving algebraic equations in Chapter 15, getting rid of parentheses is often the first step toward solving a problem. In this section, I show how to handle the main four operations with ease.

Drop everything: Parentheses with a plus sign

When an expression contains parentheses that come right after a plus sign (+), you can just remove the parentheses. Here's an example:

$$2x + (3x - y) + 5y$$
$$= 2x + 3x - y + 5y$$

Now you can simplify the expression by combining like terms:

$$= 5x + 4y$$

When the first term inside the parentheses is negative, when you drop the parentheses, the minus sign replaces the plus sign. For example:

$$6x + (-2x + y) - 4y$$
$$= 6x - 2x + y - 4y$$
$$= 4x - 3x$$

Sign turnabout: Parentheses with a minus sign

Sometimes an expression contains parentheses that come right after a minus sign (–). In this case, change the sign of every term inside the parentheses to the opposite sign; then remove the parentheses.

Consider this example:

$$6x - (2xy - 3y) + 5xy$$

A minus sign is in front of the parentheses, so you need to change the signs of both terms in the parentheses and remove the parentheses. Notice that the term $2xy$ appears to have no sign because it's the first term inside the parentheses. This expression really means the following:

$$= 6x - (+\underline{2}xy - 3y) + 5xy$$

You can see how to change the signs:

$$= 6x - 2xy + 3y + 5xy$$

At this point, you can combine the two xy terms:

$$= 6x + 3xy + 3y$$

Distribution: Parentheses with no sign

When you see nothing between a number and a set of parentheses, it means multiplication. For example:

$$2(3) = 6 \qquad 4(4) = 16 \qquad 10(15) = 150$$

This notation becomes much more common with algebraic expressions, replacing the multiplication sign ($\times$) to avoid confusion with the variable x:

$$3(4x) = 12x \qquad 4x(2x) = 8x^2 \qquad 3x(7y) = 21xy$$

To remove parentheses without a sign, multiply the term outside the parentheses by every term inside the parentheses; then remove the parentheses. When you follow those steps, you're using the *distributive property*.

Here's an example:

$$2(3x - 5y + 4)$$

In this case, multiply 2 by each of the three terms inside the parentheses:

$$= 2(3x) + 2(-5y) + 2(4)$$

For the moment, this expression looks more complex than the original one, but now you can get rid of all three sets of parentheses by multiplying:

$$= 6x - 10y + 8$$

Multiplying by every term inside the parentheses is simply distribution of multiplication over addition — also called the *distributive property*.

As another example, suppose you have the following expression:

$$-2x(-3x + y + 6) + 2xy - 5x^2$$

Begin by multiplying $-2x$ by the three terms inside the parentheses:

$$= -2x(-3x) - 2x(y) - 2x(6) + 2xy - 5x^2$$

The expression looks worse than when you started, but you can get rid of all the parentheses by multiplying:

$$= 6x^2 - 2xy - 12x + 2xy - 5x^2$$

Now you can combine like terms:

$$= x^2 - 12x$$

Parentheses by FOILing

Sometimes, expressions have two sets of parentheses next to each other without a sign between them. In that case, you need to multiply *every term* inside the first set by *every term* inside the second.

When you have two terms inside each set of parentheses, you can use a process called FOILing. This is really just the distributive property, as I show you in the following steps. The word *FOIL* is an acronym to help you make sure you multiply the correct terms. It stands for *F*irst, *O*utside, *I*nside, and *L*ast.

Here's how the process works. In this example, you're simplifying the expression $(2x - 2)(3x - 6)$:

1. **Start out by multiplying the two *First* terms in the parentheses.**

   The first term in the first set of parentheses is $2x$, and $3x$ is the first term in the second set of parentheses: $(\underline{2x} - 2)(\underline{3x} - 6)$.

   F: Multiply the first terms: $2x(3x) = 6x^2$

2. **Multiply the two *Outside* terms.**

   The two outside terms, $2x$ and -6, are on the ends: $(\underline{2x} - 2)(3x - 6)$

   O: Multiply the outside terms: $2x(-6) = -12x$

3. **Multiply the two *Inside* terms.**

   The two terms in the middle are -2 and $3x$: $(2x - \underline{2})(\underline{3x} - 6)$

   I: Multiply the middle terms: $-2(3x) = -6x$

4. **Multiply the two *Last* terms.**

   The last term in the first set of parentheses is -2, and -6 is the last term in the second set: $(2x - \underline{2})(3x - \underline{6})$

   L: Multiply the last terms: $-2(-6) = 12$

Add these four results together to get the simplified expression:

$$(2x - 2)(3x - 6) = 6x^2 - 6x - 12x + 12$$

In this case, you can simplify this expression still further by combining the like terms $-12x$ and $-6x$:

$$= 6x^2 - 18x + 12$$

Notice that, during this process, you multiply every term inside one set of parentheses by every term inside the other set. FOILing just helps you keep track and make sure you've multiplied everything.

FOILing is really just an application of the distributive property, which I discuss in the section preceding this one. In other words, $(2x - 2)(3x - 6)$ is really the same as $2x(3x - 6) + -2(3x - 6)$ when distributed. Then distributing again gives you $6x^2 - 6x - 12x + 12$.

Chapter 15

Using Algebra to Solve Equations

In This Chapter

▶ Using variables (such as x) in equations

▶ Understanding the *balance scale method* for solving equations

▶ Rearranging and isolating terms in an algebraic equation

▶ Removing parentheses from an equation

▶ Cross-multiplying to remove fractions

---

*W*hen it comes to algebra, solving equations is the main event. Solving an algebraic equation means finding out what number the variable (usually x) stands for. Not surprisingly, this process is called *solving for x* and, when you know how to do it, your confidence — not to mention your grades in your maths class — will soar through the roof.

This chapter is all about solving for x. First, I show you a few informal methods to solve for x when an equation isn't too difficult. Then I show you how to solve more difficult equations by thinking of them as a balance scale.

The balance scale method is really the heart of algebra (yes, algebra has a heart, after all!). When you understand this simple idea, you're ready to solve more complicated equations, using all the tools I show you in Chapter 14, such as simplifying expressions and removing parentheses. You find out how to extend these skills to algebraic equations. Finally, I show you how cross-multiplying (refer to Chapter 6) can make solving algebraic equations with fractions a piece of cake.

By the end of this chapter, you'll have a solid grasp of a bunch of ways to solve equations for the elusive and mysterious x.

Understanding Algebraic Equations

An algebraic equation is an equation that includes at least one variable — that is, a letter (such as x) that stands for a number. Solving an algebraic equation means finding out what number x stands for.

In this section, I show you the basics of how a variable like x works its way into an equation in the first place. Then I show you a few quick ways to solve for x when an equation isn't too difficult.

Using x in equations

An equation is a mathematical statement that contains an equals sign. For example, here's a perfectly good equation:

$$7 \times 9 = 63$$

At its heart, a variable (such as x) is nothing more than a placeholder for a number. You're probably used to equations that use other placeholders: One number is purposely left as a blank or replaced by an underline or a question mark, and you're supposed to fill it in. Usually, this number comes after the equals sign. For example:

$$8 + 2 =$$
$$12 - 3 = \_\_\_$$
$$14 \div 7 = ?$$

As soon as you're comfortable with addition, subtraction or whatever, you can switch the equation around a bit:

$$9 + \_\_ = 14$$
$$? \times 6 = 18$$

When you stop using underlines and question marks and start using variables such as x to stand for the part of the equation you want to figure out, bingo! You have an algebra problem:

$$4 + 1 = x$$
$$12 \div x = 3$$
$$x - 13 = 30$$

To evaluate an algebraic expression, you need to know the numerical value of every variable. For each variable in the expression, substitute, or plug in, the number that it stands for and then evaluate the expression.

Knowing how to evaluate arithmetic expressions comes in handy for evaluating algebraic expressions. For example, suppose you want to evaluate the following expression:

$4x - 7$

Note that this expression contains the variable x, which is unknown, so the value of the whole expression is also unknown.

An algebraic expression can have any number of variables, but you usually don't work with expressions that have more than two or maybe three, at the most. You can use any letter as a variable, but x, y and z tend to get a lot of mileage.

Suppose in this case that $x = 2$. To evaluate the expression, substitute 2 for x everywhere it appears in the expression:

$4(2) - 7$

After you make the substitution, you're left with an arithmetic expression, so you can finish your calculations to evaluate the expression:

$= 8 - 7 = 1$

So given $x = 2$, the algebraic expression $4x - 7 = 1$.

Choosing among four ways to solve algebraic equations

You don't need to call an exterminator just to kill a bug. Similarly, algebra is strong stuff, and you don't always need it to solve an algebraic equation.

Generally, you have four ways to solve algebraic equations such as the ones I introduce earlier in this chapter. In this section, I introduce them in order of difficulty.

Eyeballing easy equations

You can solve easy problems just by looking at them. For example:

$5 + x = 6$

When you look at this problem, you can see that $x = 1$. When a problem is this easy and you can see the answer, you don't need to go to any particular trouble to solve it.

Rearranging slightly harder equations

When you can't see an answer just by looking at a problem, sometimes rearranging the problem helps to turn it into one that you can solve using one of the main four operations. For example:

$$6x = 96$$

You can rearrange this problem using inverse operations — in this case, changing multiplication to division:

$$x = \frac{96}{6}$$

Now solve the problem by division (long or otherwise) to find that $x = 16$.

Guessing and checking equations

You can solve some equations by guessing an answer and then checking to see whether you're right. For example, suppose you want to solve the following equation:

$$3x + 7 = 19$$

To find out what x equals, start by guessing that $x = 2$. Now check to see whether you're right by substituting 2 for x in the equation. If you're wrong, work out a few more guesses:

$3(2) + 7 = 13$ WRONG! (13 is less than 19.)

$3(5) + 7 = 22$ WRONG! (22 is greater than 19.)

$3(4) + 7 = 19$ RIGHT!

With only three guesses, you found that $x = 4$.

Applying algebra to more difficult equations

When an algebraic equation gets hard enough, you find that looking at it and rearranging it just isn't enough to solve it. For example:

$$11x - 13 = 9x + 3$$

You probably can't tell what x equals just by looking at this problem. You also can't solve it just by rearranging it, using an inverse operation. And guessing and checking would be very tedious. Here's where algebra comes into play.

Algebra is especially useful because you can follow mathematical rules to find your answer. Throughout the rest of this chapter, I show you how to use the rules of algebra to turn tough problems like this one into problems that you can solve.

The Balancing Act: Solving for x

As I show you in the preceding section, some problems are too complicated to find out what the variable (usually x) equals just by eyeballing the problem or rearranging it. For these problems, you need a reliable method for getting the right answer. I call this method the *balance scale*.

The balance scale allows you to *solve for x* — that is, find the number that x stands for — in a step-by-step process that always works. In this section, I show you how to use the balance scale method to solve algebraic equations.

Striking a balance

The equals sign in any equation means that both sides balance. To keep that equals sign, you have to maintain that balance. In other words, whatever you do to one side of an equation, you have to do to the other.

For example, here's a balanced equation:

$$\frac{1+2=3}{\Delta}$$

If you add 1 to one side of the equation, the scale goes out of balance.

$$\frac{1+2+1 \neq 3}{\Delta}$$

But if you add 1 to *both* sides of the equation, the scale stays balanced:

$$\underline{1+2+1=3+1} \atop \Delta$$

You can add any number to the equation, as long as you do it to both sides. And in maths, *any number* means x:

$$1 + 2 + x = 3 + x$$

Remember that x is the same wherever it appears in a single equation or problem.

This idea of changing both sides of an equation equally isn't limited to addition. You can just as easily subtract an x, or even multiply or divide by x, as long as you do the same to both sides of the equation:

$$\text{Subtract}: 1+2-x=3-x$$
$$\text{Multiply}: (1+2)x = 3x$$
$$\text{Divide}: \frac{1+2}{x} = \frac{3}{x}$$

Using the balance scale to isolate *x*

The simple idea of balance is at the heart of algebra, and it enables you to find out what x is in many equations. When you solve an algebraic equation, the goal is to *isolate x* — that is, to get x alone on one side of the equation and some number on the other side. In algebraic equations of intermediate difficulty, this is a three-step process:

1. **Get all constants (non-*x* terms) on one side of the equation.**

2. **Get all *x*-terms on the other side of the equation.**

3. **Divide to isolate *x*.**

For example, take a look at the following problem:

$$11x - 13 = 9x + 3$$

As you follow the steps, notice how I keep the equation balanced at each step:

1. **Get all the constants on one side of the equation by adding 13 to both sides of the equation:**

$$
\begin{array}{r}
11x - 13 = 9x + 3 \\
+13 = \quad +13 \\
\hline
11x \quad = 9x + 16
\end{array}
$$

Because you've obeyed the rules of the balance scale, you know that this new equation is also correct. Now the only non-x term (16) is on the right side of the equation.

2. **Get all the x-terms on the other side by subtracting $9x$ from both sides of the equation:**

$$
\begin{array}{r}
11x = 9x + 16 \\
-9x - 9x \\
\hline
2x = \quad 16
\end{array}
$$

Again, the balance is preserved, so the new equation is correct.

3. **Divide by 2 to isolate x:**

$$\frac{2x}{2} = \frac{16}{2}$$
$$x = 8$$

To check this answer, you can simply substitute 8 for x in the original equation:

$$11(8) - 13 = 9(8) + 3$$
$$88 - 13 = 72 + 3$$
$$75 = 75 \ \checkmark$$

This checks out, so 8 is the correct value of x.

Rearranging Equations and Isolating x

When you understand how algebra works like a balance scale, as I show you in the preceding section, you can begin to solve more difficult algebraic equations. The basic tactic is always the same: Changing both sides of the equation equally at every step, try to isolate *x* on one side of the equation.

In this section, I show you how to put your skills from Chapter 14 to work solving equations. First, I show you how rearranging the terms in an expression is similar to rearranging them in an algebraic equation. Next, I show you how removing parentheses from an equation can help you solve it. Finally, you discover how cross-multiplication is useful for solving algebraic equations with fractions.

Rearranging terms on one side of an equation

Rearranging terms becomes all-important when working with equations. For example, suppose you're working with this equation:

$$5x - 4 = 2x + 2$$

When you think about it, this equation is really two expressions connected with an equals sign. And, of course, that's true of every equation. That's why everything you find out about expressions in Chapter 14 is useful for solving equations. For example, you can rearrange the terms on one side of an equation. So here's another way to write the same equation:

$$-4 + 5x = 2x + 2$$

And here's a third way:

$$-4 + 5x = 2 + 2x$$

This flexibility to rearrange terms comes in handy when you're solving equations.

Moving terms to the other side of the equals sign

Earlier in this chapter, I show you how an equation is similar to a balance scale. For example, take a look at Figure 15-1.

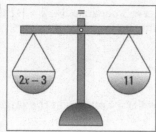

Figure 15-1:
Showing
how an
equation is
similar to
a balance
scale.

To keep the scale balanced, if you add or remove anything on one side, you must do the same on the other side. For example:

$$2x - 3 = 11$$
$$\underline{-2x \qquad\quad -2x}$$
$$-3 = 11 - 2x$$

Now take a look at these two versions of this equation side by side:

$$2x - 3 = 11 \qquad -3 = 11 - 2x$$

In the first version, the term $2x$ is on the left side of the equals sign. In the second, the term $-2x$ is on the right side. This example illustrates an important rule.

When you move any term in an expression to the other side of the equals sign, change its sign (from plus to minus or from minus to plus).

As another example, suppose you're working with this equation:

$$4x - 2 = 3x + 1$$

You have xs on both sides of the equation, so say you want to move the $3x$. When you move the term $3x$ from the right side to the left side, you have to change its sign from plus to minus (technically, you're subtracting $3x$ from both sides of the equation).

$$4x - 2 - 3x = 1$$

After that, you can simplify the expression on the left side of the equation by combining like terms:

$$x - 2 = 1$$

At this point, you can probably see that $x = 3$ because $3 - 2 = 1$. But just to be sure, move the -2 term to the right side and change its sign:

$$x = 1 + 2$$
$$x = 3$$

To check this result, substitute a 3 wherever x appears in the original equation:

$$4x - 2 = 3x + 1$$
$$4(3) - 2 = 3(3) + 1$$
$$12 - 2 = 9 + 1$$
$$10 = 10 \ \checkmark$$

As you can see, moving terms from one side of an equation to the other can be a big help when you're solving equations.

Removing brackets from equations

Chapter 14 gives you a treasure trove of tricks for simplifying expressions, and they come in handy when you're solving equations. One key skill from that chapter is removing parentheses, or brackets, from expressions. This tactic is also indispensable when you're solving equations.

For example, suppose you have the following equation:

$$5x + (6x - 15) = 30 - (x - 7) + 8$$

Your mission is to get all the x terms on one side of the equation and all the constants on the other. As the equation stands, however, x terms and constants are 'locked together' inside parentheses. In other words, you can't isolate the x terms from the constants. So before you can isolate terms, you need to remove the parentheses from the equation.

Recall that an equation is really just two expressions connected by an equals sign. So you can start working with the expression on the left side. In this expression, the parentheses begin with a plus sign (+), so you can just remove them:

$$5x + \underline{6x - 15} = 30 - (x - 7) + 8$$

Now move on to the expression on the right side. This time, the parentheses come right after a minus sign (–). To remove them, change the sign of both terms inside the parentheses: x becomes $-x$, and -7 becomes 7:

$$5x + 6x - 15 = 30 \underline{- x + 7} + 8$$

Bravo! Now you can isolate x terms to your heart's content. Move the $-x$ from the right side to the left, changing it to x:

$$5x + 6x - 15 \underline{+ x} = 30 + 7 + 8$$

Next, move -15 from the left side to the right, changing it to 15:

$$5x + 6x + x = 30 + 7 + \underline{8 + 15}$$

Now combine like terms on both sides of the equation:

$$12x = 30 + 7 + 8 + 15$$
$$12x = 60$$

Finally, get rid of the coefficient 12 by dividing:

$$\frac{12x}{12} = \frac{60}{12}$$
$$x = 5$$

As usual, you can check your answer by substituting 5 into the original equation wherever x appears:

$$5x + (6x - 15) = 30 - (x - 7) + 8$$
$$5(5) + [6(5) - 15] = 30 - (5 - 7) + 8$$
$$25 + (30 - 15) = 30 - (-2) + 8$$
$$25 + 15 = 30 + 2 + 8$$
$$40 = 40 \; \checkmark$$

Here's one more example:

$$11 + 3(-3x + 1) = 25 - (7x - 3) - 12$$

As in the preceding example, start out by removing both sets of parentheses. This time, however, on the left side of the equation, you have no sign between 3 and $(-3x + 1)$. But again, you can put your skills from Chapter 14 to use. To remove the parentheses, multiply 3 by both terms inside the parentheses:

$$11 - 9x + 3 = 25 - (7x - 3) - 12$$

On the right side, the parentheses begin with a minus sign, so remove the parentheses by changing all the signs inside the parentheses:

$$11 - 9x + 3 = 25 - 7x + 3 - 12$$

Now you're ready to isolate the x terms. I do this in one step, but take as many steps as you want:

$$-9x + 7x = 25 + 3 - 12 - 11 - 3$$

At this point, you can combine like terms:

$$-2x = 2$$

To finish, divide both sides by -2:

$$x = -1$$

Copy this example, and work through it a few times with the book closed.

Cross-multiplying

In algebra, cross-multiplication helps to simplify equations by removing unwanted fractions (and, honestly, when are fractions ever wanted?). As I discuss in Chapter 6, you can use cross-multiplication to find out whether two fractions are equal. You can use this same idea to solve algebra equations with fractions, like this one:

$$\frac{x}{2x-2} = \frac{2x+3}{4x}$$

This equation looks hairy. You can't do the division or cancel anything out because the fraction on the left has two terms in the denominator, and the fraction on the right has two terms in the numerator (refer to Chapter 14 for info on dividing algebraic terms). However, an important piece of information that you have is that the fraction equals the fraction. So if you cross-multiply these two fractions, you get two results that are also equal:

$$x(4x) = (2x + 3)(2x - 2)$$

At this point, you have something you know how to work with. The left side is easy:

$$4x^2 = (2x+3)(2x-2)$$

The right side requires a bit of FOILing (flip to Chapter 14 for details):

$$4x^2 = 4x^2 - 4x + 6x - 6$$

Now all the parentheses are gone, so you can isolate the x terms. Because most of these terms are already on the right side of the equation, isolate them on that side:

$$6 = 4x^2 - 4x + 6x - 4x^2$$

Combining like terms gives you a pleasant surprise:

$$6 = 2x$$

The two x^2 terms cancel each other out. You may be able to eyeball the correct answer, but here's how to finish:

$$\frac{6}{2} = \frac{2x}{2}$$
$$3 = x$$

To check your answer, substitute 3 back into the original equation:

$$\frac{x}{2x-2} = \frac{2x+3}{4x}$$
$$\frac{3}{2(3)-2} = \frac{2(3)+3}{4(3)}$$
$$\frac{3}{6-2} = \frac{6+3}{12}$$
$$\frac{3}{4} = \frac{3}{4} \; \checkmark$$

So the answer $x = 3$ is correct.

Chapter 16

Algebra Word Problems

- -

In This Chapter

▶ Solving algebra word problems in simple steps

▶ Choosing variables carefully

▶ Using charts to work through problems

- -

*W*ord problems that require algebra are among the toughest problems that students face — and the most common. Teachers just love algebra word problems because they bring together a lot of what you know, such as solving algebra equations (Chapters 14 and 15) and turning words into numbers (see Chapters 5 and 9). And most maths tests virtually always include these types of problems.

In this chapter, I show you a five-step method for using algebra to solve word problems. Then I give you a bunch of examples that take you through all five steps.

Along the way, I give you some important tips that can make solving word problems easier. First, I show you how to choose a variable that makes your equation as simple as possible. Next, I give you practice organising information from the problem into a chart. By the end of this chapter, you'll have a solid understanding of how to solve a wide variety of algebra word problems.

Solving Algebra Word Problems in Five Steps

Everything from Chapters 14 and 15 comes into play when you use algebra to solve word problems, so if you feel a little shaky on solving algebraic equations, flip back to those chapters for a review.

Throughout this section, I use the following word problem as an example:

> In three days, Alexandra sold a total of 31 tickets to her school play. On Tuesday, she sold twice as many tickets as on Wednesday. And on Thursday, she sold exactly 7 tickets. How many tickets did Alexandra sell on each day, Tuesday through Thursday?

Organising the information in an algebra word problem by using a chart or picture is usually helpful. Here's what I came up with:

Tuesday:	Twice as many as on Wednesday
Wednesday:	?
Thursday:	7
Total:	31

At this point, all the information is in the chart, but the answer still may not be jumping out at you. In this section, I outline a step-by-step method that enables you to solve this problem — and much harder ones as well.

Here are the five steps for solving most algebra word problems:

1. **Declare a variable.**
2. **Set up the equation.**
3. **Solve the equation.**
4. **Answer the question that the problem asks.**
5. **Check your answer.**

Declaring a variable

As you know from Chapter 14, a variable is a letter that stands for a number. Most of the time, you don't find the variable *x* (or any other variable, for that matter) in a word problem. That omission doesn't mean you don't need algebra to solve the problem. It just means that you're going to have to put *x* into the problem yourself and decide what it stands for.

When you declare a variable, you say what that variable means in the problem you're solving.

Here are some examples of variable declarations:

Let m = the number of dead mice that the cat dragged into the house.

Let p = the number of times Marianne's dad promised to take out the garbage.

Let c = the number of complaints Arnold received after he painted his garage door purple.

In each case, you take a variable (m, p or c) and give it a meaning by attaching it to a number.

Notice that the earlier chart for the sample problem has a big question mark next to Wednesday. This question mark stands for some number, so you may want to declare a variable that stands for this number. Here's how you do it:

Let w = the number of tickets that Alexandra sold on Wednesday.

Whenever possible, choose a variable with the same initial as what the variable stands for. This practice makes remembering what the variable means a lot easier, which will help you later in the problem.

For the rest of the problem, every time you see the variable w, keep in mind that it stands for the number of tickets that Alexandra sold on Wednesday.

Setting up the equation

After you have a variable to work with, you can go through the problem again and find other ways to use this variable. For example, Alexandra sold twice as many tickets on Tuesday as on Wednesday, so she sold $2w$ tickets on Tuesday. Now you have a lot more information to fill in on the chart:

Tuesday:	Twice as many as on Wednesday	$2w$
Wednesday:	?	w
Thursday:	7	7
Total:	31	31

You know that the total number of tickets, or the sum of the tickets she sold on Tuesday, Wednesday and Thursday, is 31. With the chart filled in like that, you're ready to set up an equation to solve the problem:

$$2w + w + 7 = 31$$

Solving the equation

After you set up an equation, you can use the tricks from Chapter 15 to solve the equation for *w*. Here's the equation one more time:

$$2w + w + 7 = 31$$

For starters, remember that $2w$ really means $w + w$. So on the left, you know you really have $w + w + w$, or $3w$; you can simplify the equation a little bit, as follows:

$$3w + 7 = 31$$

The goal at this point is to try to get all the terms with *w* on one side of the equation and all the terms without *w* on the other side. So on the left side of the equation, you want to get rid of the 7. The inverse of addition is subtraction, so subtract 7 from both sides:

$$
\begin{array}{rcr}
3w + 7 & = & 31 \\
-7 & & -7 \\
\hline
3w & = & 24
\end{array}
$$

You now want to isolate *w* on the left side of the equation. To do this, you have to undo the multiplication by 3, so divide both sides by 3:

$$\frac{3w}{3} = \frac{24}{3}$$
$$w = 8$$

Answering the question

You may be tempted to think that, after you've solved the equation, you're done. But you still have a bit more work to do. Look back at the problem, and you see that it asks you this question:

> How many tickets did Alexandra sell on each day, Tuesday through Thursday?

At this point, you have some information that can help you solve the problem. The problem tells you that Alexandra sold 7 tickets on Thursday. And because $w = 8$, you now know that she sold 8 tickets on Wednesday. And on Tuesday, she sold twice as many on Wednesday, so she sold 16. So Alexandra sold 16 tickets on Tuesday, 8 on Wednesday and 7 on Thursday.

Checking your work

To check your work, compare your answer to the problem, line by line, to make sure every statement in the problem is true:

> In three days, Alexandra sold a total of 31 tickets to her school play.

That part is correct because $16 + 8 + 7 = 31$.

> On Tuesday, she sold twice as many tickets as on Wednesday.

Correct, because she sold 16 tickets on Tuesday and 8 on Wednesday.

> And on Thursday, she sold exactly 7 tickets.

Yep, that's right, too, so you're good to go.

Choosing Your Variable Wisely

Declaring a variable is simple, as I show you earlier in this chapter, but you can make the rest of your work a lot easier when you know how to choose your variable wisely. Whenever possible, choose a variable so that the equation you have to solve has no fractions, which are much more difficult to work with than whole numbers.

For example, suppose you're trying to solve this problem:

> Irina has three times as many clients as Toby. If they have 52 clients all together, how many clients does each person have?

The key sentence in the problem is 'Irina has three times as many clients as Toby.' It's significant because it indicates a relationship between Irina and Toby that's based on either multiplication or division. And to avoid fractions, you want to avoid division wherever possible.

Whenever you see a sentence that indicates you need to use either multiplication or division, choose your variable to represent the smaller number. In this case, Toby has fewer clients than Irina, so choosing *t* as your variable is the smart move.

Suppose you begin by declaring your variable as follows:

> Let *t* = the number of clients that Toby has.

Then, using that variable, you can make this chart:

Irina $3t$

Toby t

No fraction! To solve this problem, set up this equation:

Irina + Toby = 52

Plug in the values from the chart:

$3t + t = 52$

Now you can solve the problem easily, using what I show you in Chapter 15:

$4t = 52$

$t = 13$

Toby has 13 clients, so Irina has 39. To check this result — which I recommend highly earlier in this chapter! — note that $13 + 39 = 52$.

Now suppose that, instead, you take the opposite route and decide to declare a variable as follows:

Let i = the number of clients that Irina has.

Given that variable, you have to represent Toby's clients using the fraction $\frac{i}{3}$, which leads to the same answer but a lot more work.

Solving More Complex Algebraic Problems

Algebra word problems become more complex when the number of people or things you need to find out increases. In this section, the complexity increases to four and then five people. When you're done, you should feel comfortable solving algebra word problems of significant difficulty.

Charting four people

As in the previous section, a chart can help you organise information so you don't get confused. Here's a problem that involves four people:

> Alison, Jeremy, Liz and Raymond participated in a canned goods drive at work. Liz donated three times as many cans as Jeremy, Alison donated twice as many as Jeremy and Raymond donated 7 more than Liz. Together the two women donated two more cans than the two men. How many cans did the four people donate altogether?

The first step, as always, is declaring a variable. Remember that, to avoid fractions, you want to declare a variable based on the person who brought in the fewest cans. Liz donated more cans than Jeremy and so did Alison. Furthermore, Raymond donated more cans than Liz. So because Jeremy donated the fewest cans, declare your variable as follows:

Let j = the number of cans that Jeremy donated.

Now you can set up your chart as follows:

Jeremy	j
Liz	$3j$
Alison	$2j$
Raymond	Liz $+ 7 = 3j + 7$

This setup looks good because, as expected, no fractional amounts are shown in the chart. The next sentence tells you that the women donated two more cans than the men, so make a word problem, as I show you in Chapter 5:

Liz + Alison = Jeremy + Raymond + 2

You can now substitute into this equation as follows:

$$3j + 2j = j + 3j + 7 + 2$$

With your equation set up, you're ready to solve. First, isolate the algebraic terms:

$$3j + 2j - j - 3j = 7 + 2$$

Combine like terms:

$$j = 9$$

Almost without effort, you've solved the equation, so you know that Jeremy donated 9 cans. With this information, you can go back to the chart, plug in 9 for *j*, and find out how many cans the other people donated: Liz donated 27, Alison donated 18 and Raymond donated 34. Finally, you can add up these numbers to conclude that the four people donated 88 cans altogether.

To check the numbers, read through the problem and make sure they work at every point in the story. For example, together Liz and Alison donated 45 cans, and Jeremy and Raymond donated 43, so the women really did donate 2 more cans than the men.

Crossing the finish line with five people

Here's one final example, the most difficult in this chapter, in which you have five people to work with.

> Five friends are keeping track of how many kilometres they run. So far this month, Mina has run 12 kilometres, Suzanne has run 3 more kilometres than Jake and Kyle has run twice as far as Victor. But tomorrow, after they all complete a 5-kilometre run, Jake will have run as far as Mina and Victor combined, and the whole group will have run 174 kilometres. How far has each person run so far?

The most important point to notice in this problem is that two sets of numbers are included: The kilometres that all five people have run up to today and their distance including tomorrow. And each person's distance tomorrow will be 5 kilometres greater than his or her distance today. Here's how to set up a chart:

	Today	*Tomorrow (Today + 5)*
Jake		
Kyle		
Mina		
Suzanne		
Victor		

With this chart, you're off to a good start to solve this problem. Next, look for that statement early in the problem that connects two people by either multiplication or division. Here it is:

Kyle has run twice as far as Victor.

Because Victor has run fewer kilometres than Kyle, declare your variable as follows:

Let v = the number of kilometres that Victor has run up to today.

Notice that I added the word *today* to the declaration to be very clear that I'm talking about Victor's kilometres *before* the 5-kilometre run tomorrow.

At this point, you can begin filling in the chart:

	Today	*Tomorrow (Today + 5)*
Jake		
Kyle	$2v$	$2v + 5$
Mina	12	17
Suzanne		
Victor	v	$v + 5$

As you can see, I left out the information about Jake and Suzanne because I can't represent it using the variable v. I've also begun to fill in the Tomorrow column by adding 5 to my numbers in the Today column.

Now I can move on to the next statement in the problem:

But tomorrow … Jake will have run as far as Mina and Victor combined …

I can use this to fill in Jake's information:

	Today	*Tomorrow (Today + 5)*
Jake	$17 + v$	$17 + v + 5$
Kyle	$2v$	$2v + 5$
Mina	12	17
Suzanne		
Victor	v	$v + 5$

In this case, I first filled in Jake's tomorrow distance $(17 + v + 5)$ and then subtracted 5 to find out his today distance. Now I can use the information that today Suzanne has run 3 more miles than Jake:

	Today	*Tomorrow (Today + 5)*
Jake	$17 + v$	$17 + v + 5$
Kyle	$2v$	$2v + 5$
Mina	12	17
Suzanne	$17 + v + 3$	$17 + v + 8$
Victor	v	$v + 5$

With the chart filled in like this, you can begin to set up your equation. First, set up a word equation, as follows:

Jake tomorrow + Kyle tomorrow + Mina tomorrow + Suzanne tomorrow + Victor tomorrow = 174

Now just substitute information from the chart into this word equation to set up your equation:

$$17 + v + 5 + 2v + 5 + 17 + 17 + v + 8 + v + 5 = 174$$

As always, begin solving by isolating the algebraic terms:

$$v + 2v + v + v = 174 - 17 - 5 - 5 - 17 - 17 - 8 - 5$$

Next, combine like terms:

$$5v = 100$$

Finally, to get rid of the coefficient in the term $5v$, divide both sides by 5:

$$\frac{5v}{5} = \frac{100}{5}$$
$$v = 20$$

You now know that Victor's total distance up to today is 20 miles. With this information, you substitute 20 for v and fill in the chart, as follows:

	Today	*Tomorrow (Today + 5)*
Jake	37	42
Kyle	40	45
Mina	12	17
Suzanne	40	45
Victor	20	25

The Today column contains the answers to the question the problem asks. To check this solution, make sure that every statement in the problem is true. For example, tomorrow the five people will have run a total of 174 miles because

$$42 + 45 + 17 + 45 + 25 = 174$$

Copy down this problem, close the book, and work through it for practice.

Part V
The Part of Tens

the
part of
tens

In this part . . .

✔ Discover useful hints and practical tips for getting the best out of basic maths.

✔ Collect tricks to help you avoid making common mathematical mistakes.

✔ Work out how to avoid the traps examiners can set for you, and ace an exam. What more could you ask for?

Chapter 17

Ten Tricks for Remembering Your Number Facts

Personally, I wish maths tests put much less emphasis on being able to do accurate, rapid-fire mental arithmetic under pressure. I think being able to estimate and feed the right sum into a calculator or computer is far more useful — but at the moment we're stuck with the tests we've got.

I suggest you learn your number facts efficiently and with the minimum of fuss. The quicker you can command total mastery of your number facts, the quicker you can stop having to learn them, and the more time you can spend on the more creative and interesting aspects of maths.

In this chapter, I list ten things you can do to make learning your number facts easier.

Playing Games

Many games, online and offline, help you practise and learn your number facts — I'm particularly fond of the Mathletics site and Manga High, because many of the alternatives are a bit patronising.

Games are a really useful way of learning anything at all, because they take the chore element out of learning and turn it into something a bit more fun. Playing a number-facts game with cards or on the computer is much less like hard work than writing down endless lists of sums. I strongly recommend games as a learning tool — let me know if you find any good ones.

Flashing Cards

Flash cards aren't so common in Australia, but in America pretty much every successful student spends hours of their revision time writing down the key facts they want to remember on index cards and repeatedly testing themselves until they have all their facts down pat. Using flash cards like this is a bit tedious but *very* effective.

You don't need to go out and buy stacks of index cards — just cut up paper or cardboard into smaller bits and write on those instead.

The traditional way to set up flash cards is to write a question on one side and the answer on the other. Then grab some cards from your 'to learn' stack and go through, reading out the question and answering aloud. Check the back of the card: If you got the question right, you put the card to one side; if you're not happy with your answer, put the card to the back of the pile. Keep on answering until you run out of questions.

The more you do this, the quicker and more accurate you get.

Sticking Stickies

At university, many people were frightened to go into my room near exam time, and not just because it smelt of damp laundry. When I was revising, I would cover every available surface with sticky notes covered with details I was meant to know for my exams, and sheets of paper full of colourful equations, diagrams, mnemonics and more.

I was pretty mean when it came to buying adhesive, so anyone who opened my door or moved a muscle a few metres away from my room would cause all of the paper to rustle and fall down, at which point I would yell at them to be more careful.

I didn't have many friends in those days.

 A more moderate version of this technique that doesn't make you the villain of your household is to put five key things you want to remember on sticky notes and put the notes somewhere you're bound to see them — say, on the bottom of your computer screen, your wardrobe, the back of the toilet door, outside of the shower screen or the bathroom mirror — anything you look at more than once a day and is a suitable surface for sticky notes is a great choice. When you can remember the info on the sticky note without even trying, replace the sticky with a new note covering something else you need to learn.

Counting on Your Fingers

Fingers are the reason we count things in tens, so using your digits to figure out questions is perfectly natural. The disadvantage is that counting on your fingers can be a lot slower than just remembering the facts — and especially in an exam, time isn't something you have a lot of.

I'm a big advocate of saying the sum and the answer aloud after you've worked it out on your fingers — for instance, after you add 6 to 9 to get 15, say, 'Nine add 6 is 15.' Repeating the sum aloud convinces your brain that the sum is an *important thing to remember*, just like when you say to yourself, 'Don't forget the excursion permission form tomorrow' over and over again on your way home from school. Or is that just something I do?

You can also use your fingers to keep track of your times tables. I suggest you say out loud, 'One six is six, two sixes are twelve' and so on, even though this is slower than counting briskly through '6, 12, 18, 24 . . .' If you're looking for the answer to 7×6, you can easily get confused if you try to keep track of the six times table — tapping your fingers as you go through saves you wondering how far you've got.

Tricking Out the Nines

In Chapter 3, I show you how to figure out your nine times table using your fingers, but that's not the only way to work with nines. Here's another way to do nine times anything (up to ten):

1. **Take one away from the number you're multiplying by.**

   Write down the answer.

2. **Take your answer to Step 1 away from nine.**

   Write this new answer to the right of your first answer — and there's your answer. For example, to do 7×9, take 1 away from 7 and write down 6. Now take 6 from 9 to get 3, and write that to the right — you get 63, which is 7×9.

A good way to check your answer to a nine times table (up to ten) question is to notice that the two numbers in the answer always add up to nine. For example, 7×9 is 63, and $6 + 3$ is 9. After ten, things get a bit trickier — for example, $11 \times 9 = 99$, and $9 + 9$ is 18 ... but if you add $1 + 8$, you then get 9. You just have to keep going until you get to a single digit.

This only works for the nine times table. Numbers in the eight times table don't always add up to eight, sadly.

Tricking Out the Other Big Numbers

In Chapter 3, I show you how to use your hands for the more difficult, bottom-right part of the times tables — 6×6 and beyond. Here are some clever tricks you can use to figure out your five, six, seven and eight times tables.

Tricks of six

Here I give you a way to work out your six times table where all you need to know is how to double and treble things (times them by three).

To times a number by six:

1. **Times the number by three.**
2. **Double the answer.**

For example, to work out 9×6, do $9 \times 3 = 27$, and then double your answer to get 54. It doesn't matter which way around you do the doubling and trebling, as long as you do them both.

Straight to eight

In this section, I show you how to work out your eight times table where all you need to know is how to double things. To times a number by eight:

1. **Double the number.**
2. **Double the answer.**

   This is now four times the original number.

3. **Double the answer again.**

For example, to do 7×8, double 7 to get 14. Double 14 to get 28. Then double 28 to get 56.

What about seven?

After you know how the sixes and eights work, you have two quick ways to work with sevens. To times a number by seven using the sixes:

1. **Work out six times your number.**
2. **Add the original number to that.**

For example, to work out 7×7, do $7 \times 6 = 42$, and add 7 to get 49.

Alternatively, you can times a number by seven using the eights:

1. **Work out eight times your number.**
2. **Take away the original number.**

So, to work out 7×7, do $7 \times 8 = 56$ and take away 7 to get 49.

Five alive!

The five times table also has an easy trick: You can times the number by ten and then divide the answer by two, or halve the number first and then times by ten. So, to work out 8×5, do $8 \times 10 = 80$ and divide by 2 to get 40; or, divide by 2 to get 4 and do 4×10 — again, the answer's 40.

If you don't like messing around with fractions, I suggest you times by ten first rather than halving.

Breaking Down and Building Up

Division tricks are pretty much the opposite of the multiplication tricks I describe in the previous section. Don't be surprised — after all, multiplying and dividing are the opposite of each other.

Eight: halving over and over

If you want to divide by eight, but doing 'proper' division bothers you, try the following method:

1. **Divide the number by two.**

2. **Divide by two again.**

   You've now divided by $2 \times 2 = 4$.

3. **Now divide by two again.**

   You've now divided by $4 \times 2 = 8$.

So, to do $72 \div 8$, halve 72 to get 36, halve again to get 18, and halve one more time to get 9. And that's right: $72 \div 8 = 9$.

Surprised by six

So, would you care to make a prediction about another way of dividing by six? Here it is:

1. **Divide by three.**

2. **Then divide your answer by two.**

You can do these steps in either order. For example, to do $42 \div 6$, you can halve 42 to get 21 and then divide by 3 to get 7. Or you can do $42 \div 3 = 14$ first and then halve the answer to get 7.

Nailing nine

Dividing by nine is just as simple:

1. **Divide by three.**

2. **Divide by three again.**

So, faced with $81 \div 9$, you can work out $81 \div 3 = 27$, and then $27 \div 3 = 9$, which is the right answer.

Finally fives

For the five times table, you can double and then divide by ten, or you can divide by ten and then double. So, to work out $85 \div 5$, you double 85 to get 170 and then divide by 10 to get 17. Or you do $85 \div 10 = 8.5$ and then double it to get 17. Doubling rather than dividing first tends to avoid the need for fractions.

Learning from Your Mistakes

To get good at anything, you have to go through a stage of feeling like you're really bad at it. And the way to get through that stage as fast as possible is to make a point of learning from your mistakes.

Whenever you make a mistake in doing a sum, take a moment to note down what you should've done. Then add this to your list of things to learn.

Go through this list as often as you possibly can; the more you practise the things you want to learn, the more quickly you'll find them sticking in your mind.

Learning from your mistakes might sound boring but it pays off really quickly.

Working from What You Know

As I show you in the section 'Tricking Out the Other Big Numbers', you can use the next times table up or down to work out the times table you want.

But wait — there's more!

You can also split up any times sum into smaller times sums. For instance, if you want to work out 12×12, you can split up the sum in several ways:

- ✔ If you know 12 is 2×6, you can do $12 \times 2 = 24$ and times that by 6 to get 144.

- ✔ If you know 12 is $10 + 2$, you can do $10 \times 12 = 120$ and $2 \times 12 = 24$ and add the two answers together to make 144.

- ✔ If you're feeling perversely smart and know that 12 is $20 - 8$, you can do $20 \times 12 = 240$, take away $12 \times 8 = 96$ and get 144. I don't recommend that one — but it does work.

You can also split up many divide sums into smaller, easier ones. You can't use all the same tricks as you use for multiplying, but here's a division recipe you can try:

1. **Look at the number you're trying to divide by and try to find two numbers that times together to make that number.**

   For example, if you want to divide by 12, you could pick either 2 and 6, or 3 and 4.

2. **Divide by each of those numbers in turn.**

   It doesn't matter which way round, as long as you use both of them.

   So, to divide 576 by 12, you can divide 576 by 2 to get 288, and divide 288 by 6 to get 48. If you prefer, you can divide 576 by 3 to get 192 and divide 192 by 4 to get 48.

This recipe doesn't work for all numbers, but it's worth trying for any number bigger than ten.

Training Yourself with Treats

Although the human brain is a marvellous and sophisticated piece of wetware, far more powerful than a supercomputer, it's also not all that dissimilar from a dog's brain. If you want to train a dog to learn a behaviour, every time the dog does the task correctly, you give the creature a treat. The dog learns to associate sitting on command with the pleasure it gets from a reward, and the next time you say, 'Sit!' it is more likely to do as it's told. Good dog.

Your mind works in much the same way: If you reward yourself with a treat after you learn to perform a task well, you do better at repeating your feat at a later time.

I recommend chocolate for humans as a treat for doing well — every time you beat your flashcards record or get a long-division sum right, give yourself a pat on the back and feel the pleasure of having made progress. You've earned it.

Chapter 18

Ten (Almost!) Pitfalls to Avoid

▶ Ensuring your answer makes sense

▶ Reading the question carefully

▶ Averting common errors

When you're under pressure in a maths test, you're bound to make some mistakes. But some mistakes are avoidable when you know how, and some mistakes you can learn to check for and put right. In this chapter, I list the top ten most common pitfalls in maths tests and explain how to avoid them.

Taking Care with Your Calculator

I had a student once who read a question, merrily tapped the numbers into his calculator, and confidently informed me that Mars was 5 centimetres away. He refused any argument to the contrary on the grounds that his calculator was always right.

Don't be like him.

A machine is only as good as what you tell it to do. Calculators can be amazingly helpful when you use them effectively, but I recommend you always work out rough answers for each step of your calculation so you can check you're doing the right thing along the way.

You're Out of Line!

When you draw a line graph, you plot a series of points on graph paper and join up the dots. Normally you get a smooth or at least smooth-ish curve.

But sometimes you go to draw the line and think, 'Hang on! That point's miles away from the others.' Check that dodgy point very carefully — it's not necessarily wrong, but be suspicious of it.

Making Sure Your Answer Makes Sense

In almost every sum you do, ask yourself whether your answer looks plausible. Here are a few questions to ask about your answer:

- ✔ **Adding:** Is your answer bigger than what you started with?
- ✔ **Taking away:** Is your answer smaller than what you started with?
- ✔ **Real-life problems:** Roughly what would you expect if you just guessed?
- ✔ **Probability:** Is your answer between 0 and 1?

You can probably come up with dozens of similar checks. Before you even begin a question, try to think of as many criteria as possible that your answer has to satisfy.

Distinguishing 'More Than' and 'At Least'

This is one that everyone trips up on at least once. If I say, 'I have to pack at least a dozen pairs of socks', 12 pairs is a perfectly acceptable number. If I say, 'I have to take more than a dozen pairs', 12 is no longer good. I have to take *more than* 12, so 13 is the smallest number I can take.

(I suppose I could take 12 pairs and an odd sock. But that's beside the point.)

Reading the Question

I'm going to be blunt: If you don't read the question correctly, you get the wrong answer. You may be tempted to rush through and do the first thing that comes into your head — even I do that sometimes. And when I do, I mess up.

Take a breath, write down all the information you have, and ponder what the question is asking. Start calculating only after you're fairly certain what you need to do.

Fathoming the Phantom 40 Minutes

Almost every unit you use in maths and science works on powers of 10: 100 centimetres make a metre, 1,000 grams make a kilogram, and so on. The only real exception is time, where 60 seconds are the order of the day. When you try to do normal maths on time, you can end up 'missing' the 40-minute gap between the 60 minutes in an hour and the 100 whatevers that you use in other sums. Check out the sections in Chapter 12 on time for more details on avoiding this gigantic elephant trap.

Getting the Wrong Percentage

A couple of things commonly go wrong when you do percentages: You work out the percentage of the wrong thing, or you add when you're meant to take away.

You can get around the 'wrong thing' problem by filling in the Table of Joy that I show you in Chapter 8. To deal with the 'add or take away' problem, simply read the question carefully to see whether your answer needs to be higher or lower than the original number in the question.

Rounding Too Early

If you want to find an answer correct to, say, two decimal places, you may be tempted to round everything as you go along. This is normally okay in day-to-day life, but in a maths test it costs you some accuracy and leaves you with a slightly wrong answer. Instead, wait until the very end to round off your numbers. If you're only working out an approximation, round early and often. Refer to Chapter 7 to discover more about rounding.

Forgetting to Convert

In 1999, one of NASA's Mars Orbiters disintegrated as it descended through the Martian atmosphere, at a cost of hundreds of millions of dollars.

The cause was traced back to a software error: One of the control programs used imperial units such as inches, and another program used scientific units such as metres. The two programs didn't understand each other's numbers and the mission went catastrophically wrong.

Oopsie.

We can take two lessons from this story:

- ✔ Whatever happens in your exam, you won't make a spaceship blow up.
- ✔ Even rocket science isn't rocket science.

Chapter 19

Ten (or so) Ways to Make Any Test Easier

Exams can be stressful and frustrating, and not many people enjoy doing them. Just knowing your stuff isn't enough to do well — being knowledgeable is just one leg of the trousers ... and you don't want to go into an exam half-dressed. You need to prepare for the exam as well. Think: What are they likely to ask? How long will I have? Will I be rushing, or will I have plenty of time to check? How will I keep calm and focused in the test situation?

But jumping through the hoops of a test doesn't have to be hard. If you can reach a point where you feel prepared, have a good, solid plan and know how to relax, tests should hold no fear for you. In this chapter, I give you some tips to get past the worst of the stress, prepare effectively, work well in the test, and then come out of the test smiling like a Cheshire cat.

Know What You're Up Against

Practising on past papers is one of the most effective ways to prepare for an exam. Past papers give you a great idea of the kinds of questions that come up. Go through some exams from previous years — under your own self-imposed exam conditions if you want — and find out which bits you spend the most time on and where you can improve your understanding.

Then focus on those areas for your next few study sessions before you try working on another past paper.

Your teacher can likely provide you with extra sample tests to work through. If you have a maths tutor, ask them to give you some questions to work through that are likely to be on the test.

Practise the Hard Parts

I remember watching *Record Breakers* as a kid and being completely baffled by footage of athlete Kris Akabusi dragging a tyre behind him as he ran. I realise now the idea went like this: If you're used to running with a tyre attached to you, when you enter a race without the tyre you can run much quicker than before.

I don't recommend revising with a tyre tied to your back. Instead, try practising slightly harder questions than those you expect to see in the test, so when you sit the real thing you think, *Wow, this is easy!* Don't beat yourself up over what you can't do. Just see what you can figure out and applaud yourself for questions you answer correctly.

Remember the Basics

Have you ever watched a football team train? Players spend hours practising handballs, short punts and other ball-handling skills that they've been able to do since they could walk. The players haven't forgotten how to run — they're just practising what they spend most of their time in a match doing. One of my coaches had the mantra 'Good players do the simple things well' — and I apply the same mantra to students.

I'm always astonished when top A-level students say things like, 'I never understood long division' or 'I haven't really looked at decimals for years.' These students are telling me they haven't practised the fundamentals of maths for so long that they've forgotten them.

Don't be like the students I describe here. Try warming up for your study sessions with something you find easy and will use over and over — perhaps some times tables or estimating exercises. Keep your hand in with the basics and you'll find the more complicated topics easier.

Use the Final Minutes before Your Exam

If you tend to forget simple things in tests, the *cheat sheet* is your friend. On a piece of paper, write a few key points you need to remember. Then spend the last few minutes before your exam reading your cheat sheet over and over again.

You can't take the cheat sheet into the exam room, but you can make notes once the test starts. So, as soon as the examiner tells you to start writing, write down as much of the cheat sheet as you can remember.

Make your cheat sheet colourful and full of pictures. Most people's brains are better at remembering pictures than lists of information.

Don't Exhaust Yourself

After every important test, you'll always see at least one all-nighter zombie — someone who looks like death warmed up and then put back in the fridge, with bags under their eyes and hair like something out of a Tim Burton movie. You can tell at a glance two things about this person: One, they've been up most of the night studying; and, two, they won't do well in the test, even with their eyes propped open.

Your brain needs sleep to function properly. I don't think many things are plain stupid, but pulling an all-nighter before a test is up there with driving while drunk and eating peanut butter. You can't expect to do high-level intelligent tasks if your brain is saying, 'I must sleep!'

Before your test, have a good breakfast and drink enough fluids. Your brain runs on this stuff. Trying to think when you're hungry, thirsty or tired is like driving on fumes with no oil in the engine and no air in the tyres. No good can come of it.

Think Positive, or 'I'll Show Me!'

One of my biggest tricks for overcoming anxiety attacks — when my brain is telling me, 'You're a loser, you can't do that, you'll mess up and everyone will laugh at you' — is to stand up straight, take a deep breath and say, 'Right! I'll show me!'

Your brain can be a bully — but it's a bully with no substance behind it. If you assert yourself and say, 'Oh yes I can!' or 'Get out of my way, brain!', you can overcome the self-doubt and low confidence that plague most people at some point.

Tell yourself, 'I'm smart, I'm capable, and I'm going to show me what I can do.' You may be surprised how much better you do than when you listen to your inner bully.

I've 'shown me' in all kinds of situations — from playing guitar on stage, to making an awkward phone call, to putting bad jokes in my thesis — and the technique's served me very well. The more you train yourself to ignore your inner bully, the less negative influence it has on your life.

POPS — posture, oxygen and positive self-talk — are fantastic tools for when you need to calm down quickly. Take a few moments to breathe and tell yourself, 'I can do this' if you find yourself blanking in a test — or anywhere else for that matter.

Have a Ritual

You may have seen certain AFL players before they take a shot on goal. Maybe they pull up their socks so they're perfectly aligned. Perhaps they pick up some grass and throw it in the air to check the wind. Then they step in and whack the ball through the posts like a machine.

I'm not prattling on about footy here so much as describing the value of a ritual. When some players take a shot on goal, they follow a set routine that they've practised over and over again. The routine prepares them mentally for the task they have to do.

I always do the same thing in tests: I open the paper, take a deep breath, tell myself to do well, and quickly read through the paper before starting the questions. This way, I know how every test starts. I know what happens in the first two minutes and that nothing bad happens in those two minutes. Having a starting ritual removes much of the worry and stress. You can create your own ritual by thinking about *exactly* what you'll do when you sit down for the test, and in what order. It doesn't have to be complicated — something as simple as, 'Take a deep breath, imagine how great I'll feel when I get my results, and then start reading the first question' would work well.

Manage Your Time

In this chapter, the phrase 'manage your time' may be the tip that gains you the most marks. The idea is not to spend too long on one question — if the answer doesn't come out quickly, mark the question with a star and come back to it later.

You have limited time in the test, so I suggest you spend that time picking up marks you can definitely get before you spend time on marks you may get eventually. Getting to the end of the test and finding you've missed three easy questions because you were looking at one hard one is a calamity.

You probably know the feeling of thinking really hard about something for ages, and then giving up, only for the answer to hit you halfway through your walk round the park later on. Leaving a question and coming back to it later can be a really efficient exam technique: As you work on the easier questions, your brain can still work on the harder questions in the background.

Here are some further tips for managing your time:

- ✔ **Read the paper:** If you prepare well, you'll know roughly what the test entails — but reassuring yourself that this test isn't different from the ones before is always a good idea. Reading through the paper first also gives your brain a chance to start its wheels turning on some of the harder questions — your subconscious can begin work on those while you rattle off the easy ones ... which you can also pick out while you read through the paper.

- ✔ **Check your answers:** With some multiple-choice questions, starting with the answers and seeing which one answers the question, rather than the other way round, is a good ploy.

  Even if the test isn't multiple choice, you can still check that an answer you reach by long division fits the question when you multiply it back.

- ✔ **Eliminate the impossible:** If you have five options, and four of them are clearly wrong, the fifth one must be right. In practice, of course, examiners aren't quite so generous as to offer only one obviously correct answer — but you can sometimes dismiss a couple of answers as obvious red herrings. For example, if the question involves cooking for more people, it's pretty likely that the new recipe calls for more of an ingredient.

Read the question carefully and make sure that what you write down answers the question.

Guess If You Need To

If time's running out and you've got a minute to answer the last five multiple-choice questions, you don't really have time to read the questions, let alone work out the answers. In this situation you have two possible approaches:

- ✔ Miss out the questions and get a guaranteed zero for those questions.
- ✔ Guess the answers and maybe pick up a few points.

Guess which of these two approaches I recommend? The clue's in the heading for this section.

Numeracy tests usually aren't negatively marked, so you don't lose points for giving a wrong answer. If you guess when you don't have time or are genuinely stuck, the worst that can happen is that you score no marks for that question.

I have a friend who once aced an economics exam by answering the first question with answer 'a', the second 'b', the third 'c' and so on. Another friend swears by picking answer 'b' every time he doesn't know the answer to a multiple-choice question, because he thinks 'b' answers come up more often than the other letters. (I don't think this is true ... but his is no worse a strategy than any other.)

Try to make guessing a last resort — and always check first to see whether you can eliminate any of the answers.

If you do a test that carries penalties for wrong answers, however, guessing wildly may not be the best strategy. Even so, if you can cross out an impossible answer and pick from the others, you generally still do better by guessing than by giving no answer.

Index

Publisher's Acknowledgements

We're proud of this book; please send us your comments through our online registration form located at dummies.custhelp.com.

Some of the people who helped bring this book to market include the following:

Acquisitions, Editorial and Media Development

Project Editor: Charlotte Duff

Acquisitions Editor: Kristen Hammond

Editorial Manager: Alice Berry

Production

Graphics: diacriTech

Technical Reviewer: Ingrid Kemp

Proofreader: Jenny Scepanovic

Indexer: Don Jordan, Antipodes Indexing

Every effort has been made to trace the ownership of copyright material. Information that enables the publisher to rectify any error or omission in subsequent editions is welcome. In such cases, please contact the Legal Services section of John Wiley & Sons Australia, Ltd.

Also available . . .